Magical Marxism

Marxism and Culture

Series Editors:
Esther Leslie (Professor in Political Aesthetics at Birkbeck, University of London) and
Mike Wayne (Reader in Film and Television Studies at Brunel University)

Magical Marxism

Subversive Politics and the Imagination

ANDY MERRIFIELD

PlutoPress
www.plutobooks.com

First published 2011 by Pluto Press
345 Archway Road, London N6 5AA and
175 Fifth Avenue, New York, NY 10010

www.plutobooks.com

Distributed in the United States of America exclusively by
Palgrave Macmillan, a division of St. Martin's Press LLC,
175 Fifth Avenue, New York, NY 10010

British Library Cataloguing in Publication Data
A catalogue record for this book is available from the British Library

ISBN   978 0 7453 3060 0   Hardback
ISBN   978 0 7453 3059 4   Paperback

Library of Congress Cataloging in Publication Data applied for

This book is printed on paper suitable for recycling and made from
fully managed and sustained forest sources. Logging, pulping and
manufacturing processes are expected to conform to the environmental
standards of the country of origin.

10   9   8   7   6   5   4   3   2   1

Designed and produced for Pluto Press by
Chase Publishing Services Ltd, 33 Livonia Road, Sidmouth, EX10 9JB, England
Typeset from disk by Stanford DTP Services, Northampton, England
Simultaneously printed digitally by CPI Antony Rowe, Chippenham, UK
and Edwards Bros in the USA

To Corinna and Lili-Rose, and their magic

Give us back our power of wonderment / I'm calling upon the magician

Aimé Césaire

The act of the imagination is an act of magic

Jean-Paul Sartre

CONTENTS

SERIES PREFACE

What if the whole edifice is not as hegemonic as it appears? What if we only need a little, perhaps, a lot more imagination, now that economic crisis has twinned with the virtual collapse of legitimacy for much of the political class that signed up to the neo-liberal paradigm? What if the Marxist critique of capitalism is already the common-sense of many activists busily building alternative models to existing society? What if these practical political projects suggest to Marxism that to move from *critique* to *practice*, it must rethink means and even some ends? The 1990s spawned a new language of resistance and Andy Merrifield's book, the latest in the *Marxism and Culture* series, reflects that, as well as an impatience with some of the traditional language and concepts of Marxism, especially the ones that block the paths from critique to practice.

Everybody knows (as Leonard Cohen once sang) that the ship is leaking and that the captain lied. Given this, the task might be to move beyond recycling ever more opaque ways of saying pretty much the same thing (the frequent fate of academic Marxism) and get on with the task of fashioning a language fit for intervention and engagement. But intervention and engagement with whom? A small and by no means the most important part of what *Magical Marxism* offers the reader, is a survey of the many who are already creating practical models of alternative living. In those alternative models lie the seeds of future visions that challenge not only capitalism's logic but some traditional Marxist thinking on the good society as well and how to get there. Marxism's traditional paradox is that to succeed in the long run it must create the conditions that destroy the means by which it at first succeeds in the short run. Party, state and labor are not ends in themselves. At best they can only be the means to begin a journey that must at some point diminish these motors of change if something really *new* is to emerge. Perhaps, as is argued in this book, the journey cannot begin at all with these motors. Lots of things that augur the genuinely new are in fact to be found outside the traditional terrain of the left.

Integration and intimidation muzzled the traditional political agent of Marxism (the organized workers) after the tumult of the 1960s and 1970s—but resistance is mobile and it simply relocated and mobilized in different forms. The language of liberation is increasingly one of *living* differently, a rather broader and many would argue a more radical vision than the more narrow workerist focus of Marxism's traditional political imaginary. To live differently requires breaking the ossified husk of the old society and kick-starting the imagination as the creative wellspring from which real change comes. In the traditional Marxist imaginary, workers taking control of the means of production—usually the factory—was the powerful prefigurative projection into the future that served as the springboard for what a different society would look like. But what if the embryonic outlines of a different society are being drawn in many different ways outside the traditional model? A Marxism open to these initiatives would indeed be "magical."

The prefigurative dynamic of culture thus looms large here as a resource for a new political imagination, inspired in large part by the culture and politics of Latin America, which has, since the 1990s, been the epicenter for resistance to neo-liberal capitalism. There are many cultures of living, of living cultures, that seed values, perspectives, habits, etc., that are explicitly antithetical to corporate capitalism, state power, and more broadly, institutional life, with its bureaucracies and hierarchies. If the participants of these new ways of living appear in the west to be overwhelmingly white and middle class, this does not in itself torpedo the validity of the politics, not least because similar political themes crop up in the global South where political agency is brown, black, and poor.

A new language of liberation is a risky project and as with everything new, it will make mistakes, go up blind alleys and fall flat on its face once in a while. In this new language, a more "orthodox" Marxism might with reason wonder where the state is in all this talk of imminent transformation? For perhaps the edifice is not as shaky as it appears? Perhaps the timber is being happily colonized by the woodworm of alternative projects, but the concrete and steel remains sturdy and strong and will not be eaten away from within? And perhaps in many cases, these alternative projects, these alternative ways of living are content to remain "autonomous zones", various escape routes that will never converge, never seeking broader social transformation?

Yet for all the difficulty in coming up with answers to such hard political questions, a more orthodox Marxism must let itself be infused by the utopian energies and aspirations, politics, and practical ideas flowing from the movement of movements. It must ask the hard questions to itself as much as to these multiple alternatives flourishing independently of corporate and state surveillance and power (independent for now, but what of tomorrow?). This is so if Marxism does not want to imitate what it seeks to overthrow.

The gap between the multiple political subjects today and the political subject of Marxism's traditional imagination may still one day close in unexpected ways. And one suspects that such a prospect would truly frighten the life out of our rulers. As general strikes roll across Europe as the economic crisis unfolds, it is obvious that such a convergence cannot be ruled out. For the moment it is in this gap that any revitalization of Marxism and socialism will be found. It is not the project of this book to attempt to close this gap and reconfigure both sides of the equation, the old political subject and the new political subjects. But arguably this is what the coming revolutions *must* accomplish and will only do so with the help of intelligently optimistic, imaginative and poetic works like Andy Merrifield's *Magical Marxism*.

Esther Leslie (Professor in Political Aesthetics at Birkbeck, University of London) and Mike Wayne (Reader in Film and Television Studies at Brunel University)

PREFACE

This book attempts to make mischief with Marxism, tries to subvert and refresh it, tries to shake it up from *within*. It pits a fantastical, dreaming Marxism in comradely opposition to scientific and staid versions of Marxism, doing so as it denounces the criminality of bourgeois society. It's a book that will doubtless fall between two stools, appalling the purists for its revisionist meanderings, turning off others with its Marxist pretensions, because it remains *too* Marxist. Yet what's on offer here isn't a deeper, more profound Marxism so much as a broader, more versatile one, a more supple Marxism that happily falls between these two stools because it bounces right back up again; and, besides, down there, in the space in between, between the stools, lurks a great big shady world of other mischief makers, young radical people, and maybe a few older ones, too, all of whom fall between two stools themselves. This book hopes to find its audience in this shady world of the unaffiliated, suggesting that they're actually more Marxist than they might think, and that we who call ourselves Marxists might become less Marxist than we think while still remaining good communists, while still keeping the red flag flying. Together, we might be able to do dangerous subversive things, mischievous things. What this book puts before its readers, then, isn't perhaps a "bad Marxism," as John Hutnyk might have it,[1] but a "mad" Marxism, a mad *magical* Marxism that calls upon the magician, that invokes a magical madness as the necessary nemesis of the chaos of our crazy times.

The book has arisen out of a double dissatisfaction: an obvious dissatisfaction with the world and a more delicate dissatisfaction with actually existing Marxism, out of a belief that the two are intimately related, that the understandable pessimism of the era has equally contaminated Marxism itself, has turned it inward and defensive, made it safe and cautious because it justifiably feels under threat, because it fears itself crumbling into dust like the Berlin wall. Here, though, I want to propose a corrective to Marxism's serial pessimism, to its perennial bad faith. Here, too, my dissatisfaction also embraces certain Marxist journals and scholarly publications, which, for a long time now, have seemed unreadable to me, too dry and predictable, too *exclusive* to insiders. Perhaps I'm not alone in thinking this? The many long, detailed articles and analyses of crises and disasters, of capitalist catastrophes, never seem to excite or inspire me, even when they are almost always right: as Marx said of the bourgeoisie, they all appear to be happy in their alienation, or at least happy in their assessments of capitalist alienation, reveling in the one-way streets they've consecrated, in the dead-ends and no exits their portrayals have built around themselves.

For years and years, I've been content to call myself "amongst other things" a Marxist,[2] even in the United States where it was sometimes awkward, and even though I've never found a Marxist party or organization to subscribe to, any mouthpiece I felt I could really associate myself with or could wholeheartedly endorse. I've always felt like a fellow-traveler somehow, like Sartre's Mathieu in *The Age of Reason* who, despite Brunet's constant urgings, never could quite commit himself "institutionally" to the cause, never could sign up "officially" to any Marxism—not that anybody has ever asked me to officially sign up. Nor was this necessarily because I feared relinquishing my freedom; more because in refusing, in not participating institutionally, I could cling onto my membership card of the Imaginary Party, the one I knew existed out there, somewhere, the one I knew *had to exist* out there, and whose ranks are swelling. The present book is really written for this imaginary constituency, for those card-carriers I know really exist. To that degree, *Magical Marxism* will, I hope, appeal to all those stray, non-aligned mischief makers who want to do something radical, who want to invent another world because they know this one sucks. I have the distinct feeling—an inkling, really—that there are a lot of us about, a lot of people sneaking about between two stools, plotting and waiting for news of what's going on above ground.

*

Prefaces are frequently the last thing authors pen to their books and this effort is no exception. It's in doing so that a writer can retrace his or her steps through their book, figure out what it might be, why it came about, now that the heat is off, now that the work itself has been done. One can reflect with a certain peace of mind, and then re-present the text as if it had been an a priori construct all along. In writing this preface, retrospectively, there are three key factors that now strike me as important in the book's genesis. The first was the decision I made back in 2003 to quit my life as an academic and go off to live in rural France, burying myself away initially in the Haute-Savoie, in the mountains, and then, a couple of years later, in an upland hideaway in the Massif Central, in the Auvergne, one of France's poorest regions. In fleeing urban life (New York), as well as the world of steady paid work, I wasn't sure if I was affirming my frustrated Marxist spirit or running away from it. I'd hitherto thought that radical Marxism meant engagement from within, from inside places of power like big cities, not opting out, downing tools and running to the outside, to some shadowy marginal world far away from urban life. Ironically, my choice of refuge was largely inspired by another Marxist, and a former metropolitan one, Guy Debord, who had himself tried to flee the spectacle during the 1970s—the "repugnant seventies" as he called them—and bivouacked in this self-same Auvergne, in a farmhouse behind a high stone wall. The house, he was fond of saying, "opened directly onto the Milky Way."[3]

It turned out that this house became, after Clausewitz, a sort of post-'68 fortress for Debord, a block of ice in the course of river whose torrential current was either tossing people aside or forcing you to go with its flow. Clausewitz said that the effectiveness of defense—the effectiveness of any fortress—hinged on two distinct elements, one passive, the other active. The latter, he said, can't be imagined without the former. Passive fortresses act as "real barriers," like barricades: they block roads, immobilize movement, dam rivers. Accordingly, they become "oases in the desert," "shields against enemy attack," "buttresses for a whole system of defense."[4] Passive fortresses try to prevent an enemy's advance, making it both difficult and hazardous: from there you can launch an active attack and dispatch garrisons to intercept or seek out any enemy.

Not long after I'd arrived in the Auvergne, I realized that Debord's ghost lived on: not only in its physical proximity, but also in its political reincarnation. All around me, often hidden away in small hamlets and tiny communities, were and are groups of people who've constructed active and passive fortresses for themselves, and who are creating whole new collective defense systems against spectacular society and its culture of consumption. And from these outposts, from these "new undergrounds," these "new reserves," they're sometimes launching frontal attacks on this degenerative system. The idea of a "new underground" or "new reserve" is the mystical surrealist André Gregory's idea, from Louis Malle's film *My Dinner With André*: people are coming together, Gregory said, presciently, in their desire to create new practical concepts about how to live and function in our neo-Dark Age. We're glimpsing, he said, "new islands of safety where history can be remembered and the human being can continue to dream and function."[5] And these islands are cropping up not only in my adoptive Haute-Loire but also in neighboring *départements* like Lozère, Aveyron and Corrèze, to name just a few, where people are struggling to affirm *terra novas* and new magical geographies of the imagination, new islands of safety inspired by dream, by the normative desire to do something more autonomous, something more meaningful in our own neo-Dark Age.

Against all odds, they're seeking out a more "authentic life" than contemporary capitalism, with its fast food and supermarkets, its labor markets and world market, can offer. Against an erstwhile deadening of the spirit at work, and a pollution of the mind at home, these people in their new communes, in their assorted ways, with their different links and survival systems, now farm organically, make honey and bake bread, raise goats and fabricate cheese, do small-scale, ostensibly trivial things that hang together as something larger, as a social movement in the making, one that has political awareness as well as practical savvy and technical know-how, one that doesn't necessarily think of itself as class-based, yet knows all-too-well where it stands within the global system of capital accumulation. These people are forming collective micro-movements against the totalitarian mega-machine, disparate groups who often ally themselves with struggles worldwide, with the *Conféderation Paysanne* and *Via Campesina*, with global landless struggles, fair trade issues, and food sovereignty in defiance of neo-liberal orthodoxies. The list is almost endless. It's as if they've read what the young Marx wrote in his *Economic and Philosophical Manuscripts*, as if they're trying to shrug off alienating forces, trying simply to be themselves, trying to liberate themselves in their external, objective world at the same time as they free themselves in their internal, subjective worlds. Their authenticity is thus an authenticity of action and consciousness, something both real and ideal, a positive energy that creates pockets of light—"pockets of resistance," to use Subcomandante Marcos's term—pockets of affirmation. "Pockets of resistance are multiplying," says Marcos. "Each has its own history, its specificities, its similarities, its demands, its struggles, its successes. If humanity wants to survive and improve, its only hope resides in these pockets made up of the excluded, of the left-for-dead, of the disposable."[6]

And so what at first seemed to me an escape from politics, I've since come to consider as a *reframing* of politics; and its testing ground has been right before me, in my own everyday life. What I've seen emerge, and what is still emerging, still taking shape ever so steadily, and what I'll explore further in this book, is a new brand of Marxism that has at its core a neo-communist impulse: more and more people are electing themselves into office, subscribing to a new Imaginary Party, to the degree that now, rather than involve a fleeing to the outside, to the margins of society, this activism has transformed itself into a sufficiently large critical mass of people to be edging its way back *inside* society.

And it's assaulting society as it strengthens its rank-and-file. At least I think it is, hope it is, have to hope that it is...

The idea for a book called specifically *magical* Marxism came in a strange, unforeseen place, in a flash, and in somewhat bizarre circumstances: in a hammock in the Portuguese colonial coastal town of Paraty, mid-way between São Paulo and Rio de Janeiro, along Brazil's "Green Coast." There, amid a tropical downpour, listening to the rain dance off the palm trees, for about a week solid I read *One Hundred Years of Solitude* and began to believe, believe in another reality, in another possible world, in a magical one. It's not that I didn't believe before, of course; it's just that the *surreality* of where I found myself somehow let me glimpse another aspect of everyday life, a fantastical one. I should say *re*-read *One Hundred Years of Solitude*, because for several years I had tried in vain to grapple with Gabriel García Márquez's epic saga of the Buendias, of Ursula and José Arcadio and their many, many offspring in the village of Macondo, hacked out of the middle of the damp jungle, not far from a sunken Spanish galleon. But I'd always been distracted by something, interrupted along the way, overwhelmed by the array of characters all bearing more or less the same name; I was never really able to get beyond the opening sequences with the gypsy magician Melquiades' mad inventions. Yet in Paraty, at the *pousada* "Caminho do Ouro," surrounded by fabulous plants, exotic flowers and little hummingbirds, all next to a gushing river, I was dazzled by García Márquez's vision of the world, by the vivacity of his human spirit, by our obsession with offsetting death, by life's emptiness without love, by our never-ending quest for adventure, for magic, for fantasy—for true fantastic reality.

Soon, after having the chance to spend a year in Brazil—to spend a whole year thinking about, conceiving and writing this book—I had a burning desire to enter into García Márquez's magical world myself, to let us all enter into his magical world, all those mischief makers out there, to become one his protagonists, to be Colonel Aureliano Buendia, *One Hundred Years of Solitude*'s principal character, to spend time like him "sneaking about through narrow trails of permanent subversion."[7] But I needed some point of entry, some trail to sneak through, and before long realized that "the political" offered this entry point, realized too that the magical was also urgently needed in politics itself. Accordingly, *Magical Marxism* is an invitation to a voyage, an invitation to enter a magical realm, to learn how to take a looking-glass perspective on life and politics. The book asks would-be readers to sneak about in this magical world with me, a world many readers actually know better than the author himself, because they've already broken out of ordinary daily life, because, through their own active volition, they've entered into another everyday life, one where everything is possible, where all is permitted for people with imagination. As such, this magical world is already real, if we look hard enough around us; it's just a question of changing one's perception about what reality is, about what politics is, about what it can be, ought to be, and about how we can follow the white rabbit down a hole into another political realm, and how we can do so while still staying solid Marxists.

This leads directly on to the third factor in the book's genesis: the magical dialogue that unfolds here is really a dialogue between Marxism as realism and Marxism as romantic dreaming, where the latter's ontological basis differs significantly to the former's. It is a dialogue that explores the respective efficacy of each camp for trying to transform the world, and for trying to transform Marxism. Hugely influential in this regard is the film—or rather *anti*-film—*My Dinner with André*, and the strange encounter between the skeptical realist "Wally," who worries about making the next rent check, and the loose-cannon romantic dreamer André, who's searching for new philosophical principles, for a new meaning to life.[8] Everybody believes André has cracked up and gone mad, and Wally presents him as a cranky freak. The dialogue starts off lightly, even whimsically, but steadily the intensity and gravity gets ratcheted-up, until it is André's existential voyage that dominates; he could talk all day and night if need be.

André bemoans the modern world's incapacity to feel anymore, overwhelmed as it is by electric blankets, central heating and air-conditioning. People no longer have time to think, no longer want to think—are no longer allowed to think. At one point, André even sounds like a young Situationist: "We're bored, we're all bored; we've turned into robots." "But has it ever occurred to you, Wally," he confronts his incredulous friend, "that the process which creates this boredom that we see in the world now may very well be a self-perpetuating unconscious form of brainwashing created by a world totalitarian government based on money?" "Somebody who is bored is asleep," André follows up, "and somebody who's asleep will not say no!"[9] As far as he's concerned, the 1960s were "the last burst of the human being before he was extinguished. And that this is the beginning of the rest of the future ... and that from now on there will simply be all these robots walking around, feeling nothing, thinking nothing. And there will be almost nothing left to remind them that there once was a species called a human being, with feelings and thoughts."[10]

But as darkness closes in, and as peoples' lives become dominated by neo-liberalism's society of spectacle—"the guardian of sleep"— there will be others, like André, like millions of people the world over, who'll see things differently, who'll try to reconstruct a new future for the planet, who'll invent "new pockets of light," as André calls them. They'll resist by "creating a new kind of school or a new kind of monastery," a new kind of "'reserve'—islands of safety where history can be remembered and the human being can continue to function, in order to maintain the species through a Dark Age. In other words," André insists, "we're talking about an underground, which did exist during the Dark Ages in a different way ... And the purpose of this underground is to find out how to preserve the culture. How to keep things living."[11]

Perhaps above all else, then, this book is an attempt to explore the development of this new underground—Marxist style. It's a book that tries to dialogue and empathize with all progressives who, like André, are out on the road of life, wandering, believing in where they're headed, even if their exact destination is nowhere yet in sight, who are unable to turn back, and who honestly believe that the shortest distance between two points—between capitalism and communism—just may not be a straight line.

For that reason, this book isn't only dedicated to the magic of my loving wife and angel of a young daughter; it's equally dedicated to all twisted people everywhere, to those who yearn to do magic, who don't live the world of the straight and narrow, but who wend and weft their way forwards and sideways, and who conjure up, in their own special ways, their own revolutionary magic. Collectively, you're ensuring that this fragile little planet of ours becomes ever so slightly a better place to be in.

Andy Merrifield
São Paulo, Brazil
April 2010

INTRODUCTION

THE CIRCULATION OF REVOLT—
REAL AND FICTITIOUS MARXISM

A life devoted to the service of dangerous belief is more interesting than one confined to waiting piously for some sacks of flour.

Alejo Carpentier

Imagining

Imagine a Marxism that's not just critical analysis, that's liberated from debates about class and the role of the state, about the dictatorship of the proletariat. Imagine a Marxism that no longer calls itself "scientific" and has given up on the distinction between form and content, between appearance and essence. Imagine a Marxism that stakes out the contours of a new dream-like reality, a materialist fantasy, a fantastic materialism, a Marxism that utters sighs of disenchantment with the present yet affirms the most tenacious nostalgia for dreams of the future. Imagine a Marxism that doesn't so much abandon materialism as move on from it, shifting gear to advocate a more free-floating and ethereal political vision, a more phantasmal radicalism. Imagine a Marxism that opens up the horizons of the affirmative and reaches out beyond the dour realism of critical negativity.

In imagining all that, a lot of people would doubtless no longer be imagining Marxism. I think these people would be wrong, however, and in this book I will try to illustrate why. I want to show how Marxism can become more magical, how with imagination it can break out of a formalist straightjacket, how it can draft a more raw, more positive conception of life that ups the ante of mere critique and analysis, of yet another study showing how messed up our world is, how exploitative and degenerative its ruling class, how grotesque its economic system. All this can surely be taken as given nowadays, all that gloom and oppression smart people know to be characteristic of our society; they don't need highfalutin theory to tell them what they live out and work with each day. *Magical Marxism* demands something more of Marxism, something more interesting, perhaps even something more *radical*.

A Tale of Two Marxisms

Long before the spectacular collapse of the Soviet Bloc, people invoked the horrors of that system to dismiss the Marxist tradition *tout court*; for a while after the fall of the Berlin Wall Marxism's ideological credibility was below rock bottom. Moscow State University quickly erased Marxist-Leninist philosophy from its curriculum, and professors still teaching Marx in the Anglophone world were slim pickings; those few who did were easily sidelined as aging dinosaurs. Thinking people—even people thinking critically—suddenly reduced Marx's complex thought to a series of caricatures; a hammer and sickle going-out-of-business-sale was in motion and increasingly Marx was being dispatched to the dustbin of history.

But then, bit by bit, from the late 1990s onwards, around the time of the East Asian and Latin American crises, the big freeze began to thaw somewhat. Marx's bad rap gave way to a fresh reincarnation, to a revisionism in which his thought is taken to be more relevant than ever before: wrong, needless to say, about the revolutionary hopes of the working class, whose ranks are fast disappearing anyway and whose dreams of revolution tumbled down along with those giant statues of Lenin; yet right about the perils and crises of capitalism. Condé Nast's glossy *New Yorker* magazine embraced this kind of reasoning back in 1997, hailing "The Return of Karl Marx." Marx, the article claimed, lives on as a savvy "student of capitalism, and that is how he should be judged."[1]

These days, it's this sort of residual Marxism that prevails, if it prevails at all, a Marxism reduced to a rather effete framework for analyzing bourgeois political economy—a Marxism that helps keep World Bank and assorted financial bigwigs on their toes. To a certain degree, this is the Marxism that continues to be peddled by skeptics *and* believers alike. Even those who invoke Marxism as a theory of social change adopt a mode of thinking that pivots on the notion of critique, on a critical analysis that is often overly economic and technical, frequently rendered wooden by arcane debates amongst its aficionados. The net result is a Marxism that's systematic yet sterile, rigorous yet stilted, a Marxism much too boring to appeal to younger people, to a post-Seattle generation of radicals—even a *post*-post-Seattle generation who still want to change the world. Instead, Magical Marxism will be more fresh-faced and inquisitive, perhaps even more naive; it will be leaky not seamless, seeing possibilities and posing questions afterwards, mobilizing around instinct as much as intellect. It comes *without* a gray bushy beard. Many young people have no difficulty grasping why workers get ripped off and how capital accumulates in the hands of the wealthy. They know capitalism rarely lives up to its promises, to its supposed potential. Yet knowing this already means that they want more, want more from Marxism for inspiring their activism.

What's interesting about my generation of Marxists—forty-something Marxists—is how few of us there are. Prominent Marxists today seem to be a lot older, ex-hippies and Yippies and SDSers, those who came of age during the 1960s. Younger folk, younger left-leaning scholars and activists a generation down from me, perhaps even two generations down, are, on the other hand, often fazed by Marxism. If they're into critical theory, it's to Foucault, Derrida, and other "post-Marxist" thinkers they'll turn. If they're active, they'll likely be apart of a *new*-New Left—an array of disparate autonomous organizations like Global Exchange, the Ruckus Society, Critical Mass, and Reclaim the Streets, comprising young footloose campaigners against the World Bank, the International Monetary Fund and the World Trade Organization; then there are environmentalists with

Friends of the Earth, Greenpeace, the Sierra Club, and Rainforest Action Network; and still more battle against genetically modified foods and struggle for local organic food systems, fight for the preservation of indigenous rights and peasant democracy movements, or are black-masked anarchists and free-spirit rebels with a cause; all these people, however, are much more likely to root for Che or the Zapatistas than for Karl Marx.

The generational rift between the "used" New Left and the *new*-New Left is apparent, as are their organizational platforms and ideological bases. Marrying Marxism with this new school of post-Seattle activism remains very challenging, especially for sustaining resistance to neo-liberalism and against the corporatization of everyday life. Interestingly, my generation's Marxism is a tale of two Marxisms, because we're both young and old enough to have our feet in both camps: we understand the need to read *Capital* as well as the desire to put bricks through Starbucks' windows; we forty-somethings understand the political purchase of sober critique *and* slightly mad destructive acts.

Whattya Rebelling Against?

I was eight years old in 1968. I was a product of the 1970s and inherited the '60s generation's failings more than its successes. Growing up in drab, working-class Liverpool, I came of age with punk rock and in 1976 left school with barely enough qualifications to allow me access to a series of dead-end and deadening clerical jobs down at Liverpool's docks. It was an era when things were falling apart, when people were leaving the city, when companies were folding. I suppose I was lucky to be in work. I remember entering the labor market just as a new band cut a record, "Anarchy in the UK," which sounded fun, sounded good, seemed the right path to follow. Besides, the band's lead singer, Johnny Rotten, was practically the same age as me. He said he didn't know what he wanted, but knew what to do: "I wanna destroy, what's the point!" The refrain struck not just as a line from a song; it was more a political anthem, something I endorsed, perhaps even personified. The 1970s was a decade of lostness and crises and breakdowns, and when the Sex Pistols said there's NO FUTURE! NO FUTURE FOR YOU! I sort of believed them.

This anarchic spirit of dissatisfaction, of plague-on-your-house radicalism, has never really left me; I'm sure I'm not alone, that my generational peers feel it too. It was an impulse that actually brought me to Marxism, got tempered by Marxism, was softened by Marxism, a decade after I'd heard the Sex Pistols' NO FUTURE clarion call; and it was reading Marx during the UK miners' strike, and during Militant's grip over Liverpool's municipal politics,[2] that I began to believe there could be a future, that spontaneous destruction didn't have to be self-destruction, that it could be channeled intelligently, used to dramatize sensitive Marxist thought and activism.

One of the first Marxist texts I remember trying to read, trying to grapple with, was a 1960s classic: *One Dimensional Man* by the German émigré Herbert Marcuse, whose Hegelian-Freudian-Marxism saw a sinister "Total Administration" possessing the body and minds of everyday people, pacifying dissent, and instilling in them a delusional "happy consciousness."[3] Back in 1964, Marcuse claimed that the Total Administration permeated all reality; it didn't. But it almost did in the 1980s and certainly does now, circa 2010: it exists in defense laboratories, in executive offices, in governments, in machines, among timekeepers, managers, and efficiency experts, in mass communications, in publicity agencies, in multinational corporations and supranational organizations, in schools and universities. Via these consenting means, said Marcuse, all opposition is liquidated or else absorbed; all potential for sublimation, for converting sexual energies into political energies (and vice versa) is repressed and *desublimated*. The Reality Principle vanquishes the Pleasure Principle, convincing people that Reality is the *only* principle.

The other staple read from those long lost days was Guy Debord's *Society of the Spectacle*, from 1967, discovered quite by chance on a very dull wet day in Liverpool's "News from Nowhere" cooperative bookstore.[4] And even though I didn't get it all at first, bit by bit, thesis by thesis, I devoured it, and it devoured me, helping me learn why, exactly, I felt so ill suited for a normal life; the lesson would never be forgotten. What I loved about Debord back then is something I still love: his completely uncompromising radicalism—as well as his lyric poetry.

It was several years later that I got hooked on Marx himself, because then I was at college as a second-chance student, a "mature student," taking a class on Marx's *Capital* given by the eminent Marxist geographer David Harvey. Discovering Marx also revealed to me a passion for studying I never knew I had, one which hadn't been encouraged at school, a passion for learning and for reading *theory*. Harvey was (and still is) a master theoretician, and went through volume one of Marx's great book with a fine toothcomb, meticulously line-by-line, chapter-by-chapter, explaining its dense method of inquiry and complex mode of presentation probably better than Marx himself could have explained.[5]

Ten years on again, in 1999, just as Seattle's streets smoldered during demos against a World Trade Organization meeting, when not a few windows of Starbucks were reduced to shards, I taught my own class on Marx's *Capital* at Clark University in the United States, to a small group of impatient radical students, to those who'd inherited *my* generation's failings.[6] On the front page of the "syllabus" I reproduced an enlarged version of a postcard of Marx, his great gray mane superimposed onto a famous shot of Marlon Brando from *The Wild One*, of Johnny clad in biker's leather jacket. Karl, whattya rebelling against? Whaddya got? Very few partaking students had read Marx before, and fewer still had seen Brando's film from the early 1950s. But everybody in class soon agreed that Marx's analysis was brilliantly expressed and ominously familiar. The participants knew how those smug prophets of globalization closely follow Marx's prognosis, forever exerting their despotism over labor at the workplace at the same time as they champion, in daily life, the anarchy of unregulated markets. The entire globe seems to dance to the demands and caprices of capital, while "it converts the worker into a crippled monstrosity through the suppression of a whole world of productive drives and inclinations... The individual himself is divided up, transformed into the automatic motor of a detail operation."[7] You only have to ask any bank-teller, factory worker, clerk, hamburger-flipper or hired hand how this detailed operation feels, and what this despotism and market anarchy really means.

Students were looking at Marx with both fresh eyes and a healthy disdain for free-market mystification. They were also practically energized, inspired by the participation that seemed to be gathering steam back then; people were joining hands again, and direct action was alive and apparently quite well; not only in Seattle, but in Washington, in Genoa, and in Quebec City, especially as the batons flailed and the tear gas swirled. The streets were getting politicized, radicalized, filling in the void left by institutional politics; a more militant form of contestation was taking hold, mixing disciplined high-tech organizing with rambunctious carnivalesque spontaneity.

It was, that is, until September 11, 2001, when two planes sailed into the World Trade Center and 2,800 people lost their lives in a spectacular act of insanity, a tragic loss, and a disaster for New York, but a gift-horse for the Bush administration. Suddenly, bombs rained down on Afghanistan, later on Iraq; and then a new round of neo-conservative revanchist politics took hold against a backdrop of "get Osama Bin Laden"; almost overnight it dowsed post-Seattle political passions. In fact, a "new imperialism" was taking hold, characterized by what David Harvey calls "accumulation by dispossession," a giant jamboree of looting and fraud, force and finagling, putting a twenty-first-century Bushian spin on Marx's theory of "primitive accumulation."[8]

Too many examples abound to doubt Harvey's thesis, each with their own place-specific particularities, yet signaling everywhere fresh terrains for profitable speculation and market expansion: asset-stripping through mergers and acquisitions, corporate fraud, credit and stock manipulation, raiding of pension funds, biopiracy, massive "corporatization and privatization of hitherto public assets, to say nothing of the wave of privatization of water and public utilities that has swept the world."[9] Meanwhile, the

rolling back of regulatory frameworks designed to protect labor and the environment from degradation has entailed the loss of rights. The reversion of common property rights won through years of hard class struggle to the private domain has been one of the most egregious of all policies of dispossession pursued in the name of neo-liberal orthodoxy.[10]

What has likewise been inaugurated is "the death of politics," the death of politics as we once knew it, just when it seemed to be getting going, just when political subjects were voicing their discontent out on the streets, arguing and shouting in the public agora. Dissent and malcontent henceforth have no agora in which to be heard; the agora is walled off, privatized, managed by a private security company, subcontracted at the behest of some faceless corporation. Now, there's no place left where people can discuss realities that concern them, no place where they can be free of the crushing presence of mass media. Now, too, state and economy have congealed into an indistinguishable unity, managed by spin-doctors, spin-doctored by managers. Technocrats placate through anodyne consensus and broker disagreement—if there is anything still resembling disagreement. Now everybody is at the mercy of the expert or the specialist, and the most useful expert is the one who best serves his master.

With consummate skill, ruling elites have manufactured consent, organized ignorance of what is about to happen, and, immediately afterwards, the forgetting of whatever has been understood. The present is all that matters. In fashion, in music, everything has come to a halt: you must forget what came before, or else reinvent it as merchandise. Meanwhile, it's no longer acceptable to believe in the future. All usurpers, as Guy Debord says in his *Comments on the Society of the Spectacle*, usually have a common aim: "to make us forget that *they have only just arrived*."[11] And, seemingly above all else,

our perfect democracy constructs its own inconceivable foe: terrorism. Its wish is *to be judged by its enemies rather than by its results*. The history of terrorism is written by the state; it is therefore instructive. People can certainly never know everything about terrorism, but they must always know enough to persuade them that, compared with terrorism, everything else must be acceptable, or in any case more rational and democratic.[12]

With barely half a century behind it, Debord says in *Comments on the Society of the Spectacle*, "spectacular" society—spectacular for all the wrong reasons—has become even more powerful, perfecting its media extravaganzas, raising a whole generation who know nothing else and who are molded by its laws. In different circumstances, he'd have considered himself altogether satisfied with his first work on this subject from 1967, and left others to consider future developments. But, Debord claimed, in the present situation, in which his darkest prognostications have been outstripped, it seemed unlikely anyone else would do it.

More than ever do we need not only a new politics but a new politics that has a touch of the magical, that brews up some new radical moonshine, a new potion for stirring up our critical concepts, for making us practically intoxicated, that dreams the unimaginable, that goes beyond merely what is, beyond all accepted rules and logic, a politics that plays by its own rules, rules that have little to do with rationality or economic reason. In García Márquez's *One Hundred Years of Solitude*, Macondo's patriarch, José Arcadio Buendia, says he doesn't understand the sense of a political contest in which adversaries agree upon the rules.[13] I'm inclined to concur: agreeing upon the rules necessarily means engagement on *their* terms, which predictably means cooptation, institutionalization, defeat; moderation means *losing* even before you've begun to get going. As *The Coming Insurrection* recently voiced: "The specter of political representation has come to a close. From left to right, it's the same nothingness striking the pose of an emperor or a savior ... We're beginning to suspect that it's only *against voting itself* that people continue to vote."[14] So why not aim higher, why not reach for the stars, think vaster, and engineer something *wilder*? Perhaps the gulf between the professional world of politics and "the political" can be bridged magically, by a wilder, more magical activism? Perhaps this can prevent us from freefalling into the vacuous political chasm widening before us? Or perhaps down in this chasm, we magical mischief makers can rise up together?

Poetry of the Future

In *The Book of Embraces*, another Latin American scribe, Eduardo Galeano, celebrates "continual rebirth."[15] The book is a suggestive parable for progressives, because through it Galeano keeps hope alive, within the pages, within the heart; he drinks another round of rum with Miguel Mármol to commemorate, or *corummerate*, the fiftieth anniversary of the latter's execution by fascist forces. Miguel, you see, has undergone eleven deaths and eleven resurrections during the course of his combative life; he says that now, each morning, he's in the habit of getting up before dawn, and, as soon as his eyes are open, "sings and dances and hops around, which neighbors below don't like one bit." As the rum flows, they both propose a new venture: why not, they say, found "Magical Marxism: one half reason, one half passion, and a third half mystery"? "*Not a bad idea*," says Miguel.[16]

Not a bad idea indeed: *Magical Marxism* will try to turn these three halves into a whole, emphasizing the passionate and mysterious halves of a reality pushed beyond all reason—or nearly beyond. *Magical Marxism* explicitly reaches out towards the utopian, towards an affective politics of hope, at the same time as it delves into the heady subcontinent of dream, of latent desire; it will take to flight and fight like a latter-day Colonel Aureliano Buendia—who, remember, asserted to the death, with a fiery passion, a magical liberal cause. Marxism and Marxists have little choice these days but to do as the colonel did: to sneak about though narrow trails of permanent subversion, trails that reveal themselves in both theory and practice. Yet there are some *pistes* of magical possibility and mystery we can map out anew, conjure up and conceive in our imagination and then struggle to make real.

Marxism has a prodigious magical power to invent, to create its own values and ethics—an ethics higher, better and more durable than the hollow values that insist upon the sacrosanctity of free-market individualism. Marxism, in short, has at its disposal the power of struggle, of struggling to invent what Marx in *The Eighteenth Brumaire* deemed a new "poetry of the future."[17] The social revolution of the twenty-first century, paraphrasing one of Marx's most vital political insights, "cannot draw its poetry from the past, but only from the future." Those who partake in revolution, Marx cautions, must criticize themselves constantly, come back to what has already been accomplished in order to begin afresh, "deriding with unmerciful thoroughness the inadequacies of their earlier attempts," until, he says, "the situation has been *created* which makes all turning back impossible."[18]

The double determination of *poetry* and the *future* is legion in Magical Marxism. Not least because it's best adherents are perhaps lyric poets, people who don't necessarily write poetry but who somehow lead *poetic lives*, who literally *become-poets*, who *become-intense*, as Deleuze might have said, who internalize powerful feelings and poetic values, spontaneous values with no holds bared. The key point here is that Marxists make life a poem, adopt a *creative* as well as critical attitude towards living.[19] Walter Benjamin, for one, saw nothing so magical for finding an exit to a one-way street as the "profane illumination," as thinking about a new ideal, as dreaming in an ecstatically sober state; a "dialectical fairytale," Benjamin called it, something which disrupts "sclerotic ideals of freedom" and pushes the poetic life to its utmost limits of possibility—which is to say, towards a *poetic politics*. Subcomandante Marcos, in the jungle of Mexico's Chiapas, likewise advocates a poetic politics; ditto French and Caribbean surrealists during the 1940s, intellectuals like André Breton and Benjamin Péret but equally the Martinique Marxist poet Aimé Césaire, who, in the pages of journal *Tropiques*, claimed that "true civilizations" are "poetic shocks: the shock of the stars, of the sun, the plant, the animal, the shock of the round globe, of the rain, of the light, the shock of life, the shock of death."[20] Politics should be like poetry: something *hot*, the voice of hotness from the margins, libertine excess, anti-science, red-hot bubbling *altermarxisme*.

Poetry, accordingly, becomes something ontological for Magical Marxists, a state of Being- and Becoming-in-the-world, the invention of life and the shrugging off of tyrannical forces that are wielded over that life. Poetic lives destabilize accepted notions of order and respectability, of cool rationality and restraint. Magical Marxism shows little restraint to the status quo, and proclaims what André Breton and the surrealists proclaimed in the 1920s: the power of absolute nonconformity and marvelous unreality. It's a credo that helps propel Magical Marxism into the future, a future invented out of a spontaneous overflow of powerful feeling, of dragging present reality along with it, of leaping across the ontological gap between the here and the there, between the now and the time to come.

Plato, that ancient Greek ideologue, was the first to recognize the danger of dreamy poets in our midst, disrupting the dignified harmony of a "naturally ordered" society. In Book Ten of *The Republic*, he rightly reminds us how poets arouse the part of the spirit that destroys good reason, implanting an "evil constitution in the soul of each individual," terribly debilitating if it reaches audiences in the public square, since there it can incite mass disorder and civic disobedience. What are basic ingredients for Magical Marxists—desire, dream, and pleasure—thus have no place in any Platonic republic: "If you receive the pleasure-seasoned Muse of song and epic, pleasure and pain will be kings in your city instead of law."[21]

Serial Dreams and Insomnia Plagues

Magical Marxism will attempt to mimic the fantasy world of Magical Realism and will posit an intellectual and political project in which resistance entails a poetic transformation of reality, in which power isn't so much taken as neutralized, in which society isn't so much overthrown as reinvented. Magical Realism has as its muse actual reality, yet converts this often stark reality into fantasy, into fantastic and phantasmal subjective visions that become more real than objective reality itself. These visions are like little fibs that bizarrely tell the truth, that invent new truths or lay bare truths we somehow relate to, almost instinctively, almost without being able to see them. Indeed, few Magical Realist truths are measurable or quantifiable. Who could believe, as readers of *One Hundred Years of Solitude* are asked to believe, that people are born with tails or are followed around by dainty yellow butterflies? And who levitates up to heaven or habitually lives to well over a hundred?

The insomnia plague that afflicts the inhabitants of Macondo is another weird, magical realist construct in *One Hundred Years of Solitude*. The insomnia plague meant not only that nobody could sleep, but also, when it struck, that nobody ever needed to sleep. At first, everyone is happy in this jetlagged, hallucinogenic state and no one is alarmed because there is always so much work to do and barely enough time to do it. "If we don't ever sleep again, so much the better," José Arcadio Buendia says. "That way we can get more out of life" (p. 43). But soon people traipse about busying themselves with all sorts of inane activity and converse endlessly with each other, fidgeting around and telling the same old jokes over and over again, jokes that nobody seems to remember having already been told before, sometimes just minutes ago. So it goes for a while, until there are a few in Macondo who slowly begin to yearn for sleep again. Not so much because they need sleep, nor out of fatigue: more out of a desperate nostalgia for dreams. And yet, with the insomnia plague, very slowly, ever so progressively and subtly, the insomniac forgets about dreaming and, in the end, loses their memory entirely. All that now persists is an eternal present, a contaminated present, a repressive situation accepted as a perfectly natural reality, as the only reality.

In Macondo, the insomnia plague was transmitted by mouth, by contaminated food and drink, and there's a sense in which processed food is doing the same today, deadening our ability to remember where anything comes from, offering us instant salty and sugary stimulation that maintains us in a state of soporific wakefulness. Meanwhile, mass media disinformation has us sink almost irrevocably into a quicksand of forgetfulness, rendering us decrepit well before we've grown old, turning us into people who no longer remember even the recent past or have any capacity to see beyond what immediately is, what exists right in front of our noses, often on some banal, two-dimensional high-tech screen. Our bodies don't feel fatigue even as our minds switch off. We're exhilarated by the dizzy delights of endless work, of being permanently online, of talking endlessly on portable telephones, of perpetual TV with hundreds of channels, of endless news and endless sound-bites, endless stores that never close, endless commodities along endless supermarket aisles, of throwaway "serial dreams" we know are there, there at a price. Our dreams are cold wide-awake realities created by somebody else, at our expense.

Of course, we've always had our Colonel Aureliano Buendias who, inspired by strange gypsies, have been hell bent on staving off the insomnia plague, who've upheld the power of dreams, dreams of a new future, of new Macondos arising out of damp swampland. Notwithstanding them, the insomnia plague has been persistent and recalcitrant and perhaps it's only now, only quite recently, in this crisis-ridden age, that the plague is beginning to wear off, that we're prepared to fight against our memory loss, against our inability to dream of the future. Perhaps our contaminated present is giving way at last, and we're on the cusp of a new era in which people might even dream again, and which maybe, just maybe, might become a magical one?

Real and Fictitious Marxism

In *The Interpretation of Dreams*, Freud says things are always better "slept on."[22] I want to use this metaphor to emphasize the power of dreams, of dream-works and political wish-fulfillment. For Freud, the mental forces contesting "the reality principle" operate in the unconscious, in a non-repressive realm where fantasy and desire retain a high degree of freedom. Needless to say, the reality principle tries to bring this free will into line, because, like all ruling powers, it insists that fantasy and pleasure are both useless and untrue. Reality obeys only the laws of reason never the language of dream. Yet imagine a Marxism scripted by the language of dream, a Marxism that valorizes tabooed images of freedom. Imagine a Magical Marxist pleasure principle.

To what extent, though, can anything like this be true, actually be real? Well, that depends upon what you dream up, what your dream-thought and dream-content bestows upon wide-awake reality, how it re-appropriates that reality. And that depends upon your imagination: whether you see in order to believe, or whether you believe in order to see. It's incredible, for instance, how much of the bourgeois order is based upon fantasy, upon a dream world in which ruling fantasies become true because those who rule really believe they're true, because they *make* these fantasies come true. Through active will and not a little force, the bourgeoisie turns its economic pleasure principle into a political reality principle, and vice versa.

Take the greatest bourgeois fantasy of all, the world's biggest pipedream we all know is somehow true: the stock market. How much of that is predicated on fantasy and wishful-images of the future, on hope and desire, on the capacity of rampant imagination to create a purely fictitious looking-glass realm of riches? Here, participants recognize such a reality because they believe in it, because they *see what they believe.* Moreover, they do so despite linguistic differences and national frontiers; they speak a "standard language" everybody understands, have a common convergence, without forsaking their own native tongues, often never relinquishing their specific currencies. What an amazing human utopia this is, what an effective transnational localism! What a pity the left can't dream up its own equivalent fictitious life-form and then make it real.

True, this financial system is a reality *necessary* for the functioning of capitalist society, for collapsing temporal and spatial barriers to accumulation, for lubricating the free flow of capital between different spheres of production and exchange, for financing costly "fixed capital" assets (like factories, warehouses, offices, and infrastructural developments); true, too, this fantasy world of predicting financial futures and creating imaginary stock ahead of actual commodity production is very risky. And for sure the system periodically comes unstuck—has to come unstuck—and crises prevail for a while. Optimism with regard to ever-rising stock values becomes what Marx calls "the fountainhead of all manner of insane forms."[23] Marx knows that if *all* connection with the actual expansion process of capital is "completely lost," then "the conception of capital as something with automatic self-expansion properties is thereby strengthened." At that point, he says, "the accumulation of debts appears as an accumulation of capital." At that point, "everything is doubled and trebled and transformed into a *mere phantom of the imagination*";[24] and at "the height of this distortion," without any solidity other than massive amounts of credit money and fictitious capital circulating in the economy, the bourgeois edifice crumbles, revealed as "*wholly illusory.*"[25]

But let's face it, this phantasmal system comes unstuck a lot less frequently than it should, and much less often than its critics would expect, or hope for. And even when it does come unstuck it has a handy habit of picking itself up, getting itself bailed out, usually by the state or through greater exploitation of labor. The reasons why it breaks down so relatively infrequently relate perhaps to Marx's buzzwords "mere" and "wholly": if the system becomes *merely* phantasmal or *wholly* illusory, then sooner or later it brushes up against a hardnosed reality principle, just as the realist element always conditions the magical imagination of somebody like García Márquez.

I say all this, however, as our financial system continues to stretch its credibility, and our credulity, to the limit: *fictitious* capital now sets the tone for *real* capital, pioneers the utopian frontiers of the possible, of future capital accumulation. Now it's as if the fictitious realm drags along the real realm. Isn't this a magnificent model for any Magical Marxism? Wouldn't the magical side of Marxism operate in much the same way as fictitious capital operates for the bourgeoisie? "Real" materialism would be dragged along by the will (and hope) of "fictitious" idealism, inventing a new basis for a more advanced, higher realism, raising the glass ceiling of the possible, of the believable, of real reality.

Revolt, too, can (and does) circulate like fictitious money capital: almost illusory, passing across frontiers and drifting through global space, often through cyberspace, exchanging itself, getting converted into other denominations of place-specific radicalism. Thus the materiality of revolt has an *immaterial* quality: it's a feeling, a structure of feeling, a distant solidarity, a "scream" (as John Holloway puts it), a faint wish, a weak hope that inspires, stimulates, and angers, that makes people want to organize and act where they are, any way they can. It's the rumor of the Zapatistas' struggle in the bush inspiring faraway movements in urban wildernesses; that's how fictitious revolt gets valorized, how its circulation from one moment to another can become a material future position, a grounded synthesis of the totality of particular moments. Specific campaigns here need to circulate in the overall process of global revolt the way capital circulates for Marx, as described in his introduction to the *Grundrisse*: as unique moments in a general unity of process, as dialectical movements undergoing continuous "quantity-quality" change. This image gives new meaning to the notion that capital is in fact labor, that labor is capital, production is consumption, consumption is production, etc. The circulation of immaterial revolt is a factor of production in concrete subversion.

If you look closely at Marx's analysis of the credit system, or at any discussion of today's financial system in the bourgeois press, much of the terminology resembles that of Ernst Bloch, our greatest utopian Marxist. Everywhere you encounter notions of "future positions," everything is anticipated, estimated, projected and promised, everything is future revenue, future exchange, all is intangible and nominal. In this system, we locate, from the other side of the political spectrum, our most creative and indefatigable political impulse: *the principle of hope*. In the 1930s, as Nazi flames engulfed continental Europe, Bloch undertook a mammoth study of what the Magical Marxist spirit might be. In our own war-torn times, he bequeaths us "wishful images" of the future, and a lot of what he wrote sounds like a great Homeric epic poem, a delirious siesta in a Márquezian hammock, full of Eldorados and Edens, of Münchhausen Macondos from a distant planet we call the earth-to-come, the one we've never yet seen. (Bloch loved to juggle with utopian ideas of the "Not-Yet-Conscious.") Bloch's magical mystery tour emphasizes invention, riding the sorceress's broomstick, engineering new concepts rather than discovering them, inventing a new world in which the "anticipatory element" guarantees its eventual realization—just like the world's financial markets.

Magic and Everyday Life

It's in our magical wish-images and dream-thoughts that Marxists might valorize the principle of hope, in the realm of the Not-Yet-Conscious. All of which suggests that we "Not Get Real." By "not getting real," I mean a refusal, a denial, of the "real world," of the reality imposed upon people across the globe. As such, Magical Marxism, as I'll construe it here, is no longer a Marxist "science," a science of exposing real truth hiding behind false appearance; it's rather about inventing other truths, about expanding the horizons of possibility, about showing how people can turn a project of life into a life-project that blooms. In a nutshell, the thesis I want to explore in this book is that Magical Marxism is about invention not discovery, about irrationality not rationality. There's no fetishism anymore, no absolute truth hidden behind innumerable fictions and false images of the world: Magical Marxism means creating another fantasy in light of the ruling fantasy; its critical power doesn't come from criticism but from an ability to disrupt and reinvent, to create desire and inspire hope. Here the Marxist earth spirit voyages beyond science, beyond the state, beyond debates about the "working class," into the realm of the inauthentic, into a paradise we know can only prevail as a paradise lost.

Magical Marxism airbrushes the role of the working class in social change, and, as I hope to show, does so for a good reason. Suffice it to say here that Marx set himself the task of probing the possibilities of overthrowing the economic and political system we call "capitalism." Downgrading the "historical mission" of the working class is not, then, to downgrade the historical mission of Marxism: it's to suggest that, above all else, Marxism is a theory and practice of how to live beyond capitalism, of how to undermine capitalism, of how social solidarity is forged between assorted people, irrespective of whether they belong to the "working class" or not. Activists around the world, as André Gorz has forcefully argued, don't necessarily identify themselves with "work" anymore, nor with others in the act of work. Neither do these people want to empower themselves in work, seize control of work. Rather, they want to *free* themselves from work itself, to reject the nature, content and (non-) meaning of work, as well as the traditional strategies and organizational forms of the workers' movement.[26] Once upon a time, labor movement rank and filers discovered one another in the factory; nowadays, solidarity and battle lines have opened out on a global scale, out into the totality of social space, while cutting deeper into everyday life. Now, the struggle is about taking back and redefining non-work life, about *everyday anti-capitalism and post-capitalist communality.*

"Magic plays an immense role in everyday life," the Marxist visionary of everyday life, Henri Lefebvre, claimed back in 1947, "be it in emotional identification and participation with other people or in the thousand little rituals and gestures used by every person, every family, every group."[27] For Lefebvre, everyday life is, on the one hand, the realm colonized by the commodity, undermined by all kinds of alienation; yet, at the same time, it's the primal arena for meaningful social change—the only arena—"the inevitable starting point for the realization of the possible." "The most extraordinary things are also the most everyday," says Lefebvre, bringing the two domains together, teasing out the radical dialectical force of "the magical" and "the everyday." So when, in November 2008, the French DST secret police invaded Tarnac, a sleepy village nestled in Limousin's Millevaches plateau, cracking down on a group of young "subversives" who'd transformed a moribund locality into a vibrant community, re-energizing communal life, giving it a convivial atmosphere of resistance, one can ask: is the state's fear not so much of "terrorism" as of people's desire to transform everyday life, to live differently, beyond institutional strictures, beyond a capitalism as we know it? Is it the re-conquest of everyday territory, superimposed upon the state's cartography, that gives Tarnac's activism its edge, its threatening logic, its potential magic?

Lefebvre knows plenty about the magical everyday; so do the surrealists, who spotted the poetic force of everyday objects, of everyday encounters. Yet for the surrealists, "the marvelous" is frequently found in hallucinogenic moments, often beyond (and below) everyday life, in umbrellas and lobsters, in sewing machines and on dissecting tables. Indeed, as Alejo Carpentier, a pioneering magical realist and founder member of the Cuban Communist Party, once said: such is a "poverty of the imagination."[28] What's more unsettling, more imaginative, Carpentier thinks, is when the magical isn't fabricated, isn't self-consciously exaggerated, but instead is pursued in reality itself, in the strangely commonplace. "The marvelous begins to be unmistakably marvelous," Carpentier says, "when it arises from an unexpected alteration of reality."[29] We find magic in

> the unexpected richness of reality or in an amplification of the scale and categories of reality, perceived with particular intensity by virtue of an exaltation of the spirit that leads it to a kind of extreme state. The phenomenon of the marvelous presupposes faith. Those who do not believe in saints cannot cure themselves with the miracles of saints, nor can those who are not Don Quixotes enter, body, soul, and possessions, into the world of Amadís of Gaul or Tirant le Blanc.[30]

This passage from Carpentier is important for the construction of Magical Marxism because it emphasizes the *concreteness* of the magical state, an idealism that isn't hyper-idealism, a transformative politics that isn't just a politics of occultism: the realm of the magical is a raw, latent, and omnipresent reality before one's own eyes, awaiting exalted alteration, there for believers to take. It's curious, for example, how practically all the magical realism of *One Hundred Years of Solitude* occurs within the four walls of Ursula Buendia's house. Everything flows through this building: all the extravagant binges and pernicious wars, all the inventions and amorous affairs, all the alchemy and magic, all Colombian history and geography. (Earlier drafts of *One Hundred Years of Solitude* actually bore the title *The House*.) That's presumably why García Márquez always reckoned his appetite for fantasy and magic was only ever whetted by ordinary daily life. We Magical Marxists can take stuff from this: for us, it's everyday life that's the stake and staging of Magical Marxist politics; everyday life is the realm of *decommodification* and *remagification*, the new twenty-first-century dialectic of enlightenment.

One of the unfortunate things about contemporary capitalist society is how work life clashes with everyday life, how the former scuffs up against the latter, dislocates wide-awake time as it creates dislocations within the self. For the bulk of the world's population, working life is dead life, a meaningless waste of time, the realm of alienation and watching the clock, of yearning for weekends, for a vacation, for retirement. You work so you can afford to stay in work, afford the expenses that work entails, afford to be located near to (or far from) work. As it self-perpetuates its own nothingness, work is the realm of *anti-magic*, a nightmare that weighs heavily on the brain of the living, in which one assumes one's role in the detailed division of labor, when one obediently fulfils one's duty as *abstract labor*, as labor in general, as labor that's quantifiable, measurable, indifferent to content, indifferent to the nature and capacities of *concrete* people.

Magic is concrete: its arena is real life. Magic is an imaginary representation of one's real conditions of life. It breeds outside the tumult of capitalist modernity, beyond its cacophony of screeching automobiles and gridlocked traffic, of alarms and buzzers, of ringing and technological gadgets that get in your face, that gnaw away inside your brain, that stifle your imagination and prevent you from dreaming. Magic flourishes when everyday life is free life, time off work, time of anti-work, or of work in its *non-*money-form. As the young Marx voiced in his *Economic and Philosophical Manuscripts*:

> [a] worker does not confirm himself in his work, but denies himself, feels miserable and not happy, does not develop free mental and physical energy, but mortifies his flesh and ruins his mind. Hence the worker feels himself only when he is not working; when he is working he does not feel himself. He is at home when he is not working, and not at home when he is working.[31]

And yet, neither are workers really at home even when they're not working, given that work and home, production and reproduction—the totality of daily life—have been subsumed, colonized and invaded by exchange value. In leisure time, workers become consumers, mere bearers of money; private life thereby becomes the domain of the advertisement, of fashion, of convenience and processed foods, of pop stars and soap operas, of dishwashers and tumble dryers. Boundaries between economic, political, and private life have pretty much dissolved. All consumable time and space are raw material for new products, for new commodities, for extended money relations.

By contrast, the realm of magic isn't the kingdom of *homo economicus* or *homo industrialis*, but of *homo ludens*, of man and woman the player, an idea so dear to Henri Lefebvre's ludic concept of what everyday life *ought to be*. Everyday politics, too, necessitates fun, means creating a stir and kicking up a fuss; play nourishes politics just as political people should be themselves *homo ludens*. The idea harks back to Johan Huizinga, whose 1938 text bearing the same stamp affirmed the vitality of the "play element" in human culture. There's a primordial quality about play, Huizinga said, something radically at odds with seriousness. Play is both in and beyond "real" life, steps out of everyday life from within everyday life, and enters an ephemeral sphere of activity, where it takes on its own magical character and often expresses freedom and joy.

Play *subserves* our culture, Huizinga thought, satisfying emotional and psychological needs, fostering "play-communities" and "play-grounds," maintaining aesthetic balance and reproductive interests. At the same time, it also *subverts* culture, operates beyond its "normal" limits, within a circumscribed world, a hallowed realm that can undermine the seriousness of everyday life, and the earnestness of working life. "In this sphere of sacred play," said Huizinga, "the child and the poet are at home with the savage."[32] Despite all this, Huizinga nonetheless wondered: "To what extent does the civilization we live in still develop in play-forms? How far does the play-spirit dominate the lives of those who share that civilization? The 19th century had lost many of the play-elements so characteristic of former ages. Has this leeway been made up or has it increased?"[33] The answer, Huizinga knew, was unequivocal: it has surely *increased*. "More and more," Huizinga lamented, "the sad conclusion forces itself upon us that the play-element in culture has been on the wane ever since the 18th century, when it was in full flower.

Civilization today is no longer played, and even where it still seems to play it is false play—I had almost said, it plays false, so that it becomes increasingly difficult to tell where play ends and non-play begins."[34] To lose the play-element, however, is to lose a part of ourselves, to limit ourselves somehow, to diminish our imagination, to wish away magic, to reduce its scope. "To be a social culture-creating force," Huizinga insisted, "this play-element must be pure," that is to say, purely magical.[35]

Magical Marxism, as we'll see in the chapters to come, lodges itself somewhere within the interstices of a liberated time and liberated space, between the right to free time and the right to free space, a space of self-affirmation and "self-unfolding," a space-time of autonomous activity, of intellectual, artistic, and practical endeavor. The political stakes are different today; a new radical Marxist politics must be invented, re-imagined, willy-nilly, by actors of many diverse stripes, by people who join hands, make friends, and who organize themselves around changing life. The extinction of political economy, Marx's time-honored goal, is no longer a workplace affair: it's a question of reclaiming the totality of everyday life—of work life and daily life, of filling it with joy and magic, with play and collective struggle, with dream and imagination, with a poetry of the future.

Might Marxism ever create in real life the magical everyday of that delirious utopia of Macondo? Returning to the utopian question years later, in 1982, at his Nobel lecture, García Márquez had this to say to those of us who assume our solitude is preordained and forever:

> we, the inventors of tales, who will believe anything, feel entitled to believe that it is not yet too late to engage in the creation of a new and sweeping utopia of life, where no one will be able to decide for others how they die, where love will prove true and happiness be possible, and where peoples condemned to one hundred years of solitude will have, at last and forever, a second opportunity on earth.[36]

As our second millennia insomnia plague begins to dissipate, this is one everyday dream-state I'll happily toast and cradle in my sleep—in a hammock, somewhere warm and sunny, amid the yellow butterflies and little gold fishes...

1

LIVING AN ILLUSION:
BEYOND THE REALITY OF REALISM

Our life is a voyage—In winter and in the night—We seek our passage... There is the fatigue and cold of morning in this well traveled labyrinth, like an enigma we have to resolve. It is a reality of illusions through which we have to discover the possible richness of reality.

Guy Debord

Real nature being lost, all becomes nature.

Pascal

No carnivorous plants grow, no toucans fly, nor do you find cyclones in *The Discourse on Method*.

Alejo Carpentier

I'm much closer to Rabelais' craziness than to Descartes' discipline.

Gabriel García Márquez

Between Spectacle and Solitude

On the face of it, 1967 is a forgotten year, disappearing into relative insignificance alongside the heady 365 days that followed it—1968, the year everybody remembers as the most remarkable of that decade. Yet some pretty noteworthy things happened in 1967: the "Be-ins" at San Francisco's Golden Gate Park and the psychedelic "Summer of Love"; Che was captured and executed in Bolivia and Detroit erupted with some of America's worst race riots; Jim Morrison of The Doors sang "We want the world and we want it NOW!" and Jimi Hendrix wondered "Are You Experienced?"; The Beatles, too, released what many believe their best album, *Sgt. Pepper's Lonely Hearts Club Band*, and Allen Ginsberg levitated the Pentagon in a giant medieval carnival protesting the Vietnam War.

But perhaps *the* highlight of 1967 was something apparently more minor: the publication of two books, one ostensibly fact, the other a magical sort of fiction. People still talk about these books and with their spellbinding brilliance they continue to inspire (one still sells bundles, too). Although these books are both radical, and each radically different from the other—appearing on different continents and in different languages—they both have something important in common, and it's perhaps no coincidence that they should appear concurrently beside *Sgt. Pepper's* and Jimi Hendrix. Indeed, each succeeds in changing our perceptions about reality and about ourselves; each somehow turns the world we thought we knew upside down as well as inside out, and each, in turn, proceeds to put that world back together again, right side up. These two books are *The Society of the Spectacle* by Guy Debord and *One Hundred Years of Solitude* by Gabriel García Márquez.

Few people would probably think of Debord, the prophet of spectacular capitalism, as a magical realist, just as fewer again would likely see García Márquez, the prophet of magical realism, as a theorist of the society of the spectacle. And yet, it's possible to conceive both men in this guise and to posit their respective masterpieces as works of art that push reality somehow beyond realism.[1] In what follows, I want to bring these two texts together into dialogue—a strange dialogue that will help initially map out the ontological contours of Magical Marxism. Perhaps we can say that the four decades since the publication of these two books has been marked by both solitude and spectacle, by a spectacular solitude, and in saying this it's true that *The Society of the Spectacle* and *One Hundred Years of Solitude* remain two darkly pessimistic texts. In a way, they pinpoint the '68 generation's shortcomings as much as embody its utopian desires. Here, Colonel Aureliano Buendia, a '60s-style anarchist, an *altermondialiste avant la lettre*, sets the brooding tone: organizing 32 armed uprisings in the name of a radical liberal cause, he lost every one of them.

On the other hand, with their almost supernatural lucidity, their dazzling erudition and phantasmal and mystical ideas, *The Society of the Spectacle* and *One Hundred Years of Solitude* also transmit a strange sort of optimism, a backdoor sense of hope, and offer another take on what our lives might be. In consequence, each book shows us how reality can be represented differently, how more acute (and astute) forms of subjectivity can create a more advanced sense of realism, a different type of objectivity, a more radical and active one. Each text, in a nutshell, equips progressives with the imaginative tools for staking out new trails of permanent subversion; narrow ones, of course...

Reality *Détourned*

It's not clear exactly when Debord began writing his political prose poem, his exposé of the modern form of the commodity. In a letter to Danish artist Asger Jorn, dated January 13, 1964, Debord said: "in the book I am presently preparing I hope that one will see, more clearly than in other preceding works, that the Situationist International worked at the center of problems modern society poses."[2] At the end of 1964, Debord told another friend that his book "will not appear before the following year."[3] In fact, *The Society of the Spectacle* eventually hit Parisian bookstores in November 1967 when working-class grievances festered and when post-war capitalism was entering a new more economically prodigious and ideologically devious phase. With its 221 short, intriguing theses, aphoristic in style and peppered with irony, *The Society of the Spectacle* is quirkily Marxian, uniting a left-wing Hegel with a materialist Feuerbach, a bellicose Machiavelli with a utopian Karl Korsch, a military Clausewitz with a romantic Georg Lukács. In so doing, Debord gives us stirring crescendos of literary power, compelling evocations of a world in which unity spells division and truth spells falsity. It is, Debord says, a topsy-turvy world where everything and everybody partakes in a perverse paradox, a world in which "the true" *really is* "a moment of the false."[4]

Debord wanted to *détourn* the reality of this non-reality, this world where ugliness signifies beauty, dishonesty honesty, and stupidity intelligence. He wanted to subject it to his own dialectical inversion, inverting the inversion, flipping it with his own spirit of negation, and in the process wrote a unique work of political art, utterly without precedent. *Détournement* is a key motif in Debord's political and literary arsenal: it pillories and negates existing reality in the name of a higher reality, in the name of a reality-invented; *détournement* is a new state of reinvented consciousness that rocks people out of their slumbering torpor, out of their modern passivity, monkey-wrenching received meaning in bourgeois reality, reveling in collective feats of resistance and acts of lampooning, sometimes outrageously crude and abusive, other times stylishly nuanced and daring. Squatting and occupying buildings and streets are classic examples of *détournement*, as are graffiti and free associative art. *Détournement* twists everything around, recreates meaning out of nonsense and nonsense out of meaning, highlights absurdity through the creation of a different sort of epic absurdity.

Each thesis of *The Society of the Spectacle* is itself an explosive charge, a sequence of *détournement*, likely drafted at night, when tipsy, and honed by day, when sober. There's a lucidity and madness here only the schizophrenia of the day and night can induce: "The spectacle says nothing more than 'that which appears is good, and that which is good appears'" (Thesis #12); "the spectacle is the new map of the world, a map which exactly covers its territory" (Thesis #31); "the spectacle is *capital* to such a degree of accumulation that it becomes an image" (Thesis #34, original emphasis); "the real consumer becomes a consumer of illusions. The commodity is this factually real illusion, and the spectacle is its general manifestation" (Thesis #47). The surrealist undertow of *The Society of the Spectacle* conjures up the realm of dream, releases unconscious yearnings and sublimates deep political desire. At times, the tone reincarnates Compte de Lautréamont, the true inventor of *détournement*, whose *Maldoror* (1869) expressed similar incandescent chants, similar mental derangements. Maldoror, who curses God and hails the "old ocean," is a bandit, Lautréamont says, "perhaps seven leagues away from this land" or "maybe only a few steps from you."[5] Lautréamont wrote only at night, always at night, seated at a piano, drinking absinthe, hammering out words at the same time as he hammered out notes. *Maldoror* is infamous for deliberately opaque similes that became touchstones of Surrealism: "the chance meeting on a dissection table of a sewing machine and an umbrella"; "beautiful like the law of arrested development in the chest of adults whose propensity for growth isn't in rapport with the quantity of molecules that their organism assimilates."[6]

Following Lautréamont, chance meetings of disparate elements and their dialectical inversions give birth to terrible beauties, and to haunting magical truths, like "the epic poem" of the spectacle, "which cannot be concluded by the fall of any Troy"; like the way the spectacle "doesn't sing the praises of men and their weapons, but of commodities and their passions," and "every commodity, pursuing its passion, unconsciously realizes something higher: the becoming-world of the commodity, which is also the becoming-commodity of the world" (Thesis #66). And like the chance meeting of a boy with a crate of frozen mullet, and the ice he'd discover with his cherished grandfather, and how the whole of *One Hundred Years of Solitude* begins with this one image, gets *détourned* from this one image of wonderment and dazzling invention, so it was years later, in May 1967, a month before *Sgt. Pepper's* unleashed itself in record stores across the globe, that *One Hundred Years of Solitude* went on sale in Buenos Aires, opening with García Márquez's re-imagined childhood memory: "Many years later, as he faced the firing squad, Colonel Aureliano Buendia was to remember that distant afternoon when his father took him to discover ice" (p. 9).

Reality as Fantasy

Legend has it that García Márquez and wife Mercedes were driving with their two sons to Acapulco for a family vacation, when the novel deemed a Latin American *Don Quixote* suddenly came to him in an epiphany, beginning with the chance encounter that distant afternoon when Gabriel's grandfather took him to see the ice. Turning the car around, García Márquez returned to Mexico City and for the next 18 months tapped away on his Olivetti electric typewriter a story that had been in his head for 18 years. "All I wanted to do," he recounted, years afterwards, "was to leave a literary picture of the world of my childhood which was spent in a large, very sad house with a sister who ate earth, a grandmother who prophesized the future, and countless relatives of the same name who never made much distinction between happiness and insanity."[7]

Yet the bizarre saga of the Buendias in the village of Macondo, hacked out of the middle of damp Colombian jungle, not far from a barnacle-encrusted Spanish galleon, takes on a reality way beyond a quaint family romance: it's a tale of paradise found and lost, an everyday saga of a magnificent and miserable humanity, a mad dream of a host of damaged characters whose only goal in life was to live to the full a wonderful human adventure. And they rarely let facts get in their way of their own stories, of the emergencies of their own passions. García Márquez always claimed that the Caribbean world of magic and drama, of mythological societies and fabulous plants, of pre-Colombian cults and slavery, of crumbling colonial empires, provided a taste for fantasy that was only barely exaggerated historical reality, oral memory as conveyed through the loosely grounded realism of his grandmother and grandfather.

An adolescent penchant for bad Latin American poetry and Marxist texts (lent to him on the sly by his history teacher), together with a revelatory reading of *A Thousand and One Nights* and Kafka's *Metamorphosis*—when Gregor Samsa wakes up one morning transformed into a gigantic insect—convinced García Márquez he wanted to be a writer, that he could be a writer; "I opened it [*A Thousand and One Nights*], and I read that there was a guy who opened up a bottle and out flew a genie in a puff of smoke, and I said, 'Wow, this is amazing!' This was more fascinating to me than anything else that had happened in my life up to that point." All that, too, convinced García Márquez that writing should be a poetic transformation of reality, that the source of creation is always reality, always somehow embedded in reality, yet a reality in which imagination is an instrument in its production and re-creation. The discovery was "like tearing off a chastity belt," García Márquez said; "you can throw away the fig leaf of rationalism," provided "you don't then descend into total chaos and irrationality."[8] From this standpoint, imagination is one moment in the production of reality, a rhetorical re-description of reality, an aspect of hidden joinery in the edifice of social creation. Which itself isn't so *un*Marxist: Marx recognized how imagination is a force of production, a dynamic element in any labor process: "A spider conducts operations which resemble those of the weaver, and a bee would put many a human architect to shame by the construction of its honeycomb cells. But what distinguishes the worst of architects from the best of bees is that the architect builds the cell in his mind before he constructs it in wax. At the end of every labor process, a result emerges which had already been conceived by the worker at the beginning, hence already existed ideally."[9]

Against this methodological backdrop, *One Hundred Years of Solitude* was typed out, poetically reviving childhood memories, kick-starting a new literary genre bearing the name "Magical Realism," guided by an ever so wafer-thin line separating reality from fantasy, and fantasy from reality. Magical Realism draws artistic sustenance from reality, yet converts this reality into a reality *détourned*, into a reality of illusions. And somehow, as readers, as narrative appropriators, we live out this illusory reality ourselves, make our way through its labyrinth, believe it and believe in it, relate to it somehow, and end up joining in, wanting to participate in its folly, in its mad inventions and alchemy, in its outrageous endeavors and voracious binges, in its tenderness and compassion, in its rage. Therein, all power goes to the imagination; "things have a life of their own," Melquiades, the gypsy magician reminded José Arcadio Buendia, Macondo's patriarch. "It's simply a matter of waking up their souls" (p. 9). José Arcadio hardly needs reminding: the patriarch's "unbridled imagination always went beyond the genius of nature and even beyond miracles and magic." He taught his two wayward sons, José Arcadio and Aureliano, the wild man who'd eventually run off with the gypsies and the withdrawn child who'd become one of the nation's most fabled warriors, to read and write and do sums; "and he spoke to them about the magical wonders of the world, not only where his learning had extended, but forcing the limits of his imagination to extremes" (p. 20).

Reality Forgotten, Reality as (Non-)Separation

One of the most bizarre Magical Realist episodes in *One Hundred Years of Solitude* is Macondo's insomnia plague. As the sickness takes hold, the insomniac is in a permanent state of vigil, and soon "the recollection of their childhood began to be erased from their memory, then the name and notion of things, and finally the identity of people and even the awareness of their own being, until the person sank into a kind of idiocy that had no past" (p. 43). The expert insomniac eventually forgets about dreams entirely, and about the act of dreaming. And even though nobody sleeps a wink, the following day people feel so rested that they forget about the bad night they've had.

What's so curious about García Márquez's notion of the insomnia plague is how it captures an equally bizarre reality we ourselves have been living out for four decades now, a reality Debord labeled "the society of the spectacle," a reality where "the sun never sets on the Empire of modern passivity" (Thesis #13). Debord says that the society of the spectacle is founded on "the production of isolation" (Thesis #28), a condition that reinforces the idea of a "lonely crowd," of people bound, on the one hand, by a common economic and political system, yet, on the other hand, brought together in a "unity of separation," as spectators lost in an agglomeration of "solitudes without illusions" (Thesis #70). Spectacular media and technology, Debord says, "are the technical realization of the exile of human powers into a beyond; it is separation perfected within the interior of man" (Thesis #20). The spectacle is the "nightmare of imprisoned modern society which ultimately expresses nothing more than its desire to sleep" (Thesis #21). But we can no longer sleep, of course, because of our insomnia plague, because the spectacle "is the guardian of sleep," and because our rulers profit from a plague that keeps us simultaneously asleep and awake, that deadens our imagination through its "permanent opium war" (Thesis #44).

This spectacular insomnia nourishes a "unity of misery." Behind the thrill of hallucinated lucidity are but different manifestations of alienation, bundled together into *intensive* and *extensive* forms of domination, two forms of spectacle "depending on the necessities of the particular stage of misery which it denies and supports" (Thesis #64). The former, intensive variety, Debord calls the "concentrated" spectacle; the latter, "diffuse." Both deny and support each other. Together, they signify two rival and successive forms of spectacular power. The concentrated spectacle functions through cult of personality, through dictatorship and totalitarianism, through brute military repression; the diffuse is more ideological, and represents "the Americanization of the world," a process that simultaneously frightens and successfully seduces countries where traditional forms of bourgeois democracy once prevailed. The diffuse spectacle guarantees freedom and affluence, dishwashers and Big Macs. When the spectacle is concentrated, the greater part of society escapes it; when diffuse, only a small part.

The concentrated spectacle, Debord says, "belongs essentially to bureaucratic capitalism, even though it may be imported as a technique of state power in more backward mixed economies, or in certain moments of crisis in advanced capitalism" (Thesis #64). Bureaucratic dictatorship of the economy "cannot leave in the exploited masses any notable margin of choice, since it had to choose everything itself." It has to ensure a permanent violence. "The imposed image of the good internalizes the totality of what officially exists, and usually concentrates itself in a single man who is the guarantor of its total cohesion" (Thesis #64).[10] All Chinese once had to learn Mao and became Mao; every Soviet had to learn Lenin and Stalin, and became each man. On the other flank come different Gods: the diffuse spectacle "accompanies the abundance of commodities, the unperturbed development of modern capitalism" (Thesis #65). Mass consumption and star-commodities fill the frame and pollute the mind; different merchandise jostles on the stage and glistens in ads. The diffuse spectacle thrives off the gadget and the gimmick and indulges in the commodity, in BlackBerrys and cell-phones, in iPods and SUVs, in accumulation for accumulation's sake, production for production's sake. With the diffuse spectacle, commodity logistics reach "moments of fervent exaltation" (Thesis # 67) in which the only goal is the goal of submission.

The insomnia plague is a fantastical construct invented in the mind of García Márquez, the master storyteller. All the same, it's an invention anchored in historical reality, a reality in which often "great dramas are condemned to oblivion in advance. We suffer from the plague of loss of memory. With the passage of time, nobody remembers that the massacre of the banana company workers actually took place."[11] This spectacular massacre, occurring in Cienaga in December 1928, blurs fact and fiction, objectivity and subjectivity, and even today nobody really knows the precise number of people killed. The strike broke out at the United Fruit Company's plantation when workers demanded written contracts, an eight-hour day and a six-day week. After a month of deadlock, with the intent of ending the strike, an army regiment was dispatched from Bogotá and soon set up machine-gun emplacements in the streets and on rooftops. Then, on Sunday December 6, late morning, they opened fire on a dense crowd of workers and their wives and children, who'd assembled in the public square after Mass, apparently to hear a speech from the governor. Amid the rattle of gunfire and incandescent chaos, people were swept away by a volley of bullets. "They were penned in," writes García Márquez, "swirling about in a gigantic whirlwind that little by little was being reduced to its epicenter as the edges were systematically being cut off all around like an onion being peeled by the insatiable and methodical shears of the machine guns" (p. 249).

Perhaps 3,000 lay dead, perhaps only two or three. Perhaps there weren't any killings? Perhaps the massacre was but a dream, a popular nightmare, the ruse of history? José Arcadio Segundo, the great-grandson of José Arcadio Buendia, another of the family's anarchists, was there, and as he tried to rescue a small child in the street, he fell forward and crashed out into an unconscious state—just as the bullets were raining; hours later, he comes to, seemingly the sole survivor, covered in dried blood and face down in a darkness smelling of death, "on an endless and silent train," full of piled up corpses headed for the sea, for watery oblivion. Is he an amnesiac? Somehow, José Arcadio Segundo leaps off the train and returns to Macondo. "There must have been three thousand of them," he tells a woman afterwards. "What?" the woman replies. "The dead," José Arcadio Segundo clarifies. "The woman measured him with a pitying look. 'There haven't been any dead here'" (p. 251). When José Arcadio Segundo arrives home, the same bewildering response greets him: "There wasn't any dead."[12]

Later, José Arcadio Segundo stumbles around, frightened, traipsing through Macondo's deserted sodden streets searching for clues, for testimony, for anything that will confirm the drama he'd just seen with his very own eyes. Even José Arcadio Segundo's brother, Aureliano Segundo, doesn't believe José Arcadio's version of the massacre nor his spectral trip on the death train. And then, a few days later again, amid a tropical downpour that doesn't seem to want to relent, José Arcadio Segundo finally reads an official proclamation: the military authorities and striking workers had obtained agreement; on the Sunday of protest everybody returned home, peacefully; the workers accepted new conditions and for three days there were public festivities. This version, which was "repeated a thousand times and mangled out all over the country by every means of communication the government found at hand," put the event to bed, and bore the objective seal of approval: "there was no dead, the satisfied workers had gone back to their families, and the Banana Company was suspending all activity until the rain stopped." "'You must have been dreaming. Nothing happened in Macondo,'" an army officer insists, trying to placate a still-perplexed José Arcadio Segundo, "'and nothing ever will. This is a happy town'" (p. 252).

*

García Márquez's portrayal of the insomnia plague, and his version of the Banana workers' massacre, are particularly fascinating and effective because they pinpoint how the reality of historical truth and the reality of (possible) subjective illusion *become one and the same.* There is no *real* way to tell either apart. We never know whether José Arcadio Segundo's version is a dream, whether it rests on a figment of his own febrile imagination, nor whether he's an insomniac turned amnesiac; neither are we sure of the official version, of everybody's insistence that "nothing happened in Macondo," that there were no dead. Thus fact and fiction mutually conspire, and negate each other; the lived becomes a representation, the representation a lived. How can we accept the authenticity of one version over another? Is there such a thing as "authentic" anymore? Aren't both versions as authentic as they are inauthentic? The blurring of one with the other, the inauthentic with the authentic, fact with fiction, the real with the meditated image, also speaks volumes about Debord's society of the spectacle, about how it has possessed us body and mind, how it now begets a different agenda for Marxist politics.

Fetish Reality, the Reality of Fetishism

In *The Society of the Spectacle*, Debord uses time-honored Marxist tools to describe and analyze a new phase of capitalist reality, one that seems to have gone immaterial, to have decoupled itself from its material thing-base, and rematerialized as an image, as a spectacle. Debord's book is experimental, is itself a piece of *détournement*, so perhaps it's hardly surprising that in mobilizing Marx he'd at the same time *détourn* Marx. Debord is adamant that the spectacle lies "at the heart of the unrealism of real society" (Thesis #6). This is a difficult concept for Marxists to get their heads' around. For what it suggests is that the separation between appearance and essence (Marx's trusty definition of science) has, like a piece of elastic, been stretched to such a degree that these two opposing ends of reality have now snapped and reformed as one. An epistemological duality has recoiled into an ontological unity: essence really is appearance, and appearance really is essence. Society's image of itself *is* the real reality of society, its reality is an image; society's form is society's content, its content is its form. It says nothing more than this. It is somehow fetishistic even to believe there's a fetishism anymore. A society hyper-separated is a non-separated society, a society of "separation perfected."

Over the years, Marxists have scrambled to retain their steely grip on Marx's celebrated concept of fetishism, the notion that there's "absolutely no connection with the physical nature of the commodity and the material relations arising out of this."[13] This, we are told, is what makes us stand apart from (and above) our bourgeois antagonists: with our analysis of fetishism we Marxists—beginning with Marx himself, continuing down the line with Lukács, and more recently reinforced by John Holloway— can claim to cast a superior eye on *real* reality; indeed, we can see behind society's illusions, behind relations between things, can strip off these illusions, can *unmask* them to *reveal* the rational kernels lurking within mystical shells. But does Marxism really need to function that way anymore? Why does it still cling defensively to what is a conceptual banality? In an otherwise provocative book, *Change the World Without Taking Power*, Holloway too falls back on the solid old crutch of fetishism, devoting pages and pages of padded and largely irrelevant discussion to Marx's concept of fetishism, to the "tragic dilemma" (why "tragic"?).[14] Holloway's thesis is a good and suitably magical one: how to struggle to change the world without taking power, how "the struggle to liberate power-to is not the struggle to construct a counter-power, but rather an anti-power, something that is radically different from power-over."[15] Yet he beds his politics down in a dubious ontological realm, in the idea of "a fetishized world that confronts us," a reality in which there's a separation between the doing and the done.

Marx, for Holloway, remains someone who can expose bourgeois sleights of hand to reveal the hidden world of capitalist alienation, demonstrating the "root" cause of people's subjugation and domination. Does Holloway really believe that? Do people around the world need Marx to reveal the root of their misery, to correct the illusions and lacunas of their vision of everyday reality? Don't they know this all too well themselves? Aren't they bludgeoned by a system that's all too obvious to them, that has absolutely no desire to conceal anything because it's based on raw, naked and *highly visible* power, on a brute force that doesn't need unmasking by anyone? Isn't it more the case that this ruling force wallows in the obviousness of its shenanigans because it knows that its opposition is too weak and feeble to stand up to its power? From this perspective, radical theory and radical struggles shouldn't concern themselves with repairing what realist Marxists like Holloway tell us has been sundered: addressing the ontological separation between the doing and the done is not a matter of "screaming," nor is it anything to do with *discovering* some real truth and rationality in an irrational and perverted world; rather, it's about moving out of this system, beyond it, outside of it, attacking it for sure, but by *inventing* something else, proposing something new.

One of the problems with Marx's concept of fetishism is that it moves in exactly the opposite direction to radical politics: it's a theory that is *retrospective*, that tries to retrace and reveal *past* actions and processes, social relations that have since become materialized in things. Yet radical politics needs to operate on a different continuum: it needs to shift forwards, needs to be about trying to become at least the worst of architects, imagining something in the present tense while struggling to realize it in the future, *prospectively*. The apathy and alienation people experience and endure across the globe is rarely based on theoretical ignorance; it's based on hopelessness and disempowerment, on our very own modern form of insomnia: it's that which renders us senseless *contemplative* beings.[16]

Contemplation can sometimes be a knowing and accepting resignation, itself a quiet form of resistance, a dogged understanding that helps people survive, cope each and every day. But it can also condemn people to live the way the residents of Macondo were condemned to live when the insomnia plague broke out: in an eternal present that not only has no historical past, but, more crucially, has no dreams of any future either, of any alternative tomorrow or day after tomorrow. The spectacular society we inhabit today, then, isn't so much an opaque world of fetishized social relations as a society of overtly publicized images, beamed out everywhere and always; it's not a disguised world so much as a banal world, an obvious flattened reality in which we've all become permanent spectators, leading our lives in front of one giant television screen.

We're now passive participants in a video game we ourselves have downloaded. We're permanently gawking at two-dimensional high-tech screens that have absolutely nothing else behind them. They are simply what they are: flat and two-dimensional, bereft of content. When kids see other kids, they play and amuse themselves together through collective activity, invent games and play act using their imagination; if somebody turns on a TV and places them in front of it, all dynamic activity ceases; kids no longer relate to other kids, no longer interact creatively with their surroundings. And they always lose the sparkle in their eyes they have when playing joyously with other children. Adults are no different. When we're confronted with TV screens, with spectacular images, whether in pubs, cafés, airport lounges, living rooms, or in our brains, we tune in but really switch off. This is a social contagion: the TV screen *is* our social reality.

In response, Magical Marxism shouldn't be construed as a romantic Rousseauian plea for a lost non-separated world: it's a call to get rid of these TV screens in life, to live life not watching digital and distant images but *engaging actively with something immediate*, a call to resist the producers of these images, to *de*thingify oneself. In fact, if anything, for Magical Marxists this is quite the reverse of repairing a duality: it's again to create a separation, a separation between form and content, between surface image and real underlying texture. It's a call to bring a new content to life, to introduce deep texturing into something that's been flattened. It is to dream of and struggle for a third, fourth and perhaps even fifth dimension to reality.

It's precisely in this vein that Jacques Rancière recently criticized Debord—wrongly, I believe—suggesting that the latter's fidelity to the young Marx is but proof of his innate romanticism, of his vision of the truth based on "non-separation."[17] But Rancière caricatures Debord's critique of the spectacle without really engaging with its complexity. And he scoffs at Debord's radical model of *action*, of the cavalry charges and sweeping assaults made by proletarian warriors. In the wake of 1968, Debord released a film version of *The Society of the Spectacle*; the rapid-fire captions, disarming classical music, footage of moody Paris vistas, exaggerated parodies of battle scenes and cavalry charges from old American Westerns, make it visually stunning and jarring. Isn't Debord right to invoke action instead of contemplative distance? His invocation of action isn't predicated on overcoming separation, or on some simple romantic humanism of yesteryear; it's more because Debord knows, as we now know, that there's really no separation anymore, that image and "real" reality are essentially one and the same thing. For us sensuous beings, however, for us magical humanists, action and active practice aren't just invoked to overcome contemplation, to help us feel alive; they're mobilized as creative ways to invent new truths about the world, to give us hope against hope, and to actively create a separation in which feeling can still be felt.

Subverting Reality

Fortunately, throughout our spectacular age, our 40-year solitude, we've always had people hell bent on staving off our insomnia plague, hell bent on resisting this image reality and the reality of its images; we've had our own Colonel Aureliano Buendias who've been inspired by strange gypsies, who've tried to uphold the power of dreams, dreams of a new future, of Macondos arising out of wild swampland. Indeed, Colonel Aureliano Buendia, the introverted soul spurred into militant direct action, is something of a twenty-first-century radical role model, a character who can assist us in our fight against the slipping away of reality, against its colonization, because the colonel is somebody who invented another reality out of his own subversive will. Thus he doesn't reveal or discover anything through theory; he creates, he pioneers a new trail for a reinvigorated, less defensive kind of political practice. Even at the time of the insomnia plague, the young Aureliano conceived a formula to *resist*, to help protect against any loss of memory: a system of marking things with their respective names, using little pieces of paper pasted on every object. As a young adult, and like a lot of progressive people, he was bookishly smart and withdrawn. He absorbed himself in his workshop, making little gold fishes, and frequently lost himself in poetry composition. But because of his humanitarian feelings, Aureliano sympathized with the left-leaning Liberal Party; even so, "he could not understand how people arrived at the extreme of waging war over things that could not be touched with the hand" (p. 85).

When Aureliano sees his conservative father-in-law tamper with the ballot boxes after the town's election, he knew then he had witnessed first-hand, very palpably, the sham of party political democracy. Though again, like many leftists, Aureliano never struck anyone as a man of action; he was, it seemed, "a sentimental person with a passive character, and a definite solitary vocation" (p. 88). But then, one Sunday morning, drinking his habitual mug of black coffee, just as the Liberal opposition to Conservative rule was escalating, and just as Macondo was steadily becoming a Tory garrison town, Aureliano tells his friend Gerineldo Márquez in a voice the latter had never heard before: "Get the boys ready. We're going to war." "With what weapons," Gerineldo wonders, incredulously. "With theirs," Aureliano replies (p. 89).

From that point on, dressed in black high boots with spurs, in an ordinary denim uniform without insignia and with a rifle slung over his shoulder, Colonel Aureliano Buendia, the commander-in-chief of the revolutionary forces, the anarchist warrior and man most feared by the government, was born; he'd reinvented his own radical self. Years later:

> on his waist he wore a holster with the flap open and his hand, which was always on the butt of the pistol, revealed the same watchful and resolute tension as his look. His head, with deep recessions in the hairline, seemed to have been baked in a slow oven. His face, tanned by the salt of the Caribbean, had acquired a metallic hardness. He was preserved against imminent old age by a vitality that had something to do with the coldness of his insides. (pp. 132–3)

When Ursula, his mother, saw him then, she said to herself: "Good Lord, now he looks like a man capable of anything." "'Whatever you decide, will be done, Aureliano,' she sighed. 'I always thought and now I have proof that you're a renegade'" (pp. 133–4).

One is struck by the strange affinity between Colonel Aureliano Buendia and the young Situationist Guy Debord, the 30-something author of *The Society of the Spectacle*, with their joint penchant for militant action and muckraking, for restrained austerity and exuberant spontaneity; their melancholic dispositions and occasional ruthlessness with friend and foe alike; their elusiveness and charismatic presence; and their fervent belief that politics was another form of war, that war was political activity, an art-form of resistance, a game of strategy, of attack and defense that should be studied as well as practiced. Colonel Buendia fought with the Duke of Marlborough, the early eighteenth-century English general, in his pocket, just as Debord, like Lenin, Mao, and Trotsky before him, had recourse to the German strategist and tactician of war, Carl von Clausewitz, whose *On War* (1832–37) was much scrutinized by the Situationist revolutionary.[18] Debord agreed with, but reversed, Clausewitz's oft-cited phrase that "war is merely a continuation of politics with other means." As for Colonel Buendia, the Duke of Marlborough (1650–1722) was his great mentor on the art of war, the general who became famous in the War of Spanish Succession (1701–14), who made war more offensive, more mobile, by searching out battle, by planning surprise attacks and lightning invasions, and who inspired the colonel in the "certainty that he was finally fighting for his own liberation and not for abstract ideals, for slogans that politicians could twist left and right according to circumstances." It was this principle that "fuelled him with an ardent enthusiasm" (p. 143).

In war, defense is often the safest and strongest ploy; "an army that is hard pressed on all sides," Clausewitz says, "flees to their castle in order to gain time and wait for a better turn of events. By their fortifications ... [they] sought to ward off the storm clouds of war."[19] And yet, as important as defense is, it's usually only offense, or counter-offense, that can win the battle and destroy any adversary. Thus, "the game of war" is, perhaps above all, a game of *movement*: a game of tactics and chance, of foresight and feign, of defense and attack, just like political activism and practical militancy. "One can occasionally win," Debord reckons, "without battle or without partial combats, and even win by a sole maneuver. One can also win by a single frontal attack without maneuvers. But outside of these two extreme cases, one normally employs a series of maneuvers, combats and a principal battle followed by new maneuvers." "One must not spare troops or maneuvers," he says, "nor dispense them vainly. Those who want to keep all will lose all. However, those who let themselves lose more than their adversary will no longer be able to contain the adversary."[20]

Debord's and Colonel Buendia's penchant for battle arises from a marked dislike for career politicians and their feeble rhetoric about social change. "We're wasting time," the colonel says, trying to negotiate with mealy-mouthed officials in their suits and ties. "We're wasting time while the bastards in the party are begging for seats in congress" (p. 115). The colonel hates those soft politicians and lawyers leaving the presidential office each morning, taking refuge in their dreary cafés to speculate over what the president had meant when he'd said yes, or no, or something quite different again. For Debord, too, active engagement is the only viable alternative to the bankruptcy of representative democracy, to the paralysis of contemplation, to the alienation of the spectator: "the more we contemplate," he says, "the less we live" (Thesis #30). Action brings us to life, gives meaning to our lives, and helps us become subjects in the creation of this life, masters of our own activity and body. Debord follows Marx's Fifth Thesis on Feuerbach: "Feuerbach," says Marx, with his own emphasis, "not satisfied with *abstract thinking*, wants sensuous *contemplation*; but he does not conceive sensuousness as *practical*, as human-sensuous activity."[21]

Debord's and the colonel's modus operandi expresses itself through such human-sensual activity, through a radicalism much more extra-political, much more intensely militant at the level of everyday life, at the level of everyday being: it's a struggle and resistance that's non-negotiable, invariably romantic and innately *poetic*. Their poetic sensibility, their radical actions, their unflinching attitudes to struggle and fighting, destabilize accepted notions of respectability and restraint; both men proclaim, in their separate ways, through their respective *détournements* and fantastical transformations of reality, an absolute non-conformity, a sneaky revolutionary practice. These days, we ourselves must go about our militant business, our militant politics, furtively, sneakily, in a manner that is attentive and unobserved, forever mindful of traps, of the innumerable ways in which present society can catch us out, ambush us, seduce us, buy us off somehow and enervate us. Above all, we must permanently sneak about if we're to remain faithful to ourselves, if we're to pursue, without let up, some kind of secret war of position. And those trails we need to stake out, those passageways through which we construct our own radical life, our life-project, will always likely be *narrow*, tiny fissures, slim cracks in the fragile superstructure of the spectacle, brief moments of chance, of possibility for radical action and freedom.

What's inspiring here is how many people have never stopped sneaking about through narrow trails of permanent subversion, staking out their own trails; and these are "ordinary" men and women, too, forging a new alternative lingua franca between themselves. They're people who've had *enough* of the garbage the ad-man promises them, and they're achieving incredible things through their struggles in lonely, abandoned rural spaces as well as in teeming, over-priced urban places, in shantytowns and in raw jungles, in suburbs and downtowns and nowherevilles across the globe, re-appropriating and rebuilding worn-out properties, inventing life anew from breezeblock and the decaying and discarded jetsam of everyday life, out of things the rich throwaway, things that are no longer useable in the dumpster culture of modern market life. Moreover, practical mobilization here is invariably inspired by dream, by the normative desire for something different, for something more autonomous, beyond the mainstream, outside the repressive domain of law and order and capitalist consumerism—of doctoring ballot boxes to suit presidential ends.

Importantly, it's no longer the spirit of negativity that dramatizes permanent subversion. These people know how messed up our world is; they've got better things to do than just critique it, than gripe about it, or waste energy analyzing what is already obvious. Their desires are to move on from denunciation and affirm something *positive*, to plot something constructive, an assertive ideal about how to think and act and dream. And often they are turning normative desire into an imagined reality, into a reality transformed. Just like the colonel, they aren't struggling for abstract ideals on some remote global plane, but are taking it upon themselves to create new life from the bottom up, practically. In places like the Auvergne, these people are engaged in rehabbing ancient cottages and farms, growing their own food, reenergizing old bars and restaurants, and they're transforming entire villages through meaningful and convivial political activity, beyond the hollow sloganeering of elected politicos. These people, like their counterparts in other lands, in lands faraway, are fed up with just interpreting the world and they know how they fit in (or don't fit in) to the overall system of capitalist domination. Instead, they now voice an ideal that is global in its localism, practical in its defiance of the world market, and poetic in its yearnings for the future.

Such people are motivated to act precisely because of their dreams, dreams of wanting to return to the land, of living off the land, of farming organically without an organic label, of baking bread, raising goats, or inventing shoestring enterprises, of building housing and a new life. And in practically engaging with their dreams, these people discover other people en route, people with similar dreams who've likewise acted practically; in discovering how they share common values, and frequently a common enemy, they're devising new radical politics together, nurturing a new sort of social movement based around active, bottom-up-will rather than worthless handouts from above. These people act as much on instinct as on intellect; they are new rank-and-file foot soldiers waging war around "things they can touch with their own hands," just like the colonel said. And they're not afraid of getting their hands dirty either. In the process, their Macondos of the mind become real-life dream-states, hacked out of proverbial wild jungle, somehow beyond the spectacle, beyond the spectacular state. And in these fantastic democracies nobody ever gives orders with pieces of paper.

Reality Lived, Reality Represented

One of the most compelling lines from *The Society of the Spectacle* comes right at the beginning: "Everything that was directly lived has moved away into a representation" (Thesis #1). This idea is both easy and difficult to grasp: the idea that images are "at the heart of the unreality of real society" (Thesis #6), that lived reality—the reality one touches, smells, feels, and acts out—has been materially invaded by an image to such an extent that the image becomes as real as real reality itself. The concept is easily enough understood for those of us who recognize the seductive power of the image, of corporate logos, of Big Macs and Coca-Cola, of Disneylands and Times Squares, of monopoly global media, of images of assorted Ayatollahs and Osama Bin Ladens, images that have now somehow lodged themselves deeply, almost instinctively, in the brains of everyone everywhere. On the other hand, the concept becomes trickier and more elusive when we are told, as Debord tells us, that the spectacular world is at once real and phony. The phony is real yet it is still inferior to a reality that is lived out *directly as lived reality*. This is difficult to comprehend because it's tough to break the immanent tautology, tough because one cannot, Debord says, "abstractly contrast the spectacle to actual social activity." Indeed, "such a division is itself divided" (Thesis #8).

Breaking through a false reality that is lived as true life, Debord says, necessitates putting some kind of practical force into action, into sustained permanent subversion. It means, perhaps more than anything else now, trying to reinvent sensual connection, to struggle for a more visceral, wholesome life-form; it means converting a negative practice into an affirmative living ideal. It means that if the spectacle is both real and fake, and if it is now pointless to draw any theoretical distinction between the two (between image-reality and representation-lived), then one must create out of practical necessity a false reality for oneself, a different sort of real falsity, a fantasy life in which one is true to oneself.[22] The old Catalan bookseller near the end of *One Hundred Years of Solitude* is instructive here because he was sustained by "his marvelous sense of unreality" (p. 325). Nevertheless, once this wise old man started to get too serious, too analytical and nostalgic for a paradise lost, his marvelous state began to crumble, began to turn *cynical* and *bitter*, becoming contaminated by these twin sources of *anti*-magic.

"Fuck rationality two times over," we might say, paraphrasing Colonel Aureliano Buendia's elder brother José Arcadio. Fuck it two times over because rationality has little to offer us radicals anymore. The rationality of science and the science of rationality are feeble when confronted with the power of the ruling class with their fictions and strategic recourse to partial truths they call the only objective Truth. And science is only as good as it relays evidence of these ruling truths, of the truth of its ruling class. Accordingly, should somebody today impose from above their own "rational" sense of spectacular unreality on us, Magical Marxists should counter, like the old Catalan bookseller, with a more marvelous type of unreality. If somebody tells us that pots of paint are weapons of mass destruction, we should fabricate our own war paint, and layer it all over our own reality, fill it with sparkling spontaneous energy, like a wild magical canvas from one of García Márquez's favorite artists, Wifredo Lam. On this canvas we might glimpse, as in a mirror, our own authentic image in an inauthentic world, our own primal dream-state whilst we're wide awake.[23]

Early Macondo, before the banana company ripped it off and the colonizer reduced it to ruins, offers us clues about the pre- and post-spectacular world, about how to live beyond the spectacle and beyond the spectacular state. Macondo had been a village founded by ordinary, intrepid people; they'd communally distributed the land, built modest adobe houses, opened up roads, "and introduced the improvements that necessity required without having bothered the government and without anyone having bothered them" (p. 53). No one was upset that the government hadn't helped. On the contrary, they were happy it had let them grow in peace. They hoped it would continue leaving them that way, because people "had not founded a town so that the first upstart who came along would tell them what to do" (p. 53). That first upstart was the Magistrate, Don Apolinar Moscote, who, one day, years after its founding, turns up at Macondo and announces to José Arcadio that he's the "official" representative, that from now on he runs the show, and, moreover, he has a letter of authority from Bogotá to prove it. "In this town," José Arcadio counters, without losing his calm, "we do not give orders with pieces of paper." "And so that you know it once and for all," he continues, "we don't need judges here because there's nothing that needs judging" (p. 53).[24] If the Magistrate wants to stay in town, as an ordinary citizen, he's quite welcome. Otherwise, "officials" aren't wanted or needed. The Magistrate says he's armed, but before he can do anything José Arcadio picks him up by the lapels and physically removes him from town.

With our depersonalized institutions and mediated forms of power, it's rare that one can confront, face-to-face, one's real enemy, and rarer still that we can pick them up by the lapels and toss them out of town. Twenty-first-century power is too cowardly for that. And yet being active, immediate, and personal in one's confrontation, seeking one's enemy out and fending it off, is perhaps the best way of affirming and defending a strategy of what Henri Lefebvre called *autogestion*: a practice of self-management undertaken democratically by the community's own inhabitants, involving citizens more than just workers, and reorganizing life not only the workplace. Wherever *autogestion* exists, even if it exists only as a concept, as a hope, it stimulates and introduces its own antithesis of the state, challenges the state as a constraining force pitched above people, upon people.

Autogestion is thus anti-statist and strengthens associative ties within civil society. It doesn't play by rules laid down by the state and its ruling class because it accepts different rules. By its very nature it is *critical* since "it radically contests the existing order, from the world of the commodity and the power of money, to the power of the state."[25] *Autogestion* involves direct action, expresses militancy beyond established trade unions or parties, beyond anything purely reactive and defensive; it makes the magical imaginative leap from the narrow confines of a "political" revolution that Marx critiqued to the broader "social" revolution that he endorsed. It marks, in a word (and as we'll see in the next chapter), the coming of *the coming insurrection*. And like life at the beginning of Macondo, *autogestion* is born spontaneously and prospers under a "natural law"; it doesn't "baptize children or sanctify their festivals" (p. 73). And it has no need of holy men either, nor of their images, because "no one will pay any attention to them." People will "arrange the business of their souls directly with God, and they have lost the evil of original sin" (pp. 73–4).

Curiously, Remedios the Beauty, Macondo's most dazzlingly attractive creature, embodies all the qualities of what a beautiful self-managed society might be, stripped of all repressive conventions and morals, liberated from all mediating images and with direct access to the real. Remedios the Beauty's startling "simplifying instinct" obeys no other law than the law of spontaneity.[26] She wanders about the Buendia's house stark naked, in total liberty, and with her exceptional purity is able "to see the reality of things beyond any formalism" (p. 164). Even the colonel "kept on believing and repeating that Remedios the Beauty was in reality the most lucid being that he had ever known" (p. 195). She exists in a world of simple unmediated realities and was immune from the banana plague when it struck, from the invasion of spectacular United Fruit Company forces. Therein, perhaps, in its most basic form, resides the real solution for reclaiming the lived from the represented: the simplifying instinct, the revival of primitive, anarchic instincts which have been sacrificed in order to sustain the spectacular illusion of living in comfort, of living affluently.

Perhaps, then, the moment is now ripe for such a different take on reality, for such magical primal action, for the invocation of the supernatural lucidity of Remedios the Beauty, especially for confronting the ugliness of global power? Perhaps the 40 years since Debord and García Márquez wrote their great books now herald a new era in which people will remember, dream again, and act upon their dreams? Perhaps, in this crisis-ridden age, people are at last prepared to fight against memory loss and stake out new narrow trails of permanent subversion, to fight for their dreams like Colonel Aureliano Buendia? Perhaps, amid the dust and rubble of the hurricane that has just swept through our ridiculous financial system, it's not too late to engage in the creation of a new utopia in which self-affirmation is possible and communities busy themselves in peace?

2

SUBSCRIBING TO THE IMAGINARY PARTY: NOTES ON A POLITICS OF NEO-COMMUNISM

Je ne mange pas de ce pain-là.

Benjamin Péret

Autonomous production will develop in all those fields in which the use-value of time can be seen to be greater than its exchange-value.

André Gorz

Tarnac: L'arbre qui cache la forêt!

Graffito, Paris, June 2009

Phantoms and Specters

A specter is haunting Europe: the specter of autonomous communist activism. A new party is expanding its ranks, "The Imaginary Party," which has already unnerved the French establishment, rattled Sarkozy's government, and penned its own intriguing manifesto: *L'insurrection qui vient* [*The Coming Insurrection*]. Everybody agrees: current society is about to explode. Even the French daily, *Le Monde*, was forced to admit "one hasn't seen power become so fearful of a book for a very long time."[1] Now an English translation has rattled the Anglosphere, too, unleashing a spate of bourgeois paranoia, highlighting for all to see what intelligent people knew already: how very flimsy the ruling class's hegemony really is, how weak is their grip on political reality. This uncompromising text is in the "vanguard" of disseminating a new brand of Marxism, a non-class-based Marxism that has at its core an incipient neo-communist impulse, one currently pitting

its wits against an intransigent neo-liberalism. Not a "party" as
such, and certainly not one made to govern, this Imaginary Party
is a collectivity that is creating for itself an empowering self-gov-
ernance: its card-carrying membership thrives off non-affiliated
people, whose platform is grounded in everyday life rather than
the workplace. Importantly, these people employ a vitality of spirit
and a principle of hope, as well as the direct-action anarchism
necessary to reinvigorate classical Marxism. Yes, everyone agrees,
well, sort of everyone: the exodus from capitalism has already
begun.

"Everyone Agrees: It's About to Explode"

In 2007, a strange little book called *L'insurrection qui vient* was
released in France under the auspices of the radical publishing
house, Éditions la fabrique. No author's name appeared on
its plain-green cover; only the signature "*Comité invisible*"—
Invisible Committee—gave clues to the culprit's identity.
"Culprit," of course, implies some sort of criminal act, and in
this sense the said Invisible Committee pleads guilty as charged:
it has knowingly ruffled the French establishment and penned the
most *radical* radical book since Guy Debord's *The Society of the
Spectacle*, itself written on the eve of another great insurrection.
"The book is important," one man said in July 2009 at Union
Square's Barnes & Noble, at an impromptu New York book
party launching Sexiotext(e)'s English translation. "It's important
because *The Coming Insurrection* speaks of the total bankruptcy
of pretty much everything. We're living in a high-end aesthetic
with zero content."[2]

It was five o'clock in the afternoon, and without prior permission
a group of 100-or-so activists merrily fêted the book's US release in
the huge East 17th Street bookstore. As an employee announced
to the milling crowd that no reading was scheduled for that night,
a man jumped onto a stage and began loudly reciting the opening
words of the book's introduction: "Everyone agrees. It's about
to explode."[3] A security guard tried to break up the gathering
but failed; then the police arrived in force and the crowd exited,

clapping and yelling, only to enter the nearby Sephora cosmetics store, resuming its mantra: "All power to the communes." Black T-shirted security guards ordered revelers out, and a few minutes later the group marched into Starbucks. "I've no idea what's going on," said a young male latte-sipper sat behind his laptop. "But I like the excitement."[4]

Such was the excitement that a few weeks later it really got the goat of frothing-at-the-mouth reactionary Glenn Beck on his Fox News show, *The One Thing* (July 1, 2009). Ostensibly mild-mannered, clad in neat-cut suit and red tie, Beck, author of the bestselling book *Common-Sense*, proceeded almost apoplectically, quivering with rage, to denounce *The Coming Insurrection*: "This is a dangerous book," he cried, "that calls for violent revolution. This is an anti-*Common-Sense* book, written by the enemies within." He continued:

> As world economies go down the tank and unemployment continues to rise, disenfranchised people are set to explode ... This started in France and spread to countries like Greece, where people are out of work, out of money and out of patience. Now it's coming here ... A few years ago I said that Europe is on the brink of destruction. This is yet another sign that it's coming. Even in Japan where protests have been seen as taboo since the 1960s, young people angered over the economy and fearing for the future are taking to the streets, beginning to unionize. The Communist Party of Japan says they're getting 1,000 new members a month.

"It's important that you read this book," Beck concluded, "so that you know who your enemies are, so that you know what is coming and be ready when it does."[5]

Insurrectional Style

Much of the intrigue and bourgeois anxiety around *The Coming Insurrection* derives from the anonymity of its author(s), from the *clandestine* nature of its enterprise: The book's most radical element is, it seems, its invisibility, its veil of mystery, its ability to frighten, announcing that an opposition—an Invisible Committee—is out there somewhere, plotting something, and power isn't quite sure who or where it is. Guy Debord always said that the more obscure and subterranean he became, the greater the media feared and loathed him; they were freaked by a mystique and mystery they could little fathom.[6] In fact, the "Insurrectionary Style"—as *The New Yorker* neatly put it—of *The Coming Insurrection*, is quintessentially Debordian,[7] drier and less poetic than *The Society of the Spectacle*, yet elegant and cutting like late Debord, like his *Comments on the Society of Spectacle*. As Luc Boltanski wrote in the French journal *Tigre*: *The Coming Insurrection* has a burning style, a style that "'burns like ice'—in the words of Baudelaire."[8]

Thus the little rumor, somewhat implausible, that Debord himself wrote *The Coming Insurrection*, that he never really committed suicide and now lives on reclusively in Champot Haut, in his tiny hamlet, in lost and lonely Auvergne, under its volcanoes; that his taste for intrigue and scandal, like that of his hero Arthur Cravan,[9] meant he fabricated his own disappearance in order to better survey the world, to critique it and secretly mastermind its eventual overthrow, four decades down the line. (Didn't somebody recently spot Debord with wife Alice in the Haute-Loire, both dressed as gypsies, wandering around the summer *marché du soir* at Chomelix?) Remember what he'd said near the end of *The Society of the Spectacle* (Thesis #220): those who want to overthrow the spectacle "must know how to wait." And so, after waiting so long, here is Debord finally announcing the coming of *The Coming Insurrection*.

But if truth be told, the style of *The Coming Insurrection* is younger at heart: its voice is too fiery and naive, too innocent and agile to be crafted by any ageing, 70-something revolutionary— dead or alive. It has the stamp of somebody on the brink of mastering their art, a Young Turk who, for the time being anyway, has less to lose, and everything to gain: the world is ahead of him (or her), and it's time to act *now*, before one becomes too old, too cynical, too embittered by past failings. As such, the idea that a 33-year-old freelance rebel, a certain Julien Coupat (born 1974), was the hand behind the deed, seems the most likely, and is increasingly the most touted media thesis. A brilliant polyglot philosophy student, graduating from Paris's elite École des hautes études en sciences socials with a doctorate in Debordian thought and Situationist theory, Coupat has all the intellectual credentials, and all the subversive wit, for the job. Equally steeped in Martin Heidegger and Carl Schmitt, Michel Foucault and Giorgio Agamben, Coupat, who fervently denies he wrote *The Coming Insurrection*, also has Debord's talent for obscurity and conspiracy, for lying low while plotting high.

Since 2005, Coupat and several comrades have assumed proprietorship of a farmhouse at Le Goutailloux, a little hamlet about the size of Debord's own Champot, a couple of kilometers outside Tarnac, a prim village of 350 inhabitants in the Corrège department. There, in one of rural France's most sparsely populated corners, miles away from any discernible urban life, Coupat and his crew have created their very own eco-community and velvet underground, rehabbed an ancient cottage, re-energized a worn-out bar, reorganized as a cooperative an adjacent épicerie, helped out with the running of a mobile library and *ciné-club*, and participated in the daily affairs of the traditionally communist commune, giving it an autonomous left-wing bent, all of which unnerves the powers that be, threatening their status quo by somehow changing the dominant order of things. Power get twitchy once it loses its grip on ordinary everyday life, faced with another sort of everyday life it barely understands.

Accordingly, in the early hours of November 11, 2008, 150 heavily armed riot police, with helicopters overhead, made a sweeping raid on the sleeping hamlet; amid barking dogs, nonplussed goats, and terrified chickens, they arrested nine humans. Accused by the Sarkozy government of sabotaging a TGV train near the German border, and of illicit political activity, the so-called "Tarnac Nine" immediately faced charges in a Paris court of "criminal association for the purpose of terrorist activity," an offense that carries up to 20 years in jail. In early December 2008, with no supporting evidence, all but Coupat were acquitted under judiciary control. In May 2009, after six months of "preventive detention," Coupat too was eventually released. As he said in an interview with *Le Monde* (May 25,

2009): "anti-terrorism, contrary to what the term itself insinuates, is not a means of fighting against terrorism, but is the method by which one positively constructs the political enemy as terrorist."[10]

Several days after the Tarnac arrests, the "Anti-Terrorist Division" of the "Central Police Judiciary and Prosecutor" drafted a criminal report in Paris. It makes for a fascinating, if scary, read.[11] Apparently, secret police had now "dismantled a clandestine autonomist-anarchist structure based in France that devotes itself to destabilizing the state by violent actions." This group, "constituted around the charismatic and ideological leader Julien Coupat, keeps itself on the margins of large political events" and has hitherto been "engaged in the sabotage of transport infrastructure," "participating regularly in political demonstrations," such as at the G8 Summits at Evian in June 2003 and at Isola San Gorgio (Italy) in 2004; at assorted ecological forums; at anti-anti-immigrant legislation gatherings; at a festival of support for protesting Greek activists at Thessalonica in September 2008; and at a demonstration in Vichy in October 2008 during a meeting of 27 European Union Ministers of Interior. "These activists," the report adds, aren't just a group of reveler "*casseurs*"—rioters—but constitute "a group well versed in techniques of urban guerilla warfare and act in a planned and concerted manner." Moreover, their discourse is "very radical and they have links with foreign groups."

According to the report, secret police surveillance uncovered the Tarnac Nine's plot to sabotage a rapid train line in the Moselle—and sabotage, the prosecutor reminds the jury, is exactly what *The Coming Insurrection* advocates. Still, during the police ransacking of Coupat's house, police found no explosives or weapons of mass destruction, no Molotov cocktails or monkey wrenches, only "documents containing detailed information on railway transportation, including exact arrival and departure times of trains." As the Italian philosopher Giorgio Agamben wrote in his defense of the Tarnac Nine: "in simple language," what all that boils down to "is a SNCF [French National Train] schedule." Police also confiscated "climbing gear," which again "in simple language," Agamben says, means "a ladder, such as one might find in any country house."[12] In short, there's little there for convicting anyone of terrorism. For Agamben, the "only possible conclusion to this shadowy affair is that those engaged in activism against the way social and economic problems are managed today are considered *ipso facto* as potential terrorists. We must have the courage to say with clarity that today, numerous European countries (in particular France and Italy), have introduced laws and police measures that we would previously have judged barbaric and anti-democratic ... laws that criminalize association and that allow the classification of political acts as having terrorist 'intentions or inclinations'."[13]

Revolters Without Qualities

Giorgio Agamben's own *The Coming Community*, as its title implies, was not without influence in shaping Coupat's political imagination.[14] The coming community, Agamben says, is something that humans are and have to be. Yet the solidarity people forge amongst themselves doesn't concern any essence like a "united working class"; rather, Agamben affirms an "inessential commonality," a belief that one's existence *now* hinges on one's possibility or potentiality, on what one can become in the future. Agamben beckons us to enter with him and with others into a mystical and blurry "zone of indistinguishability," a realm of liberation and friendship, in which, in the words of Coupat's journal of political ideas and analysis, *Tiqqun*, we can become card-carrying members of "an Imaginary Party."

Tiqqun, "the Conscious Organ of the Imaginary Party"—which takes its name from the Hebrew Cabbalist *tikkun*: to repair, to transform, to heal—saw only two issues:[15] one of 162 pages at the beginning of 1999, the other of 292 pages in October 2001; yet these two book-length treatises are full of startling analysis and stinging polemic, of dense philosophical discourse and imaginative utopian desire, reminiscent of the pages of the early *Situationist International*, or of the Lettrists' home-baked *Potlatch* from the early 1950s. Perhaps Arthur Cravan's equally short-lived *Maintenant* (five issues) is also close to the heart of

Tiqqun, its goal having been a little like that of *Tiqqun*, or of the Imaginary Party: "to present itself simply as a community of defection, as the Party of Exodus, as the slippery and paradoxical reality of subversion."[16] At any rate, in *Tiqqun* the "Imaginary Party" declares war on the bourgeois status quo, and lays down a few of the theoretical and political seeds that a few years later will bloom into *The Coming Insurrection*.

Indeed, one of the most brilliantly enduring concepts from the ephemeral pages of *Tiqqun*, which reappears unnamed in *The Coming Insurrection*, is the beguiling *"théorie du Bloom"*— "theory of Bloom." Bloom suggests growing: a person, or a community, taking root somewhere, trying to assert itself, pushing up from this sad earth, out of ashes that fertilize, emerging from the decomposition of the old world, blossoming anew. Thus the theory of Bloom is the theory of the coming community, an insurrection announced, a chronicle of a capitalist death foretold. Bloom, of course, also suggests the everyman Leopold Bloom, citizen Bloom from Joyce's *Ulysses*, the outsider in a hostile sectarian land, who's mocked for his superior intellect, for his preaching of love: "I mean the opposite of hatred," he stammers.[17] Joyce's Bloom wanders through the pages of *Tiqqun* as he wanders through the streets of Dublin, almost invisibly, clandestinely, searching for reconciliation; Leopold Bloom's presence is implied, suggested, hinted at only in the epigraph to the *théorie du Bloom*, where *Ulysses* is cited, where Bloom over a breakfast of fried kidneys offers milk to his purring cat, musing on this furry friend: "They call him stupid. They understand what we say better than we understand them."[18]

They call us stupid, but we understand them better than they understand us. That's why they fear us; hence their paranoia, their mania with trying to surveil us, to infiltrate us, to criminalize us, to prosecute us. Such is the logic of the "theory of Bloom." "Bloom can be defined as what resides inside each of us beyond advertising stunts and which constitutes the form of *universal* existence common to particular people who live inside the Spectacle. In this sense, Bloom is first of all a hypothesis, but it's a hypothesis that is becoming *true*."[19] Bloom signals an inner human potentiality, the becoming of a man and woman *without qualities*, a person who determines their own worth and whose worth is not ascribed by an external force, by any institution or ruling power. Bloom is nothing, *rien*, a person without qualities simply because they are a certain quality of person, someone who is indifferent to the dominant order, who *prefers not to*. To be sure, it's evident that Bloom's kindred souls might also bear the name Ulrich, from Musil's *Man Without Qualities*, or Bartleby, from Melville's story about the passively deferring scrivener. "At the same time," *Tiqqun* says, "it is certain that Bloom bears within himself the ruin of the society of the commodity," of spectacular society, because within this character we find the vocation of the "I prefer not to," the "I prefer not to be a little reasonable" because *we* want to do something else.[20]

This spirit of "I prefer not to" refuses to lie down and die because, following Sartre in *L'existentialisme est un humanisme* (1946), "we are condemned to be free" [*"l'homme est condamné à être libre"*].[21] Liberty can't entirely be suppressed. We can forget it, unlearn it, especially through our contact with society, with its institutions and norms, with its schools and expectations; but we, as individuals, and more problematically as collectivities, have no real choice: each of us was born free and needs to be free: it's our curse, our *condition*. The "I prefer not to" merely expresses overtly the attendant slippage, the *"non-coincidence,"* between the self we are and the self that society wants us to be. It's a non-coincidence, Sartre says, between an individual subject and his or her social being, a gap that bequeaths dissent, has to breed dissent. It's a non-coincidence that means we won't be squeezed into any dominant whole, or flattened by any spectacular image; the non-coincidence is a philosophical anti-concept, an affirmation of *residue*, of remainders, of marginal leftovers, of autonomy, of the power and radicality of the ragged and the *irreducible*.

All totalizing systems that interpellate individual subjects to *coincide* strictly with their chosen role as social beings always "expulse" a certain residue; and each residue constitutes its dialectical "other," something precious and essential in its *irreducibility*, its implacability, its refusal to comply: technocracy expulses desire and imagination; state bureaucracy expulses "deviancy" and subversion; reason and rationality expulse irrationality and spontaneity. So it goes. The non-coincidence reveals the limit of power's political desire to control totally, of its quest for ultimate and indomitable mastery. No system of control can ever be total, can ever be without possibility, contingency, inconspicuous cracks, without little holes in the net, glimmers of light and pockets of fresh air. There is always leakiness to culture and society, a non-coincidence between capitalist subjects and capitalist society, always unforeseen circumstances buried within the everyday, immanent moments of prospective subversion. The "I prefer not to" thereby becomes a key progressive motif, signifying that all is not lost, that all can never be lost, not quite. The non-coincidence is there, always there, if you look hard enough, is always written between the lines, lurking within the whole, unnerving society, out of place, out of sync with time, an opportunity to be seized and invented.

Non-Class Neo-Communism

The Coming Insurrection draws us into a Dantesque inferno, yet instead of nine circles descending into a hell of fierce and hideous monsters, we plunge into seven circles of a grubby hell that's everyday and commonplace, above ground and instantly recognizable to many of us. It's the neo-liberal, anti-democratic inferno before us now. In it, the breach between the professional world of politics and "the political" has widened to such a degree that the two no longer have anything to do with one another, and it has bequeathed a new world order from which there is no way out if you follow its logic, if you accept its rules. We have to invent this way out for ourselves; we have to demonstrate that all the roads are blocked save this one, the one we make, the one we make work. The Imaginary Party asks us to desist from partaking in this hell, asks that we "prefer not to" together, that we affirm our *inadaptability* as the point of departure, as the meeting point for "new complicities": "We're not depressed; we're on strike. For those who refuse to manage themselves, 'depression' is not a state but a passage, a bowing out, a side-step towards a *political disaffiliation.*"[22] Thus unfolds a political struggle to create a community and language in which a new order can express itself, a non-coincidence and non-coincidental commonality that conveys something affirmative, that gets going, that finds itself, organizes itself, rises up. This is really the most innovative part of *The Coming Insurrection*, its utopian element, the most original path to paradise voiced for a very a long time.

"*Excuse us we don't give a damn*" sets the subversive tone of the opening sequences to *The Coming Insurrection*, updating Bartleby's discourse of quiet rebellion, turning the screw of mild effrontery and passive refusal.[23] On the one hand, comes a sensitive cry, an appeal for gentle intimacy, for "everything that has so obviously deserted contemporary social relations: warmth, simplicity, truth, a life without theater or spectacle"; on the other hand, comes an angry, seething demand, a wish to see it all blow up, a call for *wildness*, "for a wild, massive experimentation with new arrangements, new fidelities."[24] What's being offered here is a more experimental communist ideal, explicitly anarchistic in its call for autonomy and loathing of the state, and its invocations of sabotage; but implicitly Marxist, too—though in a mischievous sense, in a piratical and fruitful sense, in the sense that follows Marx through his utopian pages of the *Grundrisse*. There, Marx's yearning was to replace the realm of necessity—the grim reality of endless work and endless alienation—with the realm of freedom, with the dream of working less or even not at all. Communism, Marx says, means a state where "the overwork of the masses has ceased to be a condition for the general development of riches." Individual free development, he says, "is no more a question of reducing the time of necessary labor vis-à-vis overwork, but to reduce to an absolute minimum the necessary labor time in society. From the free-time liberated, and the means created to the benefit of all, this reduction supposes the artistic, scientific, etc. development of individuals"[25]

The Coming Insurrection's call "to get going" bases itself on a new form of Marxist organization, on a notion "of finding each other," on a solidarity that moves beyond the narrow confines of a unified "working class."[26] In fact, it offers another brand of Marxism, a more open one, certainly a more threatening version than that espoused by academic aficionados and purists. We've only to remember how little Marx himself spoke of "class," and how the foremost task he set himself was that of probing the possibilities of overthrowing the economic and political system we call "capitalism." To be Marxist is to be communist, and *The Coming Insurrection* proposes a *new* communism "elaborated in the shadows of barrooms, in print shops, squats, farms, occupied gymnasiums." Communism is "a sharing of sensibility and elaboration of sharing, the uncovering of what is common and the building of a force."[27] Once upon a time, says *The Coming Insurrection*:

> pioneers of the labor movement were able to find each other in the workshop, then in the factory. They had the strike to show their numbers and unmask scabs. They had the wage relation, pitting the party of capital against the party of labor, on which they could draw lines of solidarity and of battle ... We have everyday insubordination for showing our numbers and for unmasking cowards.[28]

You get the impression the Invisible Committee has read its André Gorz, and agrees with the man who bids farewell to the working class, and who wants to free us from work, to find a path to paradise, to tunnel narrow trails of post-industrial subversion. "It's no longer a question of winning power as a worker," Gorz says in *Farewell to the Working Class*, "but of winning the power no longer to function as a worker. The power at issue is not at all the same as before. The [working] class itself has entered into crisis."[29] Interestingly, if we believe Gorz's provocative idea that there's now no such thing as a working class, or that its ranks have shrunken (or fragmented) to an insignificant number, then the old argument between Marxists and anarchists on the exact role of the state in the "dictatorship of the proletariat" becomes largely redundant. Since there's no longer any definable proletariat, certainly one that workers identify themselves with or feel passionate about, then there's presumably no one left to assume dictatorship. Consequently, anarchists and Marxists have no real beef with one another, seemingly concurring with what Henri Lefebvre told us long ago: that there's essentially no distinction between anarchism and Marxism, at least no significant difference that precludes one practically identifying with the other.[30] All of which presents itself as a political opportunity for Marxists, as a loosening of its historical shackles, both epistemologically (in terms of its object of analysis) and politically (in terms of the agents in this object of analysis). Post-capitalist living has no need to feel threatened by the tradition of dead historical-materialist generations.

Alberto Toscano has recently attacked *The Coming Insur-rection*'s "diagnosis of the dissolution of class solidarity as a foothold for social critique," suggesting it spells "an indifference to a Marxist discourse of class struggle" and a "de-linking of anti-capitalism from class politics."[31] But Gorz himself gives a nice rejoinder to Toscano's accusation, remarking that the former doesn't necessarily imply the latter, that the dissolution of the working class doesn't necessarily mean that Marxism has dissolved as a guide for revolt. "The negativity which, according to Marx, was to be embodied in the working class has by no means disappeared," notes Gorz.

> It has been displaced and has acquired a more radical form in a new social area ... It has the added advantage over Marx's working class of being immediately conscious of itself; its existence is at once indissolubly subjective and objective, collective and individual. This non-class encompasses all those who have been expelled from production by the abolition of work, or whose capacities are under-employed as a result of the industrialization (in this case, the automation and computerization) of intellectual work. It includes all the supernumeraries of present-day social production, who are potentially or actually unemployed, whether permanently or temporarily, partially or completely. It results from the decomposition of the old society based upon the dignity, value, social utility and desirability of work.[32]

Arguably, class continues to evoke something meaningful only in the context of a *class-conscious* ruling elite; on the other hand, those who don't rule, the bulk of us, are an assorted and fragmented layering of disparate peoples who are neither conscious of class nor motivated to act in the name of any class. Nevertheless, these peoples *are* often motivated by a desire to act against a ruling class, against a system that this class so evidently props us, a system from which a non-class feels alienated and abused by. We might say that these people aren't so much class-conscious as *collectively-conscious of an enemy*, conscious of their desire to do something about that enemy, conscious about wanting no truck with that enemy's game. As Gorz remarks, this non-class "is no more than a vague area made up of constantly changing individuals whose main aim is not to seize power in order to build a new world, but to regain power over their own lives by disengaging from the market rationality of productivism."[33] The notion of a "non-class" opens up the political terrain, makes it both potentially more fruitful and decidedly more inclusive, yet clearly more uncertain, too, because nothing can be taken for granted, because it precludes Messianic dogmatism, militates against "bearers" of history in our midst. Instead, it implies a challenge, and begets a possibility: "it reminds individuals," says Gorz, "of the need to save themselves and define a social order compatible with their goals and autonomous existence."[34]

The associative connections and potential solidarities latent in the realm of everyday life are vastly larger than those made explicit in the world of work. In daily life, the balance of power is so much more even because the plane of battle is so much broader, so much more dynamic. Subversion can happen anywhere and at anytime. Strikes are willy-nilly general, and can paralyze the whole fabric of society rather than just threaten the deep pockets of the factory owners. The reserve army of labor now has the potential to become a laboring army of reservists, joining hands and merging their minds around affinity rather than occupation, cooperating in a division of labor they themselves have formulated. "*Don't back away from what is political in friendship*," says the Invisible Committee.[35] This is a novel idea that gives political muscle to a politics of *affinity*, as well as to an *affective politics*, to the non-power of *conviviality*, as Ivan Illich might have said. Affinity politics is based on such a relation of *conviviality*, and a convivial relation happens when people participate together in the creation of their social life, when they renounce technical and productive values and replace them with an ethical value.[36]

"We've been given a neutral idea of friendship," says the Invisible Committee, "understood as a pure affection with no consequences. But all affinity is affinity *within* a common truth. Every encounter is an encounter within a common affirmation. No bonds are innocent in an age when holding onto something and refusing to let go usually lead to unemployment, where you have to lie to work, and you have to keep on working in order to continue lying."[37] As such, a movement comes into being when like-minded people find each other, when they get along with each other, when they make friends, when they decide upon a common path together. They come together because they "prefer not to," because they prefer to do something else, together, because they have established a concrete convivial relation. They don't find each other because of some abstract ideal, some specific consciousness with which they *should* associate themselves, one assorted theorists, leaders and politicos tell them it is in their best interests to identify with. Instead, they wage war around "things they can touch with their own hands," as Colonel Buendia put it (p. 85).

It's the realm of affects that binds, that's causal in any social movement formation. Affinity becomes the cement that bonds people across frontiers and barriers. In desiring another reality, inventing it, dreaming it up, people find their kindred souls, perhaps nearby, perhaps faraway; and in finding one another they struggle together for the realization of their common hopes. Struggle becomes a flesh and blood practice that tries to realize a deep desire, a friendship, a collective dream, maybe even a collective fantasy. In so doing, along the way, like a rolling snowball, participants discover other people desiring likewise, and they gather both size and momentum. And in struggling together, struggling to realize common dreams, maybe beyond work relations, beyond the state, beyond working-class affiliation, political engagement becomes a real fantasy. People discover an "interpellated" group commonality hinging upon a double movement, upon a dream and a hatred; a hatred of what is done to them in today's system of circulation and accumulation of capital; a dream of opting out and releasing themselves from political subjugation, of doing their own thing. And in struggling together, in organizing themselves around their own thing, power frequently rears its ugly head in concrete form. To that degree, struggling to realize common desires usually means protagonists encounter a common enemy. In seeking to expand its own platform and to deepen its base, resistance seeks to *neutralize* this power, to subvert it, to sabotage it.

Methodology of Moving Through Walls

Some of the most oft-cited passages of *The Coming Insurrection*, used as incriminating evidence by an inquisitorial Sarkozy state, are those on the necessity of *sabotage*, on the necessary of "removing obstacles, one by one."[38] Sabotage is valid retribution for the incivilities that reign in our streets.

> The police are not invincible in the streets, they simply have the means to organize, train, and continually test new weapons. Our weapons, on the other hand, are always rudimentary, cobbled together, and often improvised on the spot. Ours certainly can't hope to match theirs in firepower, but can be used to hold them at a distance, redirect attention, exercise psychological pressure or force passage and gain ground by surprise.[39]

The power of *surprise*, of secret organization, of rebelling, of demonstrating and plotting covertly, of striking invisibly, and in multiple sites at once, is the key element in confronting a power whose firepower is vastly superior. "FLEE VISIBILITY: TURN ANONYMITY INTO AN OFFENSIVE POSITION": *anonymity* must be used to provoke fear and distraction, to spread rumor, to conspire in "nocturnal or faceless actions, creating an invulnerable position of attack." To be explicitly visible—in a maneuver, in organizing—"is to be exposed, that is to say above all, vulnerable."[40] Here black ski-masks become emblems of veritable nobodies, of invisible Bartlebys and underground men and women, of people without qualities who want to disguise their inner qualities, who shun visibility in public, who have little desire to be the somebody the world wants them to be, insists they *ought to* be: "just looking at the faces of some of this society's *somebodies*," jokes the Invisible Committee, "illustrates why there's such joy in being nobody."[41]

A black-masked Subcomandante Marcos, staked out in Chiapas jungle, comes to mind here; the hero Marcos whose Zapatistas symbolize grassroots rebellion and revolt against a dominant neo-liberal order; Marcos who keeps his cover for as long as it takes, until it's no longer necessary to wear a disguise, until it's safe to expose himself, until his "nakedness" renders him free not fair game. "Why hide your face?" a journalist once asked Marcos, just after the Zapatistas had captured key towns in Mexico's southernmost state in January 1994. "What are you afraid to show?" *El sup* thinks of removing his mask yet suddenly the people cry "No, no, no!" So the mask stays, the allure persists, and an icon is in the making.[42] Behind the mask Marcos does away with his own self and creates another self, the non-self of the everyman and everywoman in revolt: "To be socially nothing isn't a humiliating condition," concurs *The Coming Insurrection*, "the source of some tragic lack of recognition—from whom do we seek recognition?—but is on the contrary the condition of maximum freedom of action."[43]

Power, wealth, and ruling institutions reside in the metropolis, and thus the metropolis is an obvious target for covert sabotage. The technical infrastructure of the metropolis is most vulnerable to subversion, most vulnerable to hijacking and *détournement*, most vulnerable to being tampered with and scuppered. At one time, sabotaging work through organized slow-downs, machine breaking, or working-to-rule comprised a valid modus operandi, an effective weapon for hindering production and lock-jamming the economy; now, the space of twenty-first-century urban flows— of the ceaseless and often mindless *current* of commodities and people, of information and energy, of cars and communication— becomes the "whole social factory" to which the principle of sabotage can be applied. Wire networks, fiber optic channels, energy grids—all this can now be attacked, brought down in order to construct something saner than this "hopeless mobility": "Nowadays, sabotaging the social machine with any real effect involves re-appropriating and reinventing ways of interrupting its networks. How can a high-speed TGV train line or an electrical network be rendered useless? How does one find the points in computer networks, or scramble radio waves and fill screens with white noise?"[44]

Thus "jam everything" becomes a reflex principle of critical negativity, of Bartlebyism brought back to radical life, of one part of the weaponry for all those who rebel against the present order. Ironically, the more the economy has rendered itself virtual—the more value derives from the interconnectivity of circulation as well as production, the more "delocalized," "dematerialized" and "just-in-time" its infrastructural base—the easier it is to take down, to stymie, and to redirect. The recent movement in France against the CPE (*contrat première embauche*) bill, the first of a series of state laws to make job contracts for young people more insecure, "did not hesitate to block train stations, ring roads, factories, highways, supermarkets and even airports. In Rennes, only three hundred people were needed to shut down the main access road to the town for hours and cause a 40-kilometer long traffic jam."[45] Blanqui, too, during the 1871 Paris Commune, recognized that urban space isn't simply the theater of confrontation; it's also the means and stake in an insurrection, the battleground of a guerrilla warfare that builds barricades and gun turrets, that occupies buildings and employs the methodology of moving through walls.[46]

In *Instruction pour une prise d'armes* (*Manual for an Armed Insurrection*), Blanqui gives us some useful tactics for insurrection and offers handy tips for prospective barricade builders. Always critical of what he calls "inkstand radicals," Blanqui knew better than anyone else that insurrectional magic doesn't happen by magic: it is *created*, comes about through discipline and careful organization, as well as a lot of hope and will, to say nothing of a good deal of force: "something we should not count as one of the new advantages of the enemy," Blanqui writes, is the strategic thoroughfares which now furrow the city in all the directions. They are feared, but wrongly. There is nothing to be worried about. Far from having created a danger for the insurrection, as people think, on the contrary they offer a mixture of disadvantages and advantages for the two parties. If the troops circulate with more ease along them, they are also, on the other hand, heavily exposed and in the open. Such streets are unusable under gunfire. Moreover, balconies are miniature bastions, providing lines of fire on their flanks, which ordinary windows do not. Lastly, these long straight avenues deserve perfectly the name of boulevard that is given to them. They are indeed true boulevards, which constitute the natural front of a very great strength. The weapon par excellence in street warfare is the rifle ... The grenade, which people have the bad habit of calling a bomb, is generally secondary, and subject besides to a mass of disadvantages. It consumes a lot of powder for little effect, is very dangerous to handle, has no range and can only be used from windows. Paving stones do almost as much harm but are not so expensive. The workers do not have money to waste. For the interior of houses, it's the revolver, then the bayonet, the sword, saber and dagger. In a boarding house, a pike or eight-foot long halberd would triumph over the bayonet.[47]

There's no such thing as a peaceful insurrection, Blanqui said, and the Invisible Committee concurs: "weapons are necessary" they say. Still, and again like the Zapatistas, participants know

it's a question of doing everything possible to make using arms unnecessary. An insurrection is more about taking up arms and maintaining an 'armed presence' than it is about armed struggle. We need to distinguish clearly between being armed and the use of arms. Weapons are a constant in revolutionary situations, but their use is infrequent and rarely decisive at key turning points.[48]

The insurrection can triumph as a *political force*: "It's not impossible to defeat an army politically." It's important, at first, to dispose of power at the local level, to move on from there, to spread outwards like a maggot in an apple, progressively eating itself outwards, to block circulation, to fight in the streets, to sabotage and subvert, to organize and paralyze, to make every action irreversible. But what's vital in any struggle, what has to be a perpetual source of concern, is "that out of so much hatred for the military, out of fighting them so much and thinking about them so much, you end up as bad as they are. No ideal in life is worth that much baseness."[49]

Vive la Commune!

A movement's capacity to negate, to jam the machine, to orchestrate chaos, is only as effective as its ability to create something positive, something ordered and organized, to live at war while knowing how to live together in peace. At the heart of *The Coming Insurrection* lies an appeal to create new liberated territories, new communes and "multiple zones of opacity." Attach yourself to what you feel to be true, the book urges, experience the joy of encounters, of people who've shrugged off individual straightjackets and accepted modes of "normal" behavior. "What's strange," says the Invisible Committee, "isn't that people who are attuned to each other form communes, but that they remain separated. Why shouldn't communes proliferate everywhere? In every factory, every street, every village, every school?"[50] Bit by bit, communes displace the dominant institutions of society, form each time a group of people decides to rely upon themselves, to measure their collective strength against an external enemy, a reactionary force. Every commune is at once a territorial and political entity, a milieu as well as a moment, a space as well as a flow; a commune's collective force is only as strong as the "density of ties. Not by their membership, but by the spirit that animates them,"[51] that connects one commune to another, by the passion and imagination that *gels* them together.

Moreover, communes organize themselves in order that people no longer have to work. This gives a new twist to the famous Situationist mantra of *"ne travaillez jamais!"—never work!—* because it draws a distinction between working hard and *not earning a living*, not selling one's bodily and mental capacity to another, not frittering away the bulk of one's daily life doing something you hate, something stupefying, alienating. So far as exchanging oneself within a *wage relation* goes, the twenty-first-century communard *prefers not to*; instead, they want to make themselves useless, useless as a labor-powering commodity, yet *useful* as a worker, as a person who works willingly and meaningfully, productively for him or herself and for the commune.

True, a commune needs money, needs some sort of market, of dynamic exchange, even if it's only a black market; true, too, it "plunders, cultivates, fabricates"[52] any way it can; it needs to find its very own hustles and scams to keep it afloat. That its "concrete" labor has to be enacted in accordance with a plan of production and exchange is likewise acknowledged; yet here production and exchange "are transparent in their simplicity," as Marx says in *Capital*, and exist within an association of producers and distributors, all of whom buy and sell fairly amongst themselves. It's important to note that communes can interact and participate in a system of exchange based on simple reproduction not expanded accumulation, predicating itself on need rather than greed. Here, any liberation from wage-labor doesn't mean time for a vacation, for doing nothing, for hanging out; the commune isn't a hippy commune: "Vacant time, dead time, the time of emptiness and fear of emptiness—this is the time to work. There will be no more time to *fill*, but a liberation of energy."[53] Once again, Gorz is instructive:

> the abolition of work will only be emancipatory if it also allows the development of autonomous activity. The abolition of work doesn't mean abolition of the need for effort, the desire for activity, the pleasure of creation, the need to cooperate with others and be of some use to the community. Instead, the abolition of work simply means the progressive, but never total, suppression of the need to purchase the right to live by alienating our time and our lives.[54]

For the survival of any autonomous self-organizing community, relentless effort and activity, relentless determination, is necessary. Self-organization will always be in constant need of expansion, in need of a practice that can both *occupy* and *be* a territory, that can establish a solid and durable life-form. Any commune will need to increase the density of its fellow-traveler communes, and its means of circulation and modes of solidarity with them. The ideal scenario is one where a commune's own territorial demarcation becomes unreadable, is "opaque to all authority." As a basic rule, "the more territories there are superimposed on a given zone, the more circulation there is between them, the harder it will be for power to get a handle on them."[55] Bistros and bars, sports facilities and garages, wastelands and second-hand bookstores, building rooftops and improvised street markets, "can all easily be used for purposes other than their official ones should enough complicities come together in them." Eventually, this kind of local self-organization "superimposes its own geography over the state cartography, scrambling and blurring it," to the degree that the commune produces nothing else than "its own secession."[56]

How to interrupt urban flows, build new communes in the ruins, in abandoned countryside, in overbuilt cities, how to restore local food production, create urban vegetable gardens, as Cuba did to withstand an American embargo and the implosion of the USSR?[57] How can little assorted islands of Robinson Crusoes form one great big new continent of liberation? Communes will find their own answers, says *The Coming Insurrection*, or they'll get crushed mercilessly; nothing else is possible. The Imaginary Party and its adherents worldwide are starting out from a point of extreme weakness, from relative isolation. All participants know this, even if they know nothing else. The insurrection can begin only from the ground up, somewhere: "Nothing appears less likely than an insurrection, but nothing is more necessary."[58]

World Music in the Woods

There are signs, whispers, hearsay, rumors, hints that these magical ideas are getting conjured up, are taking root and taking shape somehow, that they are *present* realities as much as futuristic yearnings: from the folks at Tarnac to angry students in Greece, from disaffected youth in the French *banlieue* (the *racaille*—scum—that Sarkozy indicts) to citizens protesting the CPE law, from the eco-communities sprouting up across rural Europe to squatter and landless movements in urban Latin America, *The Coming Insurrection* seems to describe an insurrection that has already come. And in the apocalyptic devastation of post-Bush America, *The Coming Insurrection* is also creating a stir, arousing excitement about an alternative future, and this not only at the counter of Starbucks. Meanwhile, Portuguese and Spanish translations are apparently on their way, ready to hit Brazil and other parts of Latin America, perhaps engendering there another revolution in the revolution.

But, for the time being, whether *The Coming Insurrection* plots a real or imagined insurrection isn't the point; what's important is the book's unquestionable ability to motivate and provoke, to incite and excite, to inspire and to unsettle the status quo and to rile those in power—those who fear losing their power, those who have already revealed that their power is shaky, that it is threatened by the contents of a strange little book. The experimental communes the Invisible Committee evoke and invoke are radical not simply because of their reality principle but also because of their *principle of hope*: they flag up the passage through which people can come together, can find one another in a *"network of hope,"* an idea so dear to the mystical heart of German Marxist Ernst Bloch. At the beginning of his great three-volume paean to hope, Bloch describes the "naked striving and wishing" that surges within us, that expresses itself first as a "craving," as "an expectant counter emotion" which reaches outwards, urges us on, keeps us hoping. Soon this counter-emotion burns away inside us, becomes a "hunger," a source of rebellious consciousness in the making, "the No to the bad situation which exists and the Yes to the better life that hovers ahead."[59]

The Coming Insurrection has kindled passionate debate not only about the nature of insurrection, but also about the nature of *insurrectional Marxism*. There's a lot Marxists can take from this book for breaking out of a formalist straightjacket, for drafting a rawer conception of Marxism, a more dynamic, challenging, and radical one, a Marxism that abandons old trusty shibboleths, old crutches that prop up a crippled geriatric. It suggests a Marxism that no longer proposes an abstract model of revolution imposed from above, pushed onto the masses of people who may or may not identify themselves with the working class. Instead, Marxism is treated as offering a utopian vision, an expectant counter-emotion of how people might live *post-capitalistically*. From this standpoint, it's a practice that won't nor cannot be universal, applicable to everybody, everywhere—at least in the short term; it holds for some people, those who, on the basis of what they know and feel, chose to opt out, decide to live differently, to create post-capitalist communes of like-minded adventurers, people who work together, practically, energetically, while expanding their individual selves: they make their project of life a life-project that blooms. This Marxism gets nourished in everyday life and stays there, at ground level; it happens when communes make friends and connections, theorize and act in unison, expand their networks, strengthen the densities at their core, grow stronger and stronger and edge themselves outwards to embrace other communes. Soon, one commune might merge into another, as they mutually exchange know-how and concrete labor; after a while more people opt out and join in, pool their passions.

Before long, what were once particular, fragmented communes enlarge into more widespread modes of existence, denser communities, new kaleidoscopes of possibility: this is how the revolution evolves, how the magical insurrection takes hold, how the Exodus from capitalism commences. "One needs to *dare* to break with society," Gorz says, this society of ours "that is dying and which will never be reborn. One needs to dare to make the Exodus."[60] The Exodus will be intellectual and practical, an Exodus of new ideas and of determined action, a bold leap to liberation, a testament to the power of Rebellion, a journey towards a safe haven where refugees can gather, perhaps at first in small numbers, to live free of oppression. This Exodus can establish new kinds of *Quilombos*, like the fleeing slaves did in Brazil under Portuguese colonization. *Quilombos* were scattered throughout Brazil during the seventeenth century and were full of fugitive black slaves (frequently Angolans) who'd dared to rise up against the servitude of their masters and who'd set up for themselves self-sufficient plantation communities, eventually consolidating them into proto-socialist republics.[61]

This insurrection—this Exodus from capitalism, and the establishment of new *Quilombos*—isn't set alight like a forest fire, by a decisive spark that spreads linearly, as through some necessary "historical" logic, or by the storming of any winter palace; rather the magical insurrection *resonates*, takes the shape of music, like Samba, "whose focal points, though dispersed in time and space, succeed in imposing the rhythm of their own vibrations ... To the point that any return to normal is no longer desirable or even imaginable."[62] And, after a while again, people begin to dance, to sway of this music, and the groove becomes instinctive and infectious, a kind of *world music* that goes beyond any single language, even beyond words, corporeal as much as intellectual, something *absorbed* as well as understood, a giant rave organized by madmen and women living in the woods: "In 1940, Georges Guingouin, the 'first French resistance fighter,' started with nothing but the certainty of his refusal of the Nazi occupation. At that time, to the Communist Party, he was nothing but a 'madman living in the woods,' until there were 20,000 madmen living in the woods, and Limoges was liberated."[63]

3

SPONTANEOUS OVERFLOW OF POWERFUL FEELING: ACTIVISM AND IMMATERIALITY

Where there is no spontaneity, nothing happens.

Henri Lefebvre

It is the spontaneity of a movement that permits it to rapidly acquire a form frankly revolutionary.

André Gorz

Autogestion is perhaps badly suited for growth; it's an instrument of happiness.

Alain Touraine

The Radical Groove

The idea that insurrections resonate, emit a "world music," gives a more sensory tonality to Marx's old concept from *The Communist Manifesto* of a "world literature." It also shifts the emphasis away from believing that the key problem in building alliances between social movements is a spatial one—i.e. a problem of how one movement somewhere connects with another movement somewhere else, how the gap between this place and that place is to be bridged. Arguably, the issue isn't geographical at all; nor is it something that concerns "jumping scale"—like shifting from the local to the national, and then to international, thus matching the power of footloose multinational capital. Rather, what's at stake is *temporal*, concerning not linear time but the *rhythmic* feature of organization, the rippling diffusion of a militant sensibility, of struggle, of general insurrection: it's to do not so much with people connecting spatially as with the time they take to connect humanly, to *feel* the groove of insurrectional resonances around the world and around them—as, for example, when the Zapatistas won out in Chiapas, alliances were formed taking inspiration from this struggle, and various forms of activism were kick-started.

Alliances across the globe are forged through an emotional connection, through anger, pain, sympathy, admiration, etc., not because of some missing geography or spatial gap. These rhythms are sensual and affective, pre-conceptual in a certain sense, corporeal: they're geographical only in the sense that bodies occupy a space somewhere. But how could they otherwise? Radical rhythms enter us spontaneously by a vibrational frequency, like music, like dance—poly-rhythmic, to be sure, since different struggles have their own frequency, but they nevertheless coexist and yearn at some point to harmonize. But this future harmony doesn't have to equate to uniformity or mono-tonality: people hear the same music, yet sway a little differently and dance different steps depending on where they are. Though once enough people *really* hear the music, and once they start to *really* dance, no matter where you are you have to get up and start dancing yourself.

The Force of *Mística*

Another name for this slippery intuitive impulse might be *mística*, an abstract, emotional element that flows through disaffected peoples, through individuals and collectivities, "as the feeling of empowerment, love, and solidarity that serves as a mobilizing force by inspiring self-sacrifice, humility, and courage."[1] Mística is pre-cognitive praxis, mystic and deep, deriving as much from the heart as the head, a veritable "structure of feeling"[2] that asserts itself symbolically, through folklore and oral vernacular, through spiritualism and poetry, through music and dance, through getting angry about the world, and doing something about it. It emanates from the "popular" layers of society, particularly of Latin American society, where it serves as the distinctive character-istic, even as a revolutionary watchword, of one of that continent's largest and most effective social movements: the *Movimento dos Tradalhadores Ruraís Sem Terra*, the Landless Rural Workers'

Movement (MST) of Brazil, once described by Eric Hobsbawn as "probably the most ambitious social movement in contemporary Latin America."[3]

Since the late 1970s, the MST has grown into a dynamic radical force. Under the agricultural modernization program of Brazil's 1964–85 military regime, reenacting the barbarism of the eighteenth- and nineteenth-century English Enclosure Laws, 30 million family and tenant farmers were kicked off the land. By the 1990s, the MST had consolidated itself, and its ranks began to swell even more in response to President Cardoso's (1995–2002) neo-liberal policies: import tariffs were slashed from 32.2 percent to 14.2 percent while at the same time agribusiness received generous subsidies for its export trade, all of which left modest little smallholders at the mercy of the world market. Between 1995 and 1998, in Brazil's drive for "global competitiveness," as many as 400,000 farmers became severed from their earth and livelihood. Yet like the Mexican Zapatistas, the MST has successfully mobilized and organized a disparate mass of destitute farmers into a powerful and passionate agrarian army that has contested accumulation by dispossession, and retained and regained land through daring occupations and re-appropriations, risking life and limb in the process.[4]

The MST has resettled more than 400,000 families on 7 million hectares of farmland and is now one of the most vociferous opponents of Brazil's stubborn (and institutionalized) colonial legacy of *latifúndios* as well as of global neo-liberal agribusiness as championed by the likes of the WTO. It's also become a diehard promoter of food sovereignty and food security in an era of agrotoxins and transgenic seeds. In 1999, the MST participated in the "Battle of Seattle," joining hands with other indigenous movements in the Global North as well as in the Global South, like the *Confédération Paysanne* and *Via Campesina*, and has been a regular trooper in helping host the good-guy World Social Forum in Porto Alegre and Belém. Meanwhile, it has steadily moved beyond a strictly national and defensive agenda—even beyond the idea of defending rural wage-labor itself—to affirm an offensive program of empowerment through access to land, and endorsing an alternative agricultural economy and an alternative world, one more eco-sensitive, autonomous, and convivial.

Rooted in its own brand of Paulo Freirean liberation theology, the MST uses fabled mística in its *marxiant* process of "concientization," of becoming critically conscious through participation, through learning with and from others, through wrestling free of the straightjacket of received ideas, through thinking for yourself and discovering yourself within a community of other selves. A mística of resistance comes about through teaching and books, but it's really a pedagogy of "deschooling": imagination isn't bludgeoned by rote learning and grade obsessions, nor is teaching used to promote service and prompt servility; rather it poses questions, shrugs off alienation, and fosters a spirituality that's animalistic and ritualistic. Powerful mística emotions animate MST marches and rallies, rebellions, and riots, which are tightly organized yet spontaneous and felt as well, a creation of the moment as much as the mind, the moment of indignation: candles, seeds, machetes, and flags are incorporated into rituals of singing, poetry readings, and theatrics. As one MST activist put it, mística combines "dream with the political. Others on the left criticize us because mística is viewed as idealism, ritualistic ... But without mística we cannot be militants. We get nourished from this, and if you cannot feel emotion with the *lonas pretas*, with the children in school, with the MST's flag, then why continue?"[5]

"Mística touches you inside," says another rank-and-filer. "It touches our lives because it shows the mystery of struggling, of dreaming, of having hope, of the world that is out there. So through the mística we receive our life, our reality, our dreams and our history. And the místicas give us enthusiasm, give us courage."[6] Mística "gives us impulse," says someone else:

It's something you don't explain; you feel it. We inherited a lot from theory, but in the MST it is enriched in the collectivity. Why is it that these people who live under *lona preta* stay smiling, singing and happy? It's because of mística. In school, we create mística, a necessity to study more, a way of making struggle happen. There's the mística of acting out the mystical act, where we remember martyrs through poetry or in marches—and there's the mística that you live day-to-day ... The general sense of authenticity of mística is due to the fact that it has not been institutionalized. We realize that if you allow mística to become formal, it dies out. No one receives orders to be emotional; you get emotional because you are motivated as a result of something.[7]

Mística is as political and as personal as what the Spanish poet Frederico García Lorca once labeled *duende*, a militant poetic and a poetics of militancy that makes things possible even when they're impossible, even when you think that all is lost, that everybody is dead and buried; it's a deep song Marxism that yearns to find its wildest and most sensual voice against all odds. No geographical map will ever help anyone find duende or mística. No bourgeois or ruling-class elite can ever know duende or mística because they have too much to lose, because they aren't desperate enough, because, as Marx says, they're happy in their alienation. No bourgeois or ruling-class elite can ever have duende and mística either, because each, as Lorca says, burns in the blood like a poultice of broken glass; each rejects geometry and rationality, each leans on human pain. The great artists of the south of Spain, especially of Andalusia, whether they sing or dance or bullfight, all know that nothing comes unless the duende comes, just as in radical politics, or Magical Marxism. A lot of post-industrial capitalist society has killed duende, neutered it, doused its flames, destroyed it, stolen its feeling. A life of wealth and abundance for some perversely materializes into nothingness for everyone, into a life of too much work or not enough, into a reality devoid of real sensuality and guts, a hyper-commodified air-conditioned nightmare. Yet, like the force of mística, "the duende's arrival," Lorca says, "always means a radical change in forms. It brings to old planes unknown feelings of freshness, with the quality of something newly created, like a miracle."[8]

A State of Vivid Sensation

In a remarkable essay penned at the turn of the nineteenth century, the English romantic poet William Wordsworth reflects upon a series of poems he'd bundled together under the rubric, *Lyrical Ballads*. In this essay, Wordsworth tried as best and as honestly as he could to give some "rational" explanation for his verse, to pinpoint "objectively" the expressive powers that propel an emotional force into words. Of course, Wordsworth never mentions politics and his sentiments are explicitly addressed to other poets and lovers of literature. But in ways never foreseen, and never intended, he nonetheless gives us a brilliant insight into the link between feeling and thinking, sentiment and language, imagination and composition, and in so doing shows how expressive human powers are in fact the basic ingredients of a politics as well as a poetics. Indeed, in almost every place that Wordsworth mentions "poems" and "poetry," we might just as easily replace them with "politics" and "the political." "The principal object proposed in these Poems," Wordsworth says early on, "was to choose incidents and situations from common life, and to relate or describe them throughout, as far as was possible, in a selection of language really used by men, and, at the same time, to throw over them a certain coloring of imagination."[9]

Reality is the starting point of Wordsworth's poetry, just as it must be for any politics; yet imagination does special things to color the real, and poetic ideas (and ideals) can in "a state of excitement" transform this reality into a new expressive and enlightened form, conveying unelaborated elemental sentiment in pointedly elaborate ways, for all to read, for all to *feel*. Because, above all else, Wordsworth reckons that it is *feeling* which gives importance to any action and situation, and not the action or the situation that gives meaning to the feeling. All fine poetry is, says Wordsworth, "*the spontaneous overflow of powerful feelings*";[10] likewise for all fine radical politics.

True, poems of real value and merit have usually been produced through long reflection and endless conscious revision; in all fine poetry, again as in all fine politics, feelings are modified and directed by thoughts, by mental reconstitution. But these thoughts are usually themselves the representatives of past feelings, and what poetry does "is bind together this passion and knowledge"; it thinks and feels in the spirit of human passions, says Wordsworth, passions connected to our

> moral sentiments and animal sensations, and with the causes which excite these; with the operations of the elements, and the appearance of the visible universe; with storm and sunshine, with the revolutions of the seasons, with cold and heat, with loss of friends and kindred, with injuries and resentments, gratitude and hope, with fear and sorrow.[11]

Poetic thought thus gives shape to latent human passions, guides the spontaneous overflow of powerful feelings, and translates these emotions into touching empathetic sentiment. The successful poem, like successful politics, straddles the thought–feeling divide, collapses it somehow, binds each together without reducing one to the other. It's a poetic and political verse in which men are speaking to other men, women to other women, "in spite of difference of soil and climate, of language and manners, of laws and customs; in spite of things silently gone out of mind, and things violently destroyed."[12] Poetry, says Wordsworth, "binds together by passion and knowledge the vast empire of human society, as it is spread over the whole earth and over all time." Poetry, as such, uses *composition* to hone words and shape sentences much like *organizing* helps craft and direct a politics of rage. Composition retouches powerful feeling, gives it coloring and poetic form; organizing harnesses spontaneous overflowing energy and drafts a political meter, a Marxist mística, "the real language of men in a state of vivid sensation."[13]

Wordsworth didn't know he was sketching out a field manual for duende and mística users; nor did he know he was anticipating the *profane illumination* Walter Benjamin later discovered in his own magical experimental Marxism. Yet both Benjamin and Wordsworth concur that human passions and the human mind are capable of being excited without the application of artificial stimulant. Himself no stranger to the land of artificial paradises, Benjamin once wrote of his dabbling with hashish and quest for heightened forms of radical consciousness. During one hashish trip, he recounts of how "an incomprehensible gaiety came over me." "Events took place in such a way," Benjamin says, "that the appearance of things touched me with a magic wand, and I sank into a dream of them."[14] But the trance had its dark side. In fact, reflecting upon this state the next day, Benjamin knew that the hashish awakened nothing truly illuminating. During the trace, he became "an enraptured prose-being in the highest power." Yet the problem was that, if anything, he'd become a little too enraptured: in that heady state, the act of creation came a little bit too easily; it was a phony magic.

In the end, the hashish trance "cuts itself off from everyday reality with fine, prismatic edges."[15] The real magic lies much closer to home, in the "profane illumination," in "a materialist, anthropological inspiration," to which hashish, opium, or whatever else gives but an "introductory lesson"—and a "dangerous one" at that. Benjamin was adamant that "we penetrate the mysterious side of the mysterious only to the degree that we recognize it in the everyday, by virtue of a dialectical optic that perceives the everyday as impenetrable, the impenetrable as everyday."[16] The profane illumination was, then, just that: an earthly not heavenly illumination, inspired by everyday struggle and toil, by tales of ordinary doings imbued with a bit of duende, with the force of mística, with a grubby magic that stems from the human heart and human mind, and which invariably explodes on some street or in some jungle not terribly far away. In its most intoxicating, ecstatic radical form, it might spontaneously combust into a dangerous subversive politics, maybe into a truly revolutionary act.

The Explosion, or Spontaneous Combustion

The debate about feelings and thought and about spontaneity and organization has a long and checkered history within classical Marxism. In 1904 it brought Rosa Luxemburg to blows with Lenin, just as it had earlier divided Marx and the anarchist Mikhail Bakunin within the First International Working Men's Association (1864–76). Lenin belittled spontaneity, insisting it was a "subjective element" that couldn't congeal into a fully blown "objective factor." In *One Step Forward, Two Steps Back*, he wrote that the "spontaneous development of the workers' movement leads precisely to its subordination to bourgeois ideology."[17] He reckoned a "socialist consciousness" could only be brought to the people from the outside. By itself, the working class is only capable of a restrictive, "pure-and-simple trade union consciousness." As a result, the working class needed a Party, led by an elite vanguard, by dedicated intellectuals who would make revolution their calling, who would purge the movement of its spontaneity, dictate a tight, tactical program of action, especially "to rebellious students ... to discontented religious sectaries, to indignant school teachers, etc." Lenin, in short, was leery of mística, of a wilder, more emotive politics of rage, of spontaneous militancy.

The Marxist-Leninist campaign against spontaneity, waged in the name of science, in the name of insurrection viewed as technique, as organization, has had a catastrophic effect on looser, populist protesting, throwing the subjective, breathing baby out with the stagnant, objective bathwater. Indeed, certain strains of Marxism followed Lenin's edict that spontaneity was devoid of value, that is, was essentially irrational, unscientific, against the flow of historical necessity and revolutionary capacity. Spontaneity lacked the military discipline Lenin wanted, lacked his centralist take on organization, regressed into "tailism," with the tail wagging the dog, the masses steering the Party, in a "slavish kowtowing before spontaneity."

Rosa Luxemburg, on the other hand, had little sympathy with Lenin's "ultra-centralist tendency," rejecting his contempt for nonaligned working-class activism, for the "objectivity" of the Party. Different progressive and working-class federations, Luxemburg wrote in her pamphlet *Leninism or Marxism?*, needed a "liberty of action."[18] That way they could better "develop their revolutionary initiative and utilize all the resources of a situation." Lenin's line was "full of the sterile spirit of overseer. It is not a positive and creative spirit."[19] Luxemburg is more generous, more sensitive to the ups and downs of struggle in the course of which an organization emanates and grows, unpredictably pell-mell. Social democracy, she says, isn't just "invented"; it's "the product of a series of great creative acts of the often spontaneous class struggle seeking its way forward."[20]

Needless to say, a movement might not immediately recognize itself within its struggle, within its campaign, given that people often become *aware* of themselves, objectively, as it were, as activists within a broader movement, only during the course of struggle. They invariably define themselves through their opposite, through encountering a "ruling class," their Other, through agents and institutions who are different from them, who have power and wealth and authority, and whose interests are different from theirs, somehow against theirs. Affinity and affiliation (whether formal or not) becomes *acknowledged* en route, not a priori. There aren't any precisely prescribed set of revolutionary tactics, no tactical recipe books. An "air-tight partition between the class-conscious nucleus of the proletariat already in the party and its immediate popular environment" is, for Luxemburg, mindlessly sectarian. The unconscious comes forth before the conscious; the movement, she says, advances "spontaneously by leaps and bounds. To attempt to bind the initiative ... to surround it with barbed wire, is to render it incapable of accomplishing the tremendous tasks of the hour."[21]

Luxemburg should be on the reading lists of *altermondialistes* everywhere; ditto for every Marxist's. Killing spontaneous upsurge without trying to understand it, to guide it towards a coherent practice, to shape it through "composition" (in the Wordsworthian sense) and nourish a tactics that might overcome it at the right moment—neither too early nor too late—is the desperate sign of dogmatism. As Henri Lefebvre said, reflecting upon May 1968, without spontaneity nothing happens, nothing progresses; there simply is no movement, no movement that moves, nothing that has life. "For all forms of power, consequently, spontaneity is the enemy."[22] Always and everywhere spontaneity expresses itself as a subjectivity against objectivity, as a refusal to be integrated into a duff system, as an emotional release, as a state of vivid sensation, as a catharsis to domination and exploitation, to marginalization and oppression, as a moment of truth—or perhaps of delusion.

Not every spontaneous upsurge is progressive, as Weimar Germany attests; ditto Britain's "pro-hunt" rallies and in the US the recent corporate-lobbyist-inspired anti-Obama "tea parties," championed by Fox News and our old friend Glenn Beck. So, too, was one of staunchest advocates of spontaneity a free-marketeer—Friedrich von Hayek, Margaret Thatcher's bedside read. For Hayek, the "free" price system is an unconscious invention that produces its own "spontaneous order," something resulting from human action, he says, but not from human design. Many things, however, separate Hayek's radical (conservative) spontaneity from its progressive counterpart. To begin with, the spontaneity Hayek recognized arose out of social institutions organized around a market of "free individuals" asserting their "moral" right; yet, as Marx repeatedly insisted, this is a kind of freedom—"free trade," "free exchange," etc.—which is really a freedom for the relatively few at the expense of the many. Indeed, it's a freedom that militates against any autonomous action that isn't cast within the confines of a market situation, that isn't based upon exchange, money, and value relations. It's an "anarchy" of unregulated markets that produces despotism in the workplace, and in daily life. It's a Hobbesian race for the bottom-line wherein the only prevailing authority is the authority of competition, the coercion exerted by reciprocal capitalist interests. Meanwhile, Hayek also maintains that these spontaneous, anarchic markets produce an ordered rational system that tends towards equilibrium. Even on its own terms this notion is ridiculous, given the perennial breakdowns and crises of global capitalism.

From a left libertarian standpoint, on the other hand, spontaneous non-statist activity is affirmed because it wants to rid itself of the market system, because it wants to replace it with something more genuinely autonomous and communitarian. This sort of spontaneity frequently explodes in the arenas of society not occupied by institutions, such as forgotten or feared spaces of everyday life, like peripheral *quartiers* and *banlieues*, like inner cities and ghettoes, like jungles and *favelas* and assorted shantytowns the world over. Not so long ago Mike Davis pondered on the possibility of spontaneous combustion in the mega-cities of the Global South:

Perhaps there's a tipping point at which the pollution, congestion, greed and violence of everyday urban life [in the developing world] will finally overwhelm the ad hoc civilities and survival networks of the slum. Certainly in the old rural world there were thresholds, often calibrated by famine, that passed directly to social eruption. But no one yet knows the social temperature at which the new cities of poverty spontaneously combust.[23]

By 2020, 2 billion people will inhabit *favelas* and slums scattered around the edge of the world's biggest cities. A vast global *banlieue* is in the making in which landless peasants and ex-proletarians occupy not rural hinterlands but the periphery of the world-city, ruralizing the urban as much as urbanizing the countryside. Meanwhile, a global ruling class is shaping its core, at the center, "Haussmannizing" nodes of wealth and information, knowledge and power, creating a feudal dependency *within* urban life everywhere. Who knows whether those 2 billion dispossessed will ever want to *de*marginalize themselves in a giant spontaneous street uprising. Will the globalization of communication open everything up to "the eyes of the global poor"—to adapt Baudelaire's poem—inspiring indignation and organization as well as awe (with their "big saucer eyes")? Tens of thousands of poor landless Latinos have already helped reinvent the urban labor movement in California; militancy in South African townships brought down Apartheid; millions took to streets in Jakarta, Seoul, Bangkok, São Paulo and Buenos Aires, when East Asian and Latin American economies went into meltdown during 1997; revolts against IMF shock therapy programs have regularly left many developing world capitals smoldering as the most vulnerable connect global neo-liberalism with their own local street.

Once they erupt, and certainly if they spread, power and its media quickly brandish spontaneous uprisings "riots," émeutes, and their participants are dismissed as "scum," as dangerous anarchists, as unreasonable disturbers of the peace and the "moderate" social order. Institutions, above all, fear the untamed street and try to cordon it off, try to repress its spontaneity, to separate different factions of protesters in the street; they try to quell the apparent disorder and seek to reaffirm order, in the name of the law. From street level, from below, contestation can spread to institutional areas above. Spontaneous contestation can unveil power, can bring it out into the open, out of its mirrored-glass offices and black-car motorcades, out of its private country clubs, its conference rooms and seminar centers. Especially since Seattle, streets have become explicitly politicized, filling the void left by institutional politics, bringing globalization home to roost, somewhere, at some moment. Therein lies the strength of spontaneous street contestation; therein also lies its weakness: the weakness of localism, of symbolism, of "partial practice," of an impulsive nihilism.

And yet, the explosion of street politics and spontaneity in Seattle, in Washington, in New York, in Davos, Switzerland (where the World Economic Forum meets annually), as well as in Quebec City (April 2001, where tear gas and water cannons met those protesting the Free Trade Area of the Americas talks) and at numerous G8 summits, in the *banlieue* of French big cities (November 2005), in Greece (December 2008), has led to the rebirth within radicalism of the phenomenon of violence. Violence is connected with spontaneity and with contestation— "with forces," Lefebvre says, "that are in search of orientation and can exist only by exerting themselves."[24] Violence is largely unavoidable in radical struggle: breaking things up, making nonsense out of meaning (and meaning out of nonsense), throwing bricks through Starbucks windows, driving tractors into McDonald's, burning cars, daubing graffiti on walls—all are justifiable responses to state repression and corporate injustice, to the "latent violence" of power. Hence they are legitimate forms of "counter-violence." In this sense, violence expresses what Lefebvre calls a "lag" (*retard*) between "peaceful coexistence" and "stagnating social relations," symptomatic of "new contradictions super-imposed on older contradictions that were veiled, blurred, reduced, but never resolved."[25]

Lefebvre sees a certain political purchase in destructive behavior, in senseless acts of beauty—so long as they don't degenerate into "the ontology of unconditional spontaneity," into "the metaphysics of violence." Reliance only on violence leads, he says, to a "rebirth of a tragic consciousness," antithetical to the dialectic of becoming. Consequently, serious concern with contestation, spontaneity, and violence, requires at the same time a serious delineation of spontaneity and violence, done with the aid of theory "which pure spontaneity tends to ignore."[26] Frequently, spontaneous protest is summarily denounced as idiotic, juvenile, naive, and this not only by the right-wing. But "immature" young people can teach grown-ups a thing or two about mature life and politics. If anything, "maturity" in politics may be as much a stumbling block as a solution. Often "maturity" spells certitude, and a leftist certitude translates into either dogmatism or cynicism, into an endorsement of the messianic powers of the proletariat, and nothing else but. Such a vision tends to move from the relative towards the absolute, into an invocation of the authority of the founders, into a purity and *a posteriorism* that deigns to no contamination in the meanwhile. Here left-wing cynics seem happy to revel in analyzing and criticizing the increasingly bankrupt capitalist system; the worse it gets, the more crisis ridden it becomes, the better it is for them, the more depressed they can be, the more inspired they are in their theorizing and apocalyptic prognostications. This is a perverse certitude. On the other hand, incertitude and false hopes can spell nihilism and a delusional optimism that can lurch towards absolute violence, to vain and unorganized activism, to a lot of people getting hurt on the street, especially young people.

Someone like Lefebvre was cunning in his adoption of a utopian position somewhere in between, a position he labels "*cultivated spontaneity*."[27] Cultivated spontaneity centers on concrete problems that are practical and theoretical, and which require both sobriety and exuberance in resolving them, diligent organizing mixed with mad raving ideals, method as well as mística. It means, too, an "unceasing critical analysis of absolute politics and the ideologies elaborated by specialized political machines,"[28] whether on the left or the right. Cultivated spontaneity today would be neither dogmatism nor nihilism, but something else entirely different again: it would be a form of contestation as scathing of the bourgeois system as the romantic dandies of Stendhal's time, yet more experimental in its extravagant subjectivity, more battle-trained in its magical imagination. It would be an activism that is somehow at once classical and post-modern, a new retro-Marxism: angrier and more realistic than the generation that gave us surrealism, yet more humorous and breezier than Lefebvre's own generation of earnest tie-wearing communists and labor movement affiliates.

"It requires courage to be a romantic," Stendhal claimed, "because one must take risks."[29] Any new millennium romanticism of spontaneous combusters would similarly scour the future and take risks. It would march ahead of the game, exit from us, scanning the horizon in the far distance. Its presence would suggest a new attitude drifting in the breeze, and if we look hard enough this presence can be seen and felt: in the revolts, insubordinations, protests, abstentions, spontaneous rebellions that are indeed around us today. What the romantics saw around them in Stendhal's day, and what any "new romantic" sees now, is a world governed by constraints and inanities, and these need to be blasted away, brushed aside, dynamited. A new romanticism would be affirmed, is being affirmed, by disparate and desperate elements of society: young people, political rebels, exiles, intellectuals, deskilled, unemployed and/or downsized workers, self-selected downshifters, déclassé deviants, half-crazed debauchees, misfits, successive and abortive geniuses, dandies and perhaps even a few snobs. This ragged, motley array of people would live out, is living out, within the ruins of everyday bourgeois society their ideal solutions to bourgeois society, challenging its moral order, devouring society from within as it seeks to *reinvent* the world from without, using all its powers of symbolism and imagination, all its raging powers of numbers.

All spontaneous transgressions take a devastating revenge on the constraints of the language of power. Speech (in its broadest sense) manifests itself as a primary freedom, what we might also call a *primal freedom*. When protest and critique is outlawed, silenced or pilloried in the press, when it is banished from the street, agitation and indignation will spark angry contestation; and soon an explosion of unfettered speech and action may be unleashed.

We've already glimpsed such spontaneous contestation erupting on our streets, voicing indignation and agitation, coalescing around many different agendas, expressed by many different groups, pitched around many different issues: canceling Third World debt, banning child and sweatshop labor, ridding cars from our cities, keeping city life vital, shutting down the World Bank and the IMF, taming unfettered globalization, changing the world and changing life. Participation has shown and will doubtless continue to show its indignation. A re-energized militancy and spontaneity has reared its head, just a little. This contestation has posed unflinching questions while grappling for answers, while dreaming about alternatives. Equally, it has shown an amazing capacity to politicize people, particularly young people, those disgruntled with ballet-box posturing and who care about our fragile democracy and sacked society.

Some protagonists, like Global Exchange, a San Francisco-based human rights organization, comprise nomadic gadflies, young activists who travel up and down America and all over the world. They spread the anti-corporate word at hitherto unprecedented decibels, mixing painstaking planning with spontaneous militancy, clearheaded analysis with touchy-feely utopianism. Indeed, the whole ontological raison d'être of Global Exchange is *organizing*: politicking and proselytizing, conducting teach-ins and speak-outs, staging demos and boycotts and masterminding blitzes, everywhere. Their ideas and ideals address the big black hole that capitalist consumerism bequeaths young, intelligent people today. Global Exchange is also a prime mover in the umbrella group, DAN, the Direct Action Network, whose ethos is non-violent protest. DAN *détourns* high-tech media, too, working it for its own radical ends, coordinating on the Internet, initiating guerrilla action, radicalizing fellow-traveling affinity groups, like the Ruckus Society, which affirms a politics of pleasure, having fun while it gets deadly serious, performing street theater and musical happenings, dance soirées and educational seminars.

Many cities across the globe have been disrupted and re-appropriated by another dynamic spontaneous presence: Reclaim the

Streets (RTS). Over recent years, RTS demos have shutdown streets in Manhattan (at Astor Place, in the East Village and around Times Square), in Sydney, in north, south and central London, in Helsinki, in Prague and other European capitals. In the middle of major traffic thoroughfares, crowds have danced and shouted and partied—revolutionaries, students, workers, activists, and malcontents. In their "Festivals of Love and Life," they've brought cars to a standstill and defended pedestrians' and bikers' right to the city. RTS has rediscovered a "new romantic" oomph, "transforming stretches of asphalt into a place where people can gather without cars, without shopping malls, without permission from the state, to develop the seeds of the future in the present society." So said one RTS banner posted not very long ago on an East Village wall. Such prankster politics enacts lampoon, pulls tongues and raises the finger, voices satire at a rather sober and stern enemy. Turning people on has meant turning them off party-political smokescreens. Participants know the revolution will never be televised.

Smart Spontaneity

And yet those participants have nonetheless "profited" from new corporate communication technologies, turning them against their antagonists, using them as spontaneous radical weapons much like Colonel Buendia had in his long democratic crusades in *One Hundred Years of Solitude*. "Get the boys ready," the colonel had said to Gerineldo Márquez. "We're going to war." "With what weapons?" Márquez asks. "With theirs," says the colonel (p. 89). Foremost here is the cell-phone, now a redoubtable weapon for communicating *sur place*, on the spot, spontaneously; young people raised in the culture of cell-phones no longer make appointments or arrangements weeks in advance like my 40-something generation did and still do; by calling around, by passing the message on, they organize themselves in the heat of the moment and in the heat of the movement; like bourgeois production, they arrange rendezvous *just-in-time*. So, too, in politics: new technology has collapsed space and diminished the time of organizing, of rounding up troops or shifting them elsewhere, of supplying reinforcements when and where needed, of dodging heavy police presences: all that is now unprecedentedly aided by cell-phones and text messaging. Now, spontaneity can be managed and orchestrated—media staged, as it were; and via mobile calls and text messages protesters can give each other continuous and almost instantaneous updates about routes, street closures and police actions.

Cell-phones coordinated a lot of the activism and "swarming tactics" on the streets of Seattle in 1999, and were crucial weapons in outsmarting the centralized police radio system; more recently, cell-phones and mobile technologies have been able to dodge "security bubbles" and exclusion zones cropping up in the world's big cities. At the back end of 2003, mobile messaging pioneered the "Chase Bush" campaign in London; text messages, emails, and images were sent out to all activists and anti-war campaigners trying to spoil the Blairite PR and disrupt the state-managed party. Regular SMS updates, as well as on-location reports about Bush's appearances and movements, were circulated among participants, frequently young people who see themselves as "second generation Smart Mobbers."[30] Text messages sent from cell-phones have likewise enabled activists to communicate and organize themselves at assorted World Economic Forum (WEF) summits, and in July 2004 a so-called "TXTMob" was at the center of spontaneous rallies disrupting both the Democratic and Republican National Conventions in Boston and New York.

According to the *New York Times*, "TXTMob works like an Internet mailing list for cell-phones and is the brainchild of a young man who goes by the pseudonym John Henry. He's a member of the Institute for Applied Autonomy, a group of artists, programmers and others who say their mission is to develop technologies that serve the social and human need for self-determination." The software used by all registered TXTMobbers isn't intended for everyday mobile socializing: "It was created as a tool political activists could use to organize their work, from staff meetings to street protests. Most of the people using it are on the left: of the 142 public groups listed on the TXTMob site, the largest are dedicated to protesting the Bush administration, the Republican Party or the state of the world in general." At the "Critical Mass" anti-Republican rally in New York, TXTMob bikers organized themselves by dispatching messages to alert one another of route changes to avert traffic snarls. One young female participant, thumbing through her TXTMob messages, said the system kept her safe during the ride: "It told me where the cops were and where I could rest."[31]

IT and mobile media-inspired activism might even be ushering in a new "Fifth International," a qualitatively different form of left organizing and politicking from yesteryear's internationals, from those traditionally pioneered by party-based socialists and rank-and-file unionists. The current "informatized and globalized capitalism," writes Peter Waterman, the coiner of the "Fifth International" thesis, is a capitalism very different in form and content from that pervading during the era of the "International Working Men's Associations"; today, modes of solidarity and styles of praxis require other means and incorporate new non-affiliated and non-aligned protagonists.[32] According to Waterman:

> The new internationalisms are communication internationalisms, in a number of interrelated senses: a) their privileged terrain is that of communication; b) they are concerned to create new common global under-standings and communities by both the provision of otherwise repressed and unavailable information and the creation of new emancipatory meanings or understandings; c) their internal cohesion and external influence is more a matter of communication than organization.[33]

A newly forming, looser coterie of smart and concerned citizens, spanning the entire globe and dialoguing in many different languages, are thus finding their collective lingua franca in the growing array of informational technology acronyms like SMS, PDA, GPS, GPL, XML, etc., etc. And they're drawing upon their dazzling expertise to create an anarcho-communist subculture of politically minded "hackers" and virtual radicals whose activism and communication sometimes does come home to roost in bites as well as bytes.[34] In one of his last books, *L'immatériel*, André Gorz propels these hackers and their "hacker ethnic" into the forefront of a potentially revolutionary vanguard, into an anti-statist "postindustrial neo-proletariat" and "dissidents of a numeric capitalism."[35] In the informational economy of immateriality, Gorz glimpses those who are bidding adieu to the working class, and good riddance, too, he says, because at the same time this is bidding farewell to capitalist work and money relations, to profit motives and competition exigencies, to scarcity and monopoly. "With the development of the Web and of the 'Free Software' movement," Gorz writes, "this neo-proletariat has become the geometric site towards which and from where all radical contestation of global and financial capitalism disseminates."[36]

The ranks of this neo-proletariat are expanding as we speak, either by free will or by default, by the increasing obsolescence of human labor, by the continued implementation of machines and new technology in the process of capitalist production. The value base of our economy is more and more founded upon a materiality that is in reality *immaterial*, that has decoupled the link between employing labor and making money; indeed, it has decoupled itself from the essential basis of Marx's labor theory of value, too, together with any hope of a return to a full-employment economy. Capitalism has outlived its lame promise of wealth for everyone, a decent job for everyone—outlived it long ago. All of which brings new threats as well as new possibilities; all of which, as Marx knew, is "pregnant with its contrary." Yet it is those people who voluntarily align themselves with this non-aligned neo-proletariat who perhaps hold the key, who are perhaps the new agents with a world-historical anti-capitalist mission; in fact, these people, says Gorz, "are the principal future actors of an anti-productivist, anti-statist cultural mutation."[37]

Gorz cites at length the late German Social Democrat and technology analyst, Peter Glotz, who reckoned the real novelty of this immaterial economy lies in the radicality of its self-appointed neo-proletariat, "because they've refused the culture of the nanosecond. More and more these youth are refusing to climb the social ladder," preferring to reverse what Sarkozy once thought: opting for more free time rather than more money.[38] As Glotz explains further:

they want to transform their work from full-time to part-time because they want to clear away the time-served work ethic ... The more that numeric [informational] capitalism spreads its grip on our lives, the greater will become the number of *downshifters* and voluntary déclassé. From them a new conception of the world will surge. The struggle that pits the numeric proletariat against the capitalist business elite won't have at stake questions about technology and economics, but two differing principal and passionate conceptions of life. The whole social ethic of modern capitalism is now in question.[39]

Net activism and deliberate downshifting is a contra-capitalism germinating within actually existing capitalism, an auto-organization negating the system from within as it invents an alternative community from without. The means, the actors, and the weapons are now all different from the past. Still, this anarcho-communism nascent within virtual activism, dramatized and amplified by the hacker and free software network, "is but a sketch of another possible world," as Gorz admits; its promise is that it

diffuses within the social body of society and somehow catalyzes a re-composition of that society. Only if this social body carries within it a coalition of a certain type is global change possible. Revolutions are made— when they are made—by an alliance of the most oppressed with those who are most conscious of their own alienation and that of others. It's this alliance that's emerging in the manifold movement for 'another world', for another globalization. Different constituents animate this alliance: academics, economists, writers, artists, scientists linked to and radicalized by oppositional unions, post-industrial neo-proletarians, cultural minorities, landless peasants, the unemployed and the partly-employed.[40]

Experiments in other modes of life are being explored within this new community, in the interstices of a society whose monopoly and centralization of the means of production have reached a point at which they are incompatible with the socialization of labor. This capitalist integument is leaking air—deflating from within, not bursting asunder. New technology has created ever more complex and diverse divisions of labor, and, historically, capital has appropriated this as a source of relative surplus value.

Technology's prowess, Marx says, rests in its ability "to increase the productive power of the individual, *by means of cooperation,*" by creating a new productive power, "which is intrinsically a collective one."[41] But this cuts both ways, because this collective and cooperative power, hastened as it is by globalization and informatization, also opens up new potentialities for revolt and resistance—and Marx knows it. The "unavoidable antagonism," he says, is that "as the number of cooperative workers increases, so too does their resistance to the domination of capital."[42] And it's an unavoidable antagonism that's broadening the terrain for any neo-proletariat, for creating an expanded and more concentrated geopolitical network for a different kind of cooperation, for new powers of desire and imagination, for radical *mística,* for collective sharing rather than private appropriation, for self-unfolding rather than wholesale degradation.

Cooperation as "Self-Unfolding"

A society beyond the narrow confines of wage-labor, money, and exchange lies at the heart of the Oekonux project, a German list-serve that discusses the revolutionary possibility of Free Software and an Open Source economy.[43] The founder, Stefan Merten, says that Oekonux and its sister magazine *Krisis* offer contemporary readings of Marx in the light of the new information economy and transformations in work relations:[44]

> A number of people on the Oekonux mailing list have built upon Krisis' theories and carried them onto new ground. On the list, among other things, we try to interpret Marx in the context of Free Software. It's very interesting that much of what Marx said about the final development of capitalism can be seen in Free Software. In a sense, part of our work is trying to re-think Marx from a contemporary perspective, and interpret current capitalism as containing a germ form of a new society.[45]

The fundamental basis of a capitalist economy, of a society based on the profit motive, on exchange value and money relations, is scarcity—*the active creation and perpetuation of scarcity.* The digital economy, as peddled by the likes of Microsoft, is all about domination and monopoly, about closing things off for non-payers; it's an informational industry that privately accumulates capital at the same time as it feverishly protects its intellectual property rights. A Free Software society is the veritable nemesis of that. After all, free software, like all digital information, is in essence infinitely reproducible, and at extremely low cost, and thus isn't in any sense a scarce good. Contrary to intellectual property rights (IPR) people, the Free Software movement, which offers downloadable software at zero price, goes out of its way to prevent commercial monopolization and scarcity creation. And as an anti-business ethic this can be far-reaching. As Merten says:

> For most Free Software producers, there's no other reason than their own desire to develop that software. So the development of Free Software is based on the self-unfolding (from the German term 'Selbstentfaltung', similar but not completely the same as 'self-development') of the single individual. This form of non-alienated production results in better software because the use of the product is the first and foremost aim of the developer—there simply is no profit that can be maximized. The self-unfolding of the single person is present in the process of production, and the self-unfolding of the many is ensued by the availability of high quality Free Software.[46]

When information is given away rather than sold for a fee this is potentially radical; society becomes more open and less hidden; power can't as easily conceal its doings, its manipulations; radical organizations and NGOs can obtain and share data and dirt on corporate machinations and maneuverings. New forms of cooperation can promote alternative forms of self-organization and self-managed associations. Open information and free access to informational tools can help develop new "tools of conviviality," and maybe even transcend the industrial model of production in which people really can flourish because of technological change.[47] The Free Software movement describes their normative society beyond capitalism as a "GPL society"—a *General Public License* society, a society in which Marx's "general intellect" prevails, a society without commercial copyright, a copy*left* society that no longer tolerates socially produced scarcity or secret state and corporate conniving, and no longer functions through exchange value and money, nor through labor exploitation.[48]

Marx was one of the first modern philosophers to recognize the tremendous potential of new technology to transform nature and to create mass abundance, to make life fruitful and work less onerous. For him, inside every labor-saving machine, within every example of wide-scale human cooperation, lay glimmers of a future utopia. But under capitalist social relations, this radiant dream remains merely a pipedream, "another driving motive and determining purpose of capitalist production";[49] another method, that is, to achieve value-added. The "free-gift" of collective labor mobilizing ever more sophisticated machines within ever more detailed divisions of labor and modes of "cooperative" work metamorphoses into an intricate sundering, into deadening alienation. What could be light and engaging work suddenly becomes heavy and repetitious, "disturbing the intensity and flow of a man's vital forces, which find recreation and delight in change of activity."[50]

The GPL society, by contrast, is a society in which work and the notion of "worker" undergoes radical transformation, radical rethinking. Work here would permit a common self-unfolding, like it does in a hobby or in art. Today's work-society develops by rendering more and more people obsolescent in relation to the production process. If "freed from the chains of capitalism," Stefan Merten thinks, "this development would mean freedom from more and more necessities, making room for more processes of self-unfolding—be it productive processes like Free Software or non-productive ones like many hobbies. So contrary to capitalism, in which increasing automation always destroys the workplaces for people and thus their means of life, in a GPL society maximum automation would be an important aim for the whole society." For Merten,

> Free Software surpasses the older forms of self-unfolding in several ways and that's what makes it interesting on the level of social change:

a) Most products of self-unfolding are results of outmoded forms of production, like craftwork. Free Software is produced using the most advanced means of production humanity has available.

b) Most forms of self-unfolding may be useful for some persons, but this use is relatively limited. Free Software, however, delivers goods that are useful for a large number of persons—virtually everybody with a computer.

c) Most products of self-unfolding are fruits of one individual. Free Software depends upon collaborative work—it is usually developed by international teams and with help from the users of the product.

d) Most products of self-unfolding have been pushed away once the same product becomes available on the market. By contrast, Free Software has already started to push away software developed for maximizing profit.[51]

The Free Software movement is, according to another protagonist, Pekka Himanen, "hacking capitalism," and, in contradistinction to Max Weber's protestant work ethic, offers a new social ethic to boot: "the hacker ethic." This ethic recovers a more intimate relationship to work, of which the principal motivations are pleasure, play and passion.[52] For Weber's *Protestant Ethic and the Spirit of Capitalism* (1905), work is an end in itself, a finality, a natural calling, something bestowed upon us by God who insists that we live to work rather than work to live: I *have* a job rather than *I do work*. It's a possession rather than a simple act. It follows that anything deemed "non-work" (read: "non-waged work") is assimilated as laziness or idleness, as a waste of one's time, as something morally reprehensible. It's a work ethic that persists today in our own work-obsessed society, cutting deep into our culture, especially into Anglo-Saxon culture, and appropriated by capital as its God-given business ethic. It also leads to problems of self-worth and self-esteem for all those who don't or can't work. That's why unemployment is seen as a curse rather than a potential blessing; socially, it's seen as a personal failing, as being *inactive*, not just inactive in terms of capital valorization, but in terms of oneself: you're an unproductive self.[53]

The hacker ethic opposes this Weberian ideology, and is immanently subversive in its hack stance, not just in the actual activity of programming and designing free software, like Linux or

OpenOffice, but also in its different philosophy of life and lifestyle philosophy. "In the hacker version of flexible time," Himanen says, "different sequences of life, like work, family, friends and hobbies, etc., are mixed with a certain malleability to the degree that work never occupies a central place."[54] The work of Linux is directly cooperative and voluntary; its organizational structure is horizontal not vertical, and its focus is on sharing information and innovation, not patenting it; there's a total absence of private appropriation of common goods, and often an absence of a "salary of dependence."[55] Himanen emphasizes the great diversity among hackers, from hacker-journalists and hacker-artisans, to hacker-artists, hacker-screenwriters, and hacker-activists ("hacktivists"). Some "war-driving" hackers, equipped with basic wireless antenna, pass through neighborhoods in their cars trawling the airwaves for free broadband access points and for open wi-fi networks; they note them down and later store them on online databases for free use to everybody within range. All hackers are exploring new directions for human–technology relations; all, too, permit us to better understand, and come to terms with, the kinds of mutations and possibilities opening up around work relations and projects of self-unfolding—particularly as contemporary capitalism continues its own unfolding, its steady coming apart at the seams.

Autogestion and the GPL Society

Classical Marxism has a hard time accepting the rogue nature of non-aligned spontaneity, of hacker ethics, of a striving for post-capitalist *autogestion*. Classical Marxism seems incapable of seeing any of this as the legitimate doings of a class-conscious working class, thus as anything progressive. The working class remains decisive, we hear, the only force capable of changing society. It's time to break with this kind of thinking, to break the links in the chain of Marxism's Promethean moorings; it's time Marxism let itself drift more loosely, let itself float amongst the floating relative surplus population that capitalism has "set free." It's time for it to let itself lose from its structural and productivist foundation and fight with new weapons and new techniques for a materialism that's immaterial, for a laborism that's work-shy. Marxism has the software as well as the hardware needed to engineer new forms of cooperation and solidarity, new forms of spontaneous activism and self-management spanning the world, in the global village that informational technology has somehow spawn.

A smaller world remains to be won. Old debates about the role of the state in some transitional "dictatorship of the proletariat" now appear intellectually quaint and organizationally irrelevant. Since there's little hint that the shop floor continues to inspire any radicalism other than defensive union posturing, and since the class Marx hailed as revolutionary has been unmade and rendered partyless, "taking power" through traditional worker syndicalism, through a party vanguard, is both theoretically meaningless and practically impotent. What's up for grabs is something much more ambitious and potentially more rewarding: an *autogestion* of life, a spontaneous *subjectivation* from the standpoint of social reproduction, within everyday life, within civil society. Subjectivation means that people construct their own objective structures to life, that their agency and even their wishful thinking drive them forward, compel them to act, have them strive for collective autonomy. Emotional and virtual bonds somehow gel them together; the two elements aren't mutually exclusive in arousing states of vivid sensation. For Henri Lefebvre, who has spilt much ink exploring the theme of *autogestion*, "the principle contradiction that *autogestion* introduces and stimulates is its own contradiction with the state. In essence, *autogestion* calls the state into question as a constraining force erected above society as a whole, capturing and demanding the rationality that is inherent to social relations. Once aimed at ground level, in a fissure, this humble plant comes to threaten the huge state edifice."[56]

Yet when Lefebvre talked (in 1966) about the state as a "constraining force," he was identifying a state that existed in the halcyon days of "Fordism," an interventionist state whose administrative apparatus thrust itself into the general management of everyday life. Thus it was a paternalistic state that constrained ordinary people as it went about its business of ensuring the reproductive needs of capital. Nowadays, however, this state has largely withered away, though not in the Marxist sense of the term. It has withered away from the social needs of people, re-channeling its "post-Fordist" paternalism unashamedly in the direction of capital. Historically, the traditional reflex rank-and-file response was to demand that the state look after the interests of the working class. So, instead of freeing itself from state domination, overthrowing the state or taking it over, the working class became passively dependent upon it. So much so that when, in the late 1970s and early 1980s, Margaret Thatcher and Ronald Reagan foisted themselves center stage, the left faced an awkward dilemma with its thinking about the New Right state, foundering both politically and theoretically, trapped between the rock and the hard place.[57]

The backing away of the state from its "duties" of social protection and a *de*-bureaucratization of social life might have been seen as an opportunity as much as a threat, as a potential cue to exploring new activities more self-organized, more autonomous; to self-divest from work without falling into the right's ideological trap of personal responsibility and possessive individualism. But this liberation never took place—was unable to take place in the absence of the requisite political space (or imagination). As such, touting *autogestion* in the regime of Fordism and touting it under today's neo-liberal regime is a tale of two different *autogestions*, highlighting the worst and best of times for its potential enactment. Does *autogestion* challenge corporate-state power or does it subsidize it through its own self-reliance? Does it give power a break or try to break power? Does *autogestion* signal a new form of social solidarity or is it a symptom of the decomposition of solidarity? Whatever the response here, it's clear that *autogestion* cannot be all or nothing *from the outset*; it doesn't have to be global or everywhere before it can be anywhere. *Autogestion* has to germinate somewhere, somehow, and frequently a seed is scattered spontaneously. By expressing itself, asserting itself, by growing and blooming, by defining the conditions of its own survival, *autogestion* necessarily magnifies and amplifies the problems of the society that opposes it. In any place or moment in which *autogestion* manifests itself spontaneously it always carries within itself the possibility of radicalization and generalization.

Alternative communitarian forms, virtual communities, and self-organized solidarities already exist on the social (and sometimes spatial) margins of our social system while they embody a politics that's invariably in the thick of things, invariably center stage. Under *autogestion*, individual groups freely associate without any preexisting social basis or homogeneous class interest. Often these groups have no other political ethic than an anti-capitalist/anti-corporate ethic—it's that which defines their progressive self-identity and their autonomy. They reflect a human condition that writers like Gorz label "post-Marxist." The human condition "post-Marxist" is precisely the condition confronting any conception of Magical Marxism. It's the condition in which Marxists reinvent the agents of history, give another sense to Marx's thesis of historical development—though we need to do so with a twist. To be sure, we Marxists now have to pursue this grand historical drama *independently* of any single social class capable of realizing it, of making history, or of ending "pre-history" (as Marx was wont to say). This political agenda has no class interest to invoke, no rusty anchorage to keep it fixed, no crutch to prop it up. Its inspiration is itself and its goal is to give sense to the future, to pave its way, to explore new narrow trails towards its realization *in present social relations*. If this politics draws upon the past—past myths, struggles, heroes, martyrs, and ancient rituals—it does so only as a strategic device that helps better frame the contradictions of the present conjuncture, contradictions that reveal the future. If the Zapatistas invoke Zapata and the great Mexican revolutionaries of the early twentieth century, and if their practice of everyday life is "traditional," their politics and spirit nevertheless remain rooted in the twenty-first century: they remain both autonomous and high-tech.

All forms of effective *autogestion* need to deploy some transcendent criteria, need to pose questions about the nature of individual and social transcendence. One contests using tools—intellectual software and practical hardware—that have the potential to overcome existing conditions of society, that propose an alternative to those conditions; otherwise one's contestation invariably falls back not so much on a conformism (or reformism) as on utilitarianism, and utilitarianism is always in danger of being reincorporated within the system, of being reabsorbed. In this sense, contestation isn't a technique but a *paradigm* that imagines the world differently, that makes its magic a practical realism, a realism in which public goods become new civic tools, and a General Public License (GPL) society also denotes a Global Pleasure Land. It is a paradigm posed *against* societal oppression as well as *for* a libertarian society; a paradigm in which pain and pleasure don't necessarily manifest themselves as unhealthily schizophrenic.

4

MILITANT OPTIMISM AND THE GREAT ESCAPE FROM CAPITALISM

'Would you tell me, please, which way I ought to go from here,' said Alice.
'That depends a good deal on where you want to go,' said the Cat.
'I don't much care where—' said Alice.
'Then it doesn't matter which way you go,' said the Cat.
'—so long as I get *somewhere*,' Alice added as an explanation.
'Oh, you're sure to do that,' said the Cat, 'if you only walk long enough.'

Lewis Carroll

The certainty that he was finally fighting for his own liberation and not for abstract ideals, for slogans that politicians could twist left and right according to the circumstances, filled him with an ardent enthusiasm.

Gabriel García Márquez

The Castle and the Great Escape

The world that confronts us today, each and every day, is perhaps more easily critiqued than ever before using basic Marxist tools. At the level of analysis, there's nothing radical about suggesting that it has never been simpler to adopt a classical Marxist stance *and be right*. And yet, at the level of political practice, that analysis seems far too facile, far too futile to lead us anywhere *constructive*. There's little in it that leaves us with any guide to political practice, to how we might act on the insights it offers—and therein resides a permanent Marxian dilemma. One of the difficulties here is that the world we think about, the world that functions on a particular economic model, is classically *Capital-ist* in the sense of Marx's great text; yet the world we have to act and organize in is tellingly Kafkaesque. Marxists know how to analyze and criticize this reality; but we know less about how to act in it, about how to construct a practical politics from the standpoint of this theoretical knowledge. There's no direct correlation between the two. The purity of our analysis often leaves us with very little that tells us about what we should do. Our thinking seems to have stultified our instinct; our brains have paralyzed our bodies.

The present conjuncture is Kafkaesque to the degree that castles and ramparts loom over us everywhere. These castles and ramparts are usually in plain view, frequently palpable to our senses, even inside our own minds, yet at the same time distant and somehow cut off, out of reach and inaccessible; their occupants are ever more difficult to pin down when we come knocking at their doors, providing we can find the right door to knock on. Kafka was probably better than Marx at recognizing the thoroughly modern conflict now besieging us under capitalism. Marx understood the general dynamics of the production of castles and the trials this system subjects us to, but he understood less about its corridors of power and how its organizational bureaucracies function. Marx never really understood the difficulty of waging war against a process. For his part, Kafka recognized that the conflict wasn't just an us-against-other-people affair, but a matter of us against a world transformed into an immense and invariably abstract total administration. The shift Kafka makes between his two great novels, *The Trial* (1917) and the unfinished *The Castle* (1922), mirrors an equivalent shift in our own supranational administered world. In *The Trial*, Joseph K. stands accused in a world that's an omnipotent tribunal, a sort of state-monopoly capitalist system. In *The Castle*, the protagonist K. inhabits a world that's suddenly shrunken into a village whose dominating castle on the hill seems even more powerful and elusive than ever before. Perhaps in this village with its castle we can now glimpse our own "global village," a world shrunken by globalization, a world in which the psychological drama of one man confronting a castle is now really a political parable about all of us today—about our having to conceive a collective identity to resolve the dark gothic mystery we ourselves have scripted. "Direct intercourse with the authorities was not particularly difficult," K. muses,

> for well organized as they might be, all they did was guard the distant and invisible interests of distant and invisible masters, while K. fought for something vitally near to him, for himself, and moreover, at least at the very beginning, on his own initiative, for he was the attacker ... But now by the fact that they had at once amply met his wishes in all unimportant matters—and hitherto only unimportant matters had come up—they had robbed him of the possibility of light and easy victories, and with that of the satisfaction which must accompany them and the well-grounded confidence for further and greater struggles which must result from them. Instead, they let K. go anywhere he liked—of course only within the village—and thus pampered and enervated him, ruled out all possibility of conflict, and transported him into an unofficial, totally unrecognized, troubled, and alien existence ... So it came about that while a light and frivolous bearing, a certain deliberate carelessness was sufficient when one came in direct contact with the authorities, one needed in everything else the greatest caution, and had to look round on every side before one made a single step.[1]

Almost a century on, progressives of course need the greatest caution in everything we do; we need to look around on every side before we can take a single step. The gravity of the situation isn't lost on any of us. All the same, the situation nevertheless "pampers" and "enervates" us, too, and tries to rule out all possibility of conflict by absorbing us into its "light and frivolous bearing." It has *integrated* us into *its* reality, a reality that satisfies all our unimportant wishes and desires; it has integrated itself into us as an apparently *non*-alien force. The Kafkaesque castle has thus become the veritable Debordian "integrated spectacle," a phenomenon that permeates all reality; if the dynamics of *The Trial* exhibited the traits (and the leakiness) of the "concentrated" and "diffuse" spectacles that Debord outlined in *The Society of the Spectacle*, then *The Castle* is late-Debord, and tallies with his *Comments on the Society of the Spectacle* made 20-odd years later. "When the spectacle was concentrated," Debord says, "the greater part of the surrounding society escaped it; when diffuse, a small part; today, no part."[2] The society of the castle and of the integrated spectacle is like a whirlpool: it sucks everything into a singular and unified spiraling force, into a seamless web that has effectively collapsed and amalgamated different layers and boundaries. It has created a one-world cell-form. Erstwhile distinctions between the political and the economic, between form and content, conflict and consent, politics and technocracy, have lost specific gravity, have lost clarity of meaning: integration functions through a *conflating* process of cooptation and corruption, of re-appropriation and re-absorption, of blocking off by breaking down. Each realm now simply elides into its other.

Where K. goes astray, and where his quest borders on the essentially hopeless, is in his struggle to access the castle's occupants; he wants to penetrate the castle's bureaucratic formalities and the "flawlessness" of its inner circle. K. struggles for a way in rather than a way out. Using all the Cartesian tools of a land surveyor, he confronts the castle on its own terms, within its own ostensible "rational" frame of reference. K.'s demands, consequently, are too restrictive and too unimportant, too conventional and too self-conscious. He is like a scientific Marxist of the past, rather than a magical Marxist of the future: he wants to render the world of the castle *intelligible* as opposed to rendering it *unacceptable*. Where K. is undoubtedly correct is in his belief that we need the greatest caution in everything we do: we Marxists do need to look around on every side before taking a single step, before digging out our narrow trails of permanent subversion. Yet instead of trying to enter the inner recesses of the castle—trying to find doors to knock on and people to complain to—we need to burrow out under the castle's ramparts: we need to hatch our own Great Escape. We need to dig our tunnels and construct our exit trails; to disperse the soil discreetly, covertly; to organize, with great caution, an invisible committee, an escape committee; and we need to hope our tunnels are long enough to reach the woods, are ubiquitous enough to converge with other tunnels. And if enough people dig, the surface superstructure might one day give away entirely, hopefully after everybody has left. What remains will then implode into one great big heap of rubble—like the Berlin Wall.

"The Great Escape" was the mass Allied escape attempt from the German prisoner of war camp Stalag Luft III, immortalized by John Sturges' 1963 film starring Steve McQueen as Captain Hilts, the Cooler King. In real life, Stalag Luft III, built in 1942 near the Polish town of Zagan, was, like capitalist reality, considered practically escape proof. The camp housed American and British airmen whose planes had been shot down in German territory. To these captives, the Germans soldiers said: "your war is over." But the inmates had other ideas; they had a sworn *duty* to continue to fight the enemy, by surviving, by communicating information about this enemy, and, above all, by escaping. The notion of duty was and is a powerful ideal. Squadron Leader Roger Bushell, "Big X" to his comrades, coordinated the building of three tunnels, code-named "Tom, Dick, and Harry," and organized an escape committee. Alongside these three potential exit routes were also shallow "dummy tunnels," attempts to kid the enemy, to throw them off the scent. As Sturges' film and the Paul Brickhill book that inspired it emphasize, the big problem with any escape plan involving underground tunneling was twofold: how to support the tunnels so that they didn't collapse; and what to do with the earth that had been dug up, subsoil that was a different color to that in the camp grounds? To resolve the first dilemma, inmates used bed-boards as tunnel scaffolding; and for the second they devised an ingenious method involving hidden trouser bags whose neck could be discreetly opened by pocket cords; the earth fell down the prisoners' inside legs onto a patch of ground below which they'd then walk in. Of the 200 planned escapees, only 76 were able to flee on the appointed night, from hut 104; three made it scot-free; 23 were recaptured and sent to solitary confinement, "the Cooler"; the other 50 were executed on Hitler's personal orders.

Our Great Escape today must be even more carefully planned; and because there are more inmates than ever the tunnels must also be longer and more numerous. We can have some idea in advance where and how far we should tunnel, but there is no certainty that the tunnels will converge, nor that escapees will use the same routes. Dummy tunnels will doubtless be required, too. Most vital of all, perhaps, is that everybody keep digging their own tunnel, keep organizing escape committees where they can, and that trails are staked out by people who see subversion as a *duty*, as a permanent duty to themselves. The Great Escape suggests something subterranean, something organized and tactical, practical and concrete. It tries to begin below and at ground level and doesn't float up in the air, abstractly, forcing an artificial desire for unity, for all tunnels to be dug in the same way, by the same people, with the exact same aims.

If different escape committees are to come together, along diverse trails of permanent subversion, then one cannot foist an abstract ideal from above without engaging in some serious digging below. One cannot posit in advance some abstract necessity which would unite all trails, or prescribe that they be trails allowing only a "working class" to exit. Rather than dig below ground, a lot of conventional Marxists still believe that the central object of struggle isn't to build escape tunnels but to destroy the social structures and institutions that underwrite human captivity, that support privilege and authority, that define the castle on the hill. One needs to abolish the conditions of proletarian subordination, they say; one needs firstly to destroy the logic of prison camps as well as the processes that give rise to the camp mentality. One needs to negate the contradiction between inmate and warder before one can begin to create a passage to freedom. But negating and demolishing a social structure is a project always destined to undergo the trials and frustrations Kafka suffered when he tried to break into his castle, when he tried to find a secure ground for further and greater struggles that should have followed yet which always seemed to elude him.

The Prison-House of Negativity

At issue here is the problem of *negativity*, a constant bugbear of the Marxist tradition from the beginning, Marxism's very own Stalag Luft III. Historically, negative thinking has been a collective prison-house and individual straightjacket that has limited

Marxism's sphere of action and mix of actors. To a certain extent, Marxism's Hegelian origins explain a lot about why this has been so. After all, Marx took plenty from Hegel's idealist thought, a thought that suggested history hinged on "dialectical movement," an immense epic of the mind striving for unity, attempting to free itself from itself. Hegel's *Phenomenology of Spirit* (1807) generates the objective world as a wholly internal movement of the mind, the mind overcoming itself, negating each contradiction within itself, reaching out in a process of absolute dialectical unrest, a medley of sensuous and intellectual representations whose differences coincide, and whose identity is again dissolved. Unity here is the unity of contradiction, of negative force, of looking the negative in the face and living with it. Without contradictions, everything is void, nothingness. Contradictions are like internal combustion, incessantly devouring themselves, negating themselves, uprooting being from itself, animating becoming, promoting life and the annihilation of life. For Hegel, in short, world history is dramatized by the darker side of things, through what things aren't, through denying (cf. the Latin *negare*), through the predicate *not*-something.

Of course, there are in fact two Hegels, one progressive, the other conservative; two Hegels that Marx tried to pull apart in texts like the *Grundrisse*: a Hegel who embraces contradiction and confrontation, and another who's obsessed with identity, closure, and teleology, with death.[3] The problem, though, is that even the progressive Hegel sees "spirit" as magically animated by negativity, "not as something positive," not as something that "closes its eyes to the negative, as when we say of something that it is nothing or is false, and then, having done with it, turn away and pass on to something else." Instead, Hegel claims, liberation "is looking the negative in the face and tarrying with it."[4] Positivity, accordingly, is an outcome, not a starting point; something becomes its other only by denying itself, not by affirming its constructive creative powers. In this sense, to "invert" Hegel isn't somehow to trump idealism with materialism: it's rather to tarry with the positive; it's to call for the life-spirit to turn its back on negativity, on Hegel's death-spirit, and to see human liberation as *a priori* a positive impulse, as a positive "line of interruption and escape."[5]

None of which is to imply that rebellion isn't founded on acts of negation, on resisting and resistance, on refusal, on saying NO, on fighting against a force with which one disagrees, sometimes putting one's life on the line. It's an act of fending off, of fighting *against* job cuts, *against* neo-liberalism, *against* a fascist state, *against* the government, *against* bourgeois policies, *against* the WTO. Negation is quite rightly the stuff of radical politics; but it isn't the stuff dreams are made on. And there's a sense that in their negative guises a lot of battles Marxists have engaged in in the past have been either lost altogether or won only as Pyrrhic victories. So it's perhaps time to rethink the negative, not so much to look it in the face as to walk away from it, to search out sunshine rather than cower in the shadows; it's time to create something one likes rather than smash what one doesn't, denying oneself in the process.

There's another problem with the negative, too, a problem that afflicts Marxism and stems from the non-philosophical usage of negative thinking in daily life: its inherent cynicism and pessimism, its apparent reveling in contradictions and crises, in the darker, negative side of capitalism, all of which has become grist to the critical mill for Marxist analysts. One only has to leaf through pages of *New Left Review*, *Historical Materialism*, *Monthly Review*, and *International Socialism*—to name a few self-avowedly Marxist journals—to see this vividly at play. None of their analyses are necessarily wrong; in fact, almost always they are correct. But their correctness makes them somehow problematic, problematic because they're boring, because they're *obvious*, because they're of interest only to the converted, to crisis mongers, to prophets of a doom and a collapse that never happens. All of this succeeds in turning many people off rather than on. If there were no crises, Marxists would have to invent them! So, on list-serves and at conferences, we hear of "the shifting sands of crisis," of "neo-liberalism in crisis," of "critique of crisis," of "the origins of the current crisis," of "the dimensions of the present crisis," of "the crisis of capitalism," of "the financial crisis," of "the housing crisis," etc., etc. If one has time, one diligently plows through the sordid details, rolls up at the seminars, and scrolls down the emails. One reads, takes notes, and agrees, but then what? "Crisis sells well," Umberto Eco once said; he meant not only for capitalists.

One of the great strengths of a work like *Empire*, together with its sequels *Multitude* and the more recent *Commonwealth*, is how authors Michael Hardt and Toni Negri strive to reassert the *positive* in *altermondialiste* politics. For them, the shift away from negation towards affirmation owes as much to Spinoza as it does to Marx. For that reason, certain Marxists have taken the duo to task.[6] Thus, even open Marxists like John Holloway cling on desperately to the method of negativity, because "if we adopt that [positive] position," he says, "then much of the argument about fetishism and critique falls."[7] And we can't let any of that fall, can we, because it's a time-honored crutch for a hobbled man. According to Holloway:

> To treat the subject as positive is attractive but it is inevitably a fiction. In a world that dehumanizes us, the only way in which we can exist as humans is negatively, by struggling against our dehumanization. To understand the subject as positively autonomous (rather than as potentially autonomous) is rather like a prisoner in a cell imagining that she is already free; an attractive and stimulating idea, but a fiction, a fiction that leads on to other fictions, to the construction of a whole fictional world.[8]

Holloway's "scream" seems to want to reverberate everywhere, but it sounds frustrated in the mouth of its author, trapped within his realist four walls; and it plainly has trouble penetrating the sound insulation. (As for freedom in a cell, Holloway might find enlightenment reading Dostoevsky or Solzhenitsyn or even Sartre.) Negri is particularly derided because in his now-classic Spinoza study, *The Savage Anomaly* (1991), a positive foundation of struggle is developed. Holloway cites Negri, disapprovingly: "the genealogy of social forms ... implies negativity only in the sense that negativity is understood as the enemy, as an object to destroy, as a space to occupy, not as a motor of the process." "The motor of the process," says Negri, "is positive: the continuous pressure of being toward liberation." Negri's concern, according to Holloway, is "to develop the concept of revolutionary power (the *potentia* of the multitude) as a positive, non-dialectical, ontological concept. Autonomy is implicitly understood as the existing, positive drive of the *potentia* of the multitude, pushing *potestas* (the power of the rulers) onto ever new terrains."[9] Negri, the heterodox Marxist, uses Spinoza to shift the ballast away from political critique towards social liberation (or "perfection" in Spinoza's terminology). As Negri writes, the "Spinozian alternative does not have to do with the definition of the bourgeoisie but with the essence of the revolution—the radical character of the liberation of the world."[10] Here the concern isn't so much the constitutive power of capital as the constitutive power of the subject: "The actual growth of the human essence, then, is posed as a law of contradiction and expansion of being in the tension of the spontaneity to define itself as a subject."[11]

My sympathies are with Negri: it's in the struggle to liberate oneself, to affirm oneself—not necessarily to be *recognized*, as the Hegelian master and slave drama suggests—that a communist subjectivity takes hold, that a process of ideological identification with one's kindred spirits shapes up. In affirming oneself *positively*, affirming one's potentiality, one willy-nilly encounters a force resistant to this *positivization*, be it the state or capital. In any act of affirmation, one will likely be obliged to resist, to negate an antagonist or antagonism, to defend oneself; but this is more often than not an outcome of self-affirmation, not something causal, not something that determines the action. (Palestinians resist the Israeli state only insofar as they want to assert their own territoriality; it's the latter that conditions the former.) Participation comes about, if it comes about, through some form of collective self-affirmation, through self-unfolding. Affirmation, not negation, is the driving force, the impetus towards any neo-communist project, towards the "positive humanism" that Marx rallies around in "The Economic and Philosophical Manuscripts."

One instructive analogy we could draw is that between how, in the first volume of *Capital*, Marx theorizes accumulation vis-à-vis competition, and how popular liberation might resemble capital accumulation for capitalists: accumulation is an imperative that compels capitalists to compete with other capitalists, with those likewise intent on accumulating capital. Accumulation is thus a positive drive for capitalists of whatever denomination, and in their quest to accumulate they become locked in fratricidal competition. Liberation figures pretty much in the same vein for radicals: as a positive impulse of self-affirmation, as accumulation through self-valorization, which inevitably results in them encountering other radical people doing likewise; it also means they'll likely encounter the negative force of opposition, in competition with this affirmation. From this standpoint, accumulation, like liberation, is the determinant, and competition (negativity) the determined; not vice versa. While it's true that overcoming a negative, an obstacle, an enemy, is frequently what motivates people to act collectively, it's equally true that negativity pales alongside our earth-shattering affective powers, alongside our anticipatory consciousness and positive capacity to *imagine*, to *desire*, to *hope*, and to *love*. Indeed, it's clear that Marxism's analytical and pessimistic "cold stream" is but a chilly breeze compared to the tail wind of its warm front, compared to what Ernst Bloch intriguingly terms "the positive aspect of our Being-in-possibility."[12]

Warm Stream Marxism, or Militant Optimism

Bloch is the master purveyor of an upbeat Marxism, of a Marxism of "world-improving dreams" and "expectant emotions"; he's the master of a strange Hegelian-Spinozian Marxism that tarries with the positive. "Man is not solid," Bloch claims with a certain uncertainty in *The Principle of Hope*, and this uncertainty somehow provides reassurance for our utopian impulses. "If we give every mere factuality in the external world a critical right," he writes, "then we make what is fixedly existing and what has fixedly become into absolute reality per se."[13] In response, Bloch says, a different concept of reality, different to the narrow and ossified one we currently peddle, is long overdue. We need a warmer alternative; we need something Bloch calls "militant optimism." Militant optimism isn't a phony or facile optimism, but a new philosophy of "comprehended hope."[14] Militant optimism can help us down the path towards the New, Bloch says, and we must proceed along this trail, sometimes gradually, carefully, step by step, tunnel by tunnel; other times in great leaps and bounds, taking calculated risks, trusting our instincts, our guarded impulses. Importantly, "both critical caution which determines the speed of the path, and the founded expectation which guarantees a militant optimism as regards the goal, are determined through insight into the correlate of possibility."[15]

Within this "correlate of possibility" are two components that prefigure the consideration of the attainable, a *coldness* and *warmth* of concrete anticipation, two facets of the real Possible, and of the possibility of Becoming Real. On one side there is cool analysis, precise strategy, negativity and distance, a familiar Marxist materialism of the actual; from the other side comes a warm stream of Marxism, a hotter, more daring redness, a shimmering heat on the horizon. While you clearly can't have one without the other, Bloch is nonetheless candid in his preference for the sunshine, for siding with the primary-colored Macaw rather than the shady gray owl of Minerva. Militant optimism drifts in this warm stream, and sometimes squawks its merry song, repeats its cheeky wisecracks. Where cold stream Marxism appeals to the debased, enslaved, abandoned, and exploited human being, warm stream Marxism belongs to our liberating desires, to our utopian Totem; it tries to ward off disenchantment and depression. "Marxism as a doctrine of warmth," says Bloch,

> is thus solely related to that positive Being-in-possibility, not subject to any disenchantment, which embraces the growing realization of the realizing element ... The path then opens up within it as function of the goal, and the goal opens up as substance in the path, in the path explored towards its conditions, visualized towards its openness ... Forward materialism or the warm-doctrine of Marxism is thus theory-practice of reaching home or of departure from inappropriate objectification.[16]

It is this Blochian warm stream Marxism that energizes the Zapatistas' self-determination in Chiapas, energizes their "intergalactic Marxism." As an adopted Mexican himself, John Holloway often alludes to the Zapatista struggle, yet, ironically, what he fails to recognize, or perhaps prefers to deny, is how it refutes the central theme of his provocative book: the power of negativity. The Zapatistas' indigenous uprising in December 1994 was dramatized by what they wanted, not by what they didn't. It was, in the first instance, a revolutionary act of self-determination, of autonomous self-affirmation, a positive declaration that 38 municipalities now belonged to them, to rebel peasants. Later, the Zapatistas announced the creation of "Good-Government Councils" (*Juntas de Buen Gobierno*) to ensure self-management of education and health, and of resource redistribution in an agrarian-based economy. A local cultural politics of autonomous governance was very much the movement's initial radical conception.

Needless to say, achieving local autonomy in the face of state power and retaliation is an ambitious and risky business for any social movement, even if some have suggested that the Zapatistas "doing their own thing" only conforms to the Mexican state's neo-liberal dogma that demands a withdrawal from social reproduction obligations, calling for individual responsibility and self-reliance (although that self-reliance rarely stretches to capital). But, as others have countered, "Zapatista autonomy also represents a critique and a potential destabilizer of these [neo-liberal] conditions."[17] For one thing, the Zapatistas have politically sequestered and clung on to control over a big chunk of Southern Mexico, embarrassing the hell out of the federal government; for another, they've assumed the self-management of matters of everyday life, fostered participation to counteract political passivity and dependency, organized their own economic system of resource generation and distribution, and have become ideologically and symbolically one of the most vociferous critics of neo-liberal quackery anywhere.

The positive nature of struggle means that struggle is forever ongoing, forever adapting itself in a transformative process of permanent subversion. As one Zapatista militant admits:

> Land was what we were originally struggling for, but once we had it, we saw that we needed to decide how we were to organize ourselves, how we were to work the land, how we were going to make decisions, and how we were going to coordinate with other communities and other people in Mexico. We also saw that we needed to do things ourselves so as not to continue being beggars of the government. That is when we saw that what we were doing was autonomy.

Another participant adds: "Before it was the government who made the decisions. It didn't ask, it just informed. However, our autonomous government impulses and promotes rather than orders."[18]

While it's obvious that the Zapatista model has its limitations (are its tactics and autonomy conceivable in big urban areas, for instance?) as well as drawbacks ("we work and work and we still don't find good markets to sell our products"), as a modus operandi Zapatista politics are nonetheless educative. For they pivot around a notion of *action* (positive) wedded to *critique* (negation), requiring both a struggle for *autonomy* (as positive action) and a form of *resistance* (negativity) that has since become rearguard maneuvering necessary to defend this autonomy. The movement has shifted from a positive towards a negative, at least in the first instance, from attack and self-determination to defense and resistance. Critique emerged from the act, out of the action, not out of theory. Theirs was and still is a revolutionary action couched in terms of positive and permanent subversion—just like Colonel Buendia's. Only unlike Colonel Buendia, the Zapatistas won. Meanwhile, the fact that they are finally fighting for their own liberation and not for abstract ideals—for slogans that politicians can twist left and right according to circumstances—continues to fill them with an ardent enthusiasm.

Permanent and Positive Subversion

Just as, in *One Hundred Years of Solitude*, Colonel Aureliano Buendia was forever dreaming up forms of permanent subversion from his hammock in Macondo, warm stream Marxists need to do likewise from ours (remember: the inmates in Stalag Luft III slept in hammocks once their bed-boards propped up their escape tunnels). Warm stream Marxism needs to ensure that its militancy underwrites not only a permanent subversion but a positive one, too. Positive subversion isn't a dialectical theory of recognition (à la Hegel), but an *ontology of action*, action coupled with critique, autonomy coupled with resistance—the ordering is important. As such, subversion becomes a *permanent condition of action*. Neither a universal essence in human beings, nor an essence that guides human nature; rather, subversion is the *condition* of human beings in their quest for liberty, in their struggle for self-affirmation, for self-unfolding: it is a condition defined by contextualized action not by generalized resignation. It is a condition that is somehow implicitly *optimistic*, because it insists that humans can act, that humans are always compelled to act, that in the act there is always hope, and that hope always prevails in any act of subversion.

Subversion is a moral of both action and engagement, of political engagement. To a large extent, too, it is first of all an effect of individual subjectivity, of a man or woman in revolt. But subversion is equally an act of *inter*subjectivity: by acting, by engaging in the world, through subversion, human beings comprehend themselves at the same time as they discover others. And in finding other people, it becomes possible to transform a subversive intention into subversive activities, or, more notably, into subversive *situations*, situations in which activity is creative not simply destructive, a reflection of militant optimism not bad faith. In subversive situations, people can share a collective sensibility and elaborate a concept of sharing, find out what they have in common and how they might build themselves into a magical subversive force.

The subversive acts of Magical Marxism are of course progressive not reactionary ones. I say this because David Harvey has recently criticized Hardt and Negri's concept of "*jacquerie*," as outlined in their latest book *Commonwealth*, and his critique warrants further comment. According to Hardt and Negri, *jacqueries* were great acts of indignation and subversion occurring in Europe between the sixteenth and nineteenth centuries: mass peasant uprisings and spontaneous worker revolts, assorted urban rebellions and organized food riots. Hardt and Negri project this popular political history into their post-modern world of Empire and *altermondiality*.[19] Harvey, however, wonders what makes these *jacqueries* exclusively leftist? "Are all screaming right-wingers," he asks, "interrupting the health-care reformers in the United States an instance of singularities in motion as a jacquerie? They are certainly erupting in a seemingly infinite rage against the capitalist state's attempt to impose a new form of biopower on their world."[20] Harvey's question is fair enough but the answer is probably, yes, screaming right-wingers voicing their infinite rage against existing political systems are indeed *jacqueries*, actually are acts of permanent subversion. Unfortunately, the *form* of political revolt and the nature of acts of rebellion, whether on the left or the right, are difficult to tell apart. Where they differ, of course, is in their *content*, in their stated agenda, in the goals and ends that they desire.

Marxism has no unique semantic right over the concept of subversion. Left subversion has to pit its wits practically and organizationally against right subversion, just as worker and capitalist pit their wits against each other in Marx's *Capital*, and "force decides" between their respective rights, between their respective goals of subversion. Harvey seems to think that Marxist subversion *should* formally differ from right-wing subversion, perhaps akin to the way old-style Marxists once thought that communist "science" should somehow differ from bourgeois science. However, the difference isn't in the science itself, but in its application, in its objective, in its control. So too with subversion. If anything, throughout history, the subversive rage of the right has outdone that of the left: the latter has often seemed too embarrassed to affirm its rage, too embarrassed to act on it for fear of upsetting someone. The left has frequently preferred to repress what it really feels in the gut because it somehow doesn't fit with its theory.

As an existential left category, subversion will, by definition, always threaten the basis of bourgeois law. Hence, the preservation of bourgeois society requires the constant repression of subversion. We've seen the Mexican state doing so in Chiapas, and the French state in the Limousin. (And hackers, too, are on the receiving end of bourgeois state-endorsed Intellectual Property Rights.) In bourgeois circles, "subversive activities" have been defined as: "those which threaten the safety or well-being of the state, and which are intended to undermine or overthrow parliamentary democracy by political, industrial or violent means." These are the words of Britain's former Labour Home Secretary Melvyn Rees, from 1978, cited in a noteworthy article by R. J. Spjut called "Defining Subversion."[21] As Spjut says, in the British context Rees' definition of subversion contains two components: the first is that political and industrial activities are subversive "if they threaten the sovereign, the Crown and both Houses of Parliament, and are so intended"; the second is that "political and industrial activities are subversive if they disrupt—even temporarily—the operation of government policy by a person or organization whose motive in the long term is the overthrow of the state though this is not necessarily their immediate intent."[22]

Spjut highlights how, from almost every angle you consider it, left subversion is anathema to liberal democracy's power base and, in consequence, whether peaceful or otherwise, will always be brandished unlawful. Rees' first definition of subversion, Spjut says, "is incompatible with liberal constitutional government because peaceful, lawful actions to reform or abolish the sovereign are viewed as subversive"; the second definition, too,

> is incompatible with liberal constitutional government because lawful, non-violent industrial and political disruption of government policy is monitored as subversive. The first definition results in a recognition that state security requires that political freedom ought not to seek reform of the sovereign, a limitation on liberty. The second suggests that political freedom ought not to obstruct government policy, which while also a limitation, is so drastic that it implies a radical transformation of liberty.[23]

In its quest for a radical transformation of existing concepts of liberty, for a positive form of liberty stemming from a condition of positive subversion, warm stream Marxism will, accordingly, constantly need to resist state power. To be sure, those who hold power will always be protected by the government from erosion by those who don't. There's thus little to expect from the state other than repression or pacification, or both; there's little to expect other than baton blows or bribes, suppression or seduction—or various permutations of each. Thus the state, as Nietzsche once said, "is the coldest of cold monsters. Coldly it tells lies, and this lie crawls out of its mouth: 'I, the state, am the people.'"[24] In recent times, the neo-liberal state has become such an instrument in the socialization of capital that the idea of reforming it democratically is as equally utopian as abolishing it; to expect some transitional period during which the state becomes a dictatorship of the people, is, in short, as ludicrous as it is now defunct. The history of Marxism tells us that Marx, Engels, and Lenin all knew that there can be no freedom so long as there is a state apparatus. For all three, the state is incompatible with freedom, even in a democracy, and is always a force of constraint, always somehow parasitic. Yet they criticized the anarchists for wanting to leap frog, at one fell swoop, the "transitional era," the era of the infamous "dictatorship of the proletariat," even as they agreed that the state is a "parasitic excrescence" looming over society.

Nowadays, it's not so much a "leap frog" that's needed as a Marxist side step, an underground movement that ducks and dives and collectively engineers another concept of the "transitional era." Permanent and positive subversion will be the means and perhaps also its end: any post-capitalist experiment will always be in the course of transition and adaptation, always resisting something in order to affirm itself, always negotiating its own internal power play alongside its will to empower itself. The act is rarely ever finished. In its search for autonomous self-affirmation and self-organization in everyday life, permanent and positive subversion must wedge itself into state power, must create a *breach* at the interior of the neo-liberal state's integration of political and economic life, of the economic spin of its politicians and the political spin of its economists. Head-on confrontation probably won't create this breach, nor will it ever "smash" the state in one hammer blow.

Marx himself spoke of "breaking state power," of "smashing the state," when Parisian workers tried to break French state power in the autumn of 1870. Marx was pretty skeptical about whether they'd succeed in this desire; he said any attempt to smash the state was the "folly of despair." Yet the following spring, a worker and citizen uprising became a vivid reality, and Marx changed his tune, greeting this spontaneous proletarian revolt with generosity, despite its unfavorable auguries. As Lenin put it in *State and Revolution*, Marx wasn't only enthusiastic about the heroism of the Communards, who, he'd said, had "stormed heaven"; he equally regarded the event as a historic landmark in revolutionary practice, as a key experiment in advancing world proletarian revolution everywhere. It was an event to analyze and from which tactical lessons could be gleaned. Moreover, around the time of the Paris Commune, Marx wrote a letter to Kugelmann (dated April 12, 1871), in which he claimed:

> If you look up the last chapter of my Eighteenth Brumaire, you will find that I declare that the next attempt of the French Revolution will be no longer, as before, to transfer the bureaucratic-military machine from one hand to another, but to *smash* it, and this is the precondition for every real people's revolution on the Continent. And this is what our heroic Party comrades in Paris are attempting.[25]

Lenin drew a similar conclusion: "To smash the bureaucratic machine," he said, "briefly expresses the principal lesson of Marxism regarding the task of the proletariat during a revolution in relation to the state." And yet, notwithstanding Lenin and Marx's noble analytical intentions, this *smashing* of the bureaucratic state machine is something no social movement is ever likely to achieve today. The Communards discovered as much the hard way; they were, according to Lenin, working their way towards this goal of smashing the state, but they never quite reached that end. Perhaps Lenin was asking too much—or too little—of the proletarian revolution? Because *smashing* doesn't seem quite right anymore: it's too impossible a practice and too simple an analysis. What the Zapatistas are doing in Chiapas presents itself as another possible paradigm of governance. They didn't so much smash the Mexican state as make a breach within it, subvert it, decouple themselves from the state's "official" domain, and so weaken the latter's grip on civil society, loosen its political and bureaucratic straightjacket.

The virtues and the pitfalls here are both obvious enough. On the one hand, the Zapatistas planned and successfully enacted a Great Escape from neo-liberal statehood, creating their own emancipator-state en route; on the other hand, their fiefdom is open to attack from the outside, is surrounded on all sides. It's a breach, and like all breaches is a *space of slippage*, a narrow trail of permanent subversion. A space of slippage is a zone where the state's control has weakening or degenerated. It's a liberated autonomous realm in which new communes can bloom, in which the realm of the possible—another possible world—might be glimpsed. But it's a zone that must somehow be enlarged, must spread itself out, becoming stronger on all sides and more resistant in its own self-affirmation at the core. We might rename any new space of slippage *the realm of the really lived*, the kingdom of our Being-in-possibility; or, if we journey long enough, stretch it out far and wide enough, we might call it the magical wonderland of *somewhere*.

Silos and Segues

How social movements might spread and converge with other movements elsewhere, how they might cohere with each other while remaining true to themselves at their core, honest with their rank-and-filers, is the biggest left political problematic of modern times. Why should one movement fighting for, say, housing justice in Brazil be interested in housing justice issues in Europe, or in "right to the city" groups in New York, those struggling to occupy vacant condominiums during the nation's real estate slump? Why should communist municipalities in Italy or France be bothered by Zapatista communism in Mexico? The obvious response is that they can learn from one another, discover what is common and universal, as well as what is contextual and particular, in what they do. They can dialogue, pool ideas, share strategies, look at what works somewhere and fails elsewhere. Sometimes they can raise money together; other times they can mutually exchange resources as well as foot soldiers. All the time they can provide moral support, encouragement, reassurance that they're not alone, that what they experience is what others experience, and that what they do inspires. Transfer between groups may be virtual, emotional, and material, both ideological and practical. Word gets around in mysterious ways, via strange mechanisms, through vague and indirect forms of solidarity that quietly make stuff happen, nudging things along. That's what building alliances is all about, though there are, alas, no set recipes, no easy formulas for success.

In the wake of Seattle, and as a radical alternative to the annual bourgeois elite World Economic Forum gathering at Davos, the World Social Forum (WSF) was launched in 2001, hosted by the Southern Brazilian town of Porto Alegre, then controlled by the progressive Workers Party (PT). From its inception, WSF has been a potentially revolutionary project designed to bring far-flung peoples, organizations, and movements together, to provide a space for dialogue and discussion, debate and analysis, for celebration and commiseration, for making new friends while catching up with old comrades. Local groups can encounter their peers on a truly international stage, and together they can catalyze global ambitions. Spearheaded by the Brazilian Workers' Party (which, under Lula, spectacularly gained presidential power in October 2002), by the European "Association for Taxation of Financial Transactions for the Aid of Citizens" (ATTAC), and by the editorship of the monthly newspaper *Le Monde diplomatique*, the first WSF attracted 12,000 participants; in successive years this grew to 150,000; in 2004 the WSF moved to Mumbai and brought together 60,000 people; in 2007, events on a similar scale shifted to Nairobi; and in 2009, the WST returned to Brazil, to Belém, the capital of Amazonia. In January 2010, celebrating the Forum's tenth anniversary, Porto Alegre once again staged the international grassroots gathering in the depths of neo-liberal crises, during the same week as 240 banker bigwigs met in the deep-freeze of Davos to bail the financial system out.

Marx, remember, always said that there was something "strikingly revealing" about capitalist crises. For one thing, "instead of investigating the nature of the conflicting elements which erupt in the catastrophe, the apologists content themselves with denying the catastrophe itself and insisting, in the face of their regular and periodic recurrence, that if production were carried on according to the textbooks, crises would never occur."[26] The other thing is that crises present themselves not only as moments of interruption but also as moments of opportunity for invention, for disruption from below. Hence Porto Alegre's decennial round of the WSF came on the cusp of a possible transition, at a potentially vital historical moment.

With its 1.2 million inhabitants, the city of Porto Alegre, capital of the prosperous state of Rio Grande do Sul, is itself a curious example of what the British militant Hilary Wainwright once called "public power beyond the state." Always a center of popular resistance to Brazil's military rule (1964–85), due in part to its tradition of democratic neighborhood associations, for a while Porto Alegre pioneered a fascinating experiment in open grassroots democracy: the so-called "Participatory Budget" (PB). Herein, municipal government appointees invited ordinary citizens to participate in decisions about what investments should be made in the city and where. The city duly opened up its books to popular scrutiny, and decisions about public spending and public works would be debated in assemblies of the people and in popular plenaries. (Porto Alegre is also unique in Brazil because the city's water company is municipally owned, and a company owned by the city council builds most of its buses.)

According to Wainwright, "the PT's political understanding was always that it would share with the community whatever power it gained through electoral success, and would be open to their knowledge as well."[27] And it was salutary how involvement in PB meetings burgeoned, from 1,000 citizens in 1990, to 20,000 in 1997, and around 40,000 in 2003. And yet, as all this was going on at the local level, the PT under Lula began acting like a conventional political party: it steadily began to renege on its promises, to tighten its grip over public spending, centralize its control over public spending, and actually cut urban funding. City and central government were moving in opposite directions, and Porto Alegre was swimming against the dominant current. The party political route towards local democracy was once again cast in doubt. Unable to keep running a system it had set up, the curtain fell on Porto Alegre's signature Participatory Budget when, after 16 years of governance in the city, the PT lost the 2004 municipal elections. New center-right Mayor José Fogaça said he wouldn't abandon the PB concept, even though he also wanted to embrace partnerships with the private sector.

So when the World Social Forum returned to fête its tenth birthday, the city chambers of the former bastion of anti-globalization struggle were none-too-receptive. An editorial in the local *Jornal do Centro* (January 2010) lamented and lambasted this fact:

> Porto Alegre has been discriminated against. Broken down by agents that damage in exchange for their interests ... the great media role doesn't give a damn about the World Social Forum 2010 ... With information released only after the first day of the Forum, many people did not know about the event. Scorning its participants, they demonstrate the inability to live with the counterpoint, not respecting the views of diverse segments of society worldwide. In terms of globalization, a score of zero for our press. Not to mention journalist retirees who live on state coffers, writing in newspapers of dubious quality, speaking without knowledge of the discussions sponsored by the Forum. A pity.

A pity indeed, because Porto Alegre's *Usina do Gasômetro*, the focal point of WSF activities, the giant (11,300 square meters) former electricity plant, built in 1928 and renovated as a cultural space in 1989, could have been a great microcosm of another possible world, of a space of slippage, where multicolored and multicultural activists, militants, NGOs, students, the discontented and the exploited all could have really come together, really joined hands across the debris of neo-liberal devastation. (Patrick Bond has put together a typology of the hundreds of organizations who meet at the WSF, and they can be roughly divided into three types: "Political Movements for Social Change," like movements or parties representing the values/ideas of social democracy, socialism, autonomism, and anarchism; "Traditional and Cross-Sectoral Civil Society Movements," like labor, anti-racism, anti-war, women, civil rights, consumer rights, indigenous rights, etc.; and "Issue-based Civil Society Movements," like finance, trade, land, housing, food sovereignty, debt cancellation, etc.[28])

All these groups could have come together had they been able to find each other, had there had been signs letting people know what was happening, and where. Alas, rather than a possible alternative, rather than a potential space of slippage, the *Usina* on the waterfront became another castle on the hill, another impenetrable labyrinth that somehow reinforced the *divergence* rather than convergence of many social movements; it demonstrated all that is pathetic about left organization— constraints notwithstanding—pathetic about its search for a magical politics of the future, about its inability to organize itself. Umbrella organizations are important; but only insofar as they help people organize themselves, and only insofar as they organize organizations. To this extent, Walden Bello's skepticism is well taken:

> Is the WSF still the most appropriate vehicle for the new stage in the struggle of the global justice movement? Or, having fulfilled its historic function of aggregating and linking the diverse counter-movements spawned by global capitalism, is it time for the WSF to fold up its tent and give way to new modes of global organization of resistance and transformation?[29]

Even on its own terms there were other snags. Even if you could relocate yourself, find out what was happening, track down the venue,[30] you'd soon find that each separate workshop often appeared happy just knowing that their own kind knew what was happening, that their own supporters and activists were sufficient for a debate, enough for appreciative audiences. You wouldn't be wrong to think things were taking place in a dozen or so different silos, in hermetically sealed private chambers in which leaders contentedly preached to their already converted parish. Who will shape and steer a unified movement, a unified exodus? How will this steering be done? What will be the relationship between luminary intellectuals and the many ordinary participants, those struggling for their respective causes? These are big questions requiring enlightened answers; instead, business-as-usual radicalism fudged imaginative responses. Silo politics isn't going to lead to anything or lead anywhere. Neither will the same old rhetoric, the same talks listing the same litany of horrors, horrors that everybody knows about anyway. Many speeches seemed too stagy, too banal, and the anger too hollow, too well rehearsed to be convincing. It was a double whammy: a lack of real analysis combined with a lack of real imagination. Speakers lodged themselves in the realist mire, in what actually exists, in the ruins of neo-liberalism. Few spoke about the potential of the phoenix rising or explored the politics of possibility. It was as Bloch warned: The factuality of the "real world" was being accorded too much critical right. One simply lashed out in the prison-house of negativity.

A lot of people agreed that what is needed is an anti-capitalist revolutionary movement. We have to organize the anti-capital-ist transition, they insisted. It's true that this is precisely what is necessary—we live in a moment of crisis, of multiple crises, and as the term "moment" implies, this is something ephemeral, something subject to change and transition. But transition into what? The development of capitalism over the past 500 years has been nothing but transition, evolution, adaptation, destruction, nothing but different moments of production, of manufacture and machinery, of development of the productive forces, of merchant capital and industrial capital, of finance capital and fictitious capital, of Fordism and post-Fordism, of deindustrialization and deterritorialization, of class struggle and class decomposition, of the World Wide Web and weapons of mass destruction. All that is solid has melted into air. All has changed, all has aged, and yet all, at the same time, somehow seems to remain the same. For that reason it's clear that while capitalism changes and forever cannibalizes itself, forever "creatively destroys" itself (though one rarely sees this "creative" side anymore), it is highly unlikely to dissolve of itself. It needs, in other words, to be pushed, to be toppled, needs the rug pulled from underneath its feet.

People need to be convinced, too, that there are alternatives, that we can live with different social relations, with different technological capacities, with a different daily life, with different social institutions that answer to human needs and desires rather than the other way round.[31] Like capitalism itself, it's evident that the development of these different forms of life, of communes and different modes of social organization, will evolve in evolutionary movement, constantly undergoing incremental refinement and adaptation, growing and succeeding, encountering difficulties and frustrating setbacks, opening themselves up to change and transition and therefore to the risk of failure. In the current moment there are always germs of a different moment, subversions that go on inside as well as on the outside. Inside this system, a system that forces most of us to behave in a manner we might not otherwise chose to, oppositional solidarities can be and are forged when people open themselves up to their counterparts.

But solidarity and alliances are no longer straightforward affairs: no longer is it clear what solidarity actually means, what it really boils down to materially, even how it is practiced. In the workplace, traditional lines of solidarity were established with those you labored alongside; there was the physical proximity of one's fellow workers, whose material needs were usually commensurate with your own. One joined hands to struggle to reduce the working day, for decent pay and conditions, or to avoid layoffs. One drank at the same pub, met at same union hall; one was invariably male. The stakes and the terrain of combat were known, were tangible and visible everyday, for everybody, the bosses included. Today, by contrast, the stakes and the arena of combat are different, and things are a great deal less tangible, especially from the perspective of daily life. Solidarity at work continues, but the battle to save jobs or secure pay rises is a battle already lost, or perhaps a battle no longer worth winning. One continues to struggle against the state, but more particularly battles now get waged within the domain of civil society, within and against institutions some of which are supra-state-like, both political and economic, both financial and unaccountable, complex processes as opposed to simple, identifiable things.

Within civil society, too, the idea of the working class becomes much more diffuse and blurry, and to some degree much more meaningless as a radical concept. Can we have an anti-capitalist transition without a working class, a working class such as Marx defined it, posited as the agent of this transition? Of course we can. If there are disparate groups of people who all come together because of their discontent with capitalism, with neo-liberalism, does it matter one iota whether this anti-capitalist alliance is "working class"? Does it matter if we call them "the multitude," a "non-class," "the general intellect" or whatever? Do labels really matter anymore? We can call them anything we like because what they have in common is that—to a greater or lesser degree, whether alienated or dissatisfied, exploited or deprived—they all find themselves on the receiving end of the accumulation and circulation of capital; they all find themselves somehow damaged by the normal business of global capitalism, by its ordinary local madness, even when occasionally some of them might also be complicit in that ordinary madness. Why discriminate between people who fit the "category" of working class and those who don't? Why draw a distinction between people who intellectual-ize and people who can function as intellectuals? Everybody is in the same boat, everybody can learn from and teach one another. Everybody has a common enemy that few would deny.

Most people know that a small minority of the world's population controls global finance, global military power, and global governance. And everybody knows that this minority is shrinking each day as the ranks of their other, the rest of us, the millions who work or who are denied work, who have nice jobs or shitty jobs, expand. Everybody knows that this minority is accumulating more might, more money, more power; and a lot of people know that we, the masses, the multitude, whether we identify with a particular class or not, have so much in common, so many similar causes at stake, so many mutual interests, so many shared dilemmas about assuring that our culture survives, that to comport ourselves so *singularly* would cut off possible alliances. When people have a cause, it's often a single cause that prevails—even if it's global revolution. Constraints of time and of knowledge, practicality and feasibility, often mean that it can't be otherwise. One does what one can where one can, how one can. But a single-issue cause doesn't and shouldn't be a form of political singularity, a silo politics. The silo mentality precludes the development of *transitional segues*. A segue politics would allow us to valorize crises, to move onto a new stage, to move into a different moment of struggle, a higher, more advanced moment; not towards a final moment, a *telos*, but towards a moment of unity in which we might become positive agents of change together, united agents of positive progress.

Struggle and subversion within segue politics would be multifarious and issue-based, and each campaign would circulate as its own specific moment of struggle. Yet these different moments of struggle would circulate as "moments within a unity" (as Marx said in his *Grundrisse* introduction); it follows that a "concrete totality" of struggle occurs when there's a concentration of many determinations of struggle, when there's a "unity of the diverse." At that stage, each moment of struggle, each social movement, would come together in such a way that their respective degree of force arises not from their discrete strength but from the relationships they have with other groups; they take on meaning through each other and have no real political force outside of their dynamic relationship with other social movements. Within such a general "unity of the diverse," the sum of the parts becomes far, far greater than the strength of any individual part alone. Meanwhile, as they circulate in the global process of revolt, each moment of struggle will undergo a quantitative-qualitative change in the efficacy of their politics.

For a successful segue politics, those operating in silos need to drop their defensive posturing with their comrades and open themselves up, take the risk of exposure, accept the idea that solidarity comes about through what Giorgio Agamben calls "inessential commonality."[32] With an inessential commonality, a segue lets us slip into another political realm, perhaps into a more magical one, a "zone of indistinguishability" (again, the expression is Agamben's), a blurry, still-unrealized realm of liberation and global friendship. (Don't underestimate the political power of friendship, *The Coming Insurrection* told us, and Guy Debord would have concurred, despite his frequent sectarian ruthlessness.[33]) But liberty is a form of discipline, and making friends equally requires perseverance and a certain patience, taking time to get to know each other, to enter into genuine dialogue, talking as well as listening. To that end, it's perhaps time that progressives of whatever stripe develop another less jaded version of the World Social Forum, another global project to refresh our hopes that another world is possible. It still is possible. It always will be possible. We need another zone of indistinguishability, another space of slippage, a space in which there's a lot of spontaneous energy as well as a few signs indicating where to go and what time the action begins. We need a new space of slippage in which we can organize and strategize, act without self-consciously performing, encounter others without walls, and hatch en masse a daring Great Escape from capitalism.

5

MACONDO OF THE MIND: IMAGINATION SEIZES POWER

Come, whistle the sun, like a glass of white wine. Come, we'll teach you the language of tomorrow. We're men of today, we bear the weight of today; but that's not enough: we honor all that's becoming. We're in full bloom. The light of the night has conceived the morning.

Paul Éluard

He spoke to them about the magical wonders of the world in a way that not only touched the limits of his and their knowledge, but that forced to an incredible extreme the limit of his and their imagination.

Gabriel García Márquez

Man is nothing else but what he makes of himself.

Jean-Paul Sartre

Let's Hack Through the Jungle

The founder of Macondo, José Arcadio Buendia, had two aspects to his personality that are indispensable for the left activist: he was a daringly *practical* man, but also someone with an *unbridled imagination*. These twin powers made for an almost inexhaustible magical source and magical force. Indeed, *practicality* and *imagination* were two aspects of José Arcadio's personality that animated his spirit of social initiative. He was forever forward-looking, never dwelling on the past, and his insatiable curiosity and desire for adventure led him to convince his friends to cross the distant mountains, to try to found a new community next to the sea. Through sheer will and in the hope of a better life to come, they kept going, hacking their way through the jungle. Then, one morning, after two years of journeying across difficult terrain, they finally reached the cloudy summit of the mountain range, where, below, they saw not the sea but a gigantic swamp, apparently limitless. That evening, camped out near a river and lying in his hammock, José Arcadio Buendía had a dream. He dreamt of a noisy city and shipwrecked people. He asked them what city it was, and they answered him with a name he had never heard, and that had no meaning at all, "but that had a supernatural echo in his dream: Macondo" (*One Hundred Years of Solitude*, p. 9). The following day, José Arcadio urged his men to cut down the trees where they were, to make a clearing beside the river, at the coolest spot on the bank: here they would establish the new city.

From the beginning, José Arcadio became a kind of "youthful patriarch" of Macondo, with the imaginative drive and practical wherewithal to orchestrate the building of the town. He collaborated with everyone, even in the physical work, helping to plant trees, giving advice on the raising of children and animals, doing everything for the welfare of the community. His own simple adobe house had been the first and best in the village. It had "a small well-lighted living room, a dining room in the shape of a terrace with gaily colored flowers, two bedrooms, a courtyard with a gigantic chestnut tree, a well-kept garden, and a corral where goats, pigs, and hens lived in peaceful communion" (p. 15). Other houses would soon be modeled after its image and likeness. Moreover, the placement of each house was such that from all of them one could reach the river and draw water with the same effort; likewise their arrangement in Macondo's streets was so well planned that no house got more sun than any other during the hottest time of day. Within a few years Macondo became the most orderly and hardworking village in the land, and its 300 inhabitants had instigated their own style of democratic socialism. It was a village that grew happily and soon became a town; it didn't "give orders with pieces of paper" and had no need of police or priests, of meddling officials or institutions, of lawyers and judges, because there was nothing that couldn't be judged by the people themselves. Macondo was a town in which citizens organized local affairs. The people distributed land amongst themselves, opened up roads, and introduced necessary improvements without having to bother the government and without anyone having bothered them: "No one was upset that the government had not helped them. On the contrary, they were happy that it had let them grow in peace, and they hoped that it would continue leaving them that way, because they had not founded a town so that the first upstart who came along would tell them what to do" (p. 53).

Macondo isn't, of course, a bad ideal for a new organization of life, for a space in which people might realize a new subjectivity, and act and live together in relative harmony. In its initial conception, it was a utopian town with few repressive conventions and morals, and that had liberated itself from mediating images. It was a society with no intermediaries—no institutions and their agents imposing themselves between workers and their products, creating subjects out of naturally born citizens. One of the town's most interesting features was its apparent lack of a money economy, of money as an arbiter of value. To be sure, the thriving prosperity of the town was due more to the innovative spirit of its denizens than to any rapacious desire to accumulate wealth and capital. One is struck by how little money-values figure in the daily life of Macondo, at least in its pre-colonized phase: if there were markets, then people exchanged with one another in a system of fair barter; and if the law of value prevailed, then it prevailed as a measure of *necessary labor time* not *abstract* labor. A case in point is the relationship between José Arcadio Buendia and the gypsy sage Melquiades, who swapped back and forth new weird and magical objects on the basis of reciprocal trust, as if an incipient form of Local Exchange Trading (LETS) existed between them, and between the residents of Macondo.

In our own times, the system of Local Exchange Trading is a novel and growing experiment in how various goods and services can switch hands without recourse to printed money; it's a novel experiment in how people can live alternatively in a self-managed way, and in how they can go back to the future. Though still restricted to the local scale, the fact that many cities in North America, Australasia, Great Britain, and Europe now have an "open money" network and a system of direct swaps for goods and services, of interest-free credit and a full disclosure principle available to all members, means there's something truly radical about the formula. If it can be broadened—and there's no reason why it can't develop at least on a regional basis—it has revolutionary potential for the construction of a dynamic economy, of "circles of cooperation" that put an alternative spin on the notion of money as a supreme social power.[1]

LETS' radicality lies in the fact that it helps resolve the problem of money in the economy—money that, under capitalism, is a big part of all that's wrong with our culture, the foundation of the nonsensical society we've somehow created for ourselves. Money as we currently know it is printed by central banks and circulates across national borders in pernicious ways, in ways that foster scarcity and promote competition. Some people have too much, others none at all. All of us have to scramble and hustle for money to survive; we compete for it, bargain for it, beg for it, and yearn for it in a zero-sum game in which nobody can really win the ultimate existential battle. But imagine a situation in which local people can issue money themselves, in which a local currency can serve their needs, financing community undertakings. Imagine a money system that isn't based on monopoly power; money that nobody can claim or exert ownership over; a money system in which there's no profit making, no commission, no interest to be filched. Imagine a money system in which no money leaves it, and that represents a measure of personal worth rather than despotic power. Such is the promise of the LETSystem, such are the ideal criteria that the LETSystem strives to meet.

Invented in the 1920s in Germany, and developed under diverse forms in the United States during the Depression, LETS expanded most rapidly throughout the 1980s, when, in 1983, Michael Linton coined the term Local Exchange Trading Systems in Comox Valley, British Columbia, Canada.[2] Thereafter, the idea captured the imagination of a lot of people who began to set up organizations to trade between themselves. Records are kept of all members; paying for goods and services can be done by writing a LETS check or a credit note for an agreed amount of LETS units, or else by exchanging printed LETS notes. Members, too, can earn credit by doing services in kind, like child-minding for one person, and then spending the credit later, on, say, a plumber, who's also a member of the particular LETS network. Childcare, transport, DIY, food, hiring of tools and big equipment can be added to the roster of services: the list is potentially endless and vast in its spatial reach. The sway of LETS can be local and regional; as "local" the network of participating people may be restricted to just a few blocks of an urban neighborhood; but a "local" network can equally extend into a wider geographical terrain and comprise numerous independent LETS registries that cooperate to exchange goods and services with each other at commensurate rates. Good organization is necessary in order that group coordination can be maintained, and so that the relative successes (and failures) of one network don't unduly affect the growth and development of its neighbors.

Interconnected yet autonomous organizations existing within a regional network ensure that their services and activities serve the needs of each locality; this avoids the pitfalls of centralization and monopoly control yet means that organizations are collectively large enough to be effective over a broader scale. LETS money circulates within these networks and money exists purely and solely as a means of exchange, as a token used to equate one service or good with another. Money is quite literally a "promissory note," and there is no way to store it up, invest it, or profit from it by treating it as a commodity. Money circulates as an enabling use value not as a dreaded exchange value that contaminates everything and everybody. As such, small businesses can flourish without the need for big inputs of capital; marginalized communities can mutually engage in exchange of goods and services to do amazing things on a shoestring. LETS can reintegrate the unemployed, allowing people the labor-market deems worthless to finally feel self-worth. As ever, dangers of bourgeois re-appropriation lurk, dangers of social pacification and the promotion of self-reliance so handy for the neo-liberal state; but this doesn't necessarily have to be the case if the system is well organized and if participants put their hearts and energies into making the project a success, making it a community's principal economy rather than its safety net.

One of the many nice things about the LETSystem is that fosters a sense of community and community empowerment that brings consenting people freely together. (The system of course stands or falls on the level of commitment participants give to it, give to their community.) Another progressive thing about LETS is that it *de*-economizes economic life, makes a locality a voluntarily *de*-institutionalized space that shrugs off the weight of heavily centralized control, of unwieldy bureaucracies that alienate life for the many, that fail as service providers and ultimately answer only to the bottom-line, to shareholder greed, or to the perverse "rational" logic of the organization men. In a certain sense, too, LETS also *re*-politicizes social life because it *re-empowers* real people in their everyday lives; then people become aware of their power, of their re-empowerment, not a power to dominate something but an *imaginative power* to socialize an economy, to invent a different notion of political economy, an alternative politics and economy in which no upstart can ever tell you what to do.

Being and Imagination

José Arcadio Buendia wasn't constrained in his dreams by what Bloch calls "the factuality of the external world" because his imagination "went beyond the genius of nature and even beyond miracles and magic" (p. 9). José Arcadio Buendia thought it possible to do anything he willed—well, almost anything—and taught his sons from an early age to think likewise. He spoke to them of the wonders of the world, not only where his learning extended, but forcing the limits of his imagination to extremes. He pushed his imagination beyond the reality of realism, made it subordinate to his imagination, to his adventurous will, and in so doing he was able to achieve what he wanted; he was somehow able to realize his dream of Macondo because he *de*-realized reality, he speculated with reality, placed his bets squarely on a "speculative realism,"[3] one that took risks with reality, that gambled on futures, that rolled the dice and hoped for the best, just like the bourgeoisie does with its stock market.

Or perhaps José Arcadio Buendia is really a magical existentialist, grappling with deep ontological questions of Being and freedom and with the political question of collective action that Marxists still need to grapple with, that Sartre grappled with during the 1940s with mixed success. To a certain extent, the analysis Sartre undertook in his great masterpiece, *Being and Nothingness* (*L'être et le néant*) (1943), still has plenty to say to the Magical Marxist spirit, to a Being that yearns to be "for itself," that yearns to fill in the nothingness reigning between consciousness and the realm of things in the world. Sartre's epistemological point of departure here is *consciousness*, at the level of *cogito*; yet unlike Descartes the consciousness Sartre posits is always a consciousness that has an object, that is only ever conscious of something, conscious that it refers to the inert world of the inorganic, to things. Consciousness doesn't have an essence, but, following the phenomenologist Husserl, is instead a consciousness of *intending*, a consciousness that's *intentional*. In itself, consciousness is empty, is bereft of anything, is *rien*. But the issue that henceforth arises, including for any Magical Marxist, is how this consciousness relates to Being.

Sartre suggests there are two different sorts of Being, or "two regions" of Being. He calls them "Being-in-itself" (*l'être en soi*) and "Being-for-itself" (*l'être pour soi*). The former is a Being that's present in inanimate objects, a passive kind of Being that's a thing-in-itself, "a Being," says Sartre, "that is what it is."[4] The latter type, a much more dynamic and potentially progressive Being, is a Being that is both conscious of itself—i.e. self-conscious—and conscious of itself being conscious of other objects; it is a Being that is faced with an object, that confronts an object, that is conscious of this object, yet is nonetheless *not* this object. Thus, if a Being-in-itself is a simple Being, a Being that is what it is, constituted neither of possibilities nor impossibilities, then a Being-for-itself is a more complex force, because it is a Being that is conscious of the gap that exists between its own consciousness and the objects it is conscious of. It is somehow aware of the distance between its own thinking and the things in the world: it is aware, in other words, *of that which it is not.*

Importantly, it is precisely this disjuncture—this space or gap that exists between our consciousness and the objects we think about—which gives rise to what Sartre calls "nothingness": it is through being conscious of Being, conscious of being a Being-for-itself, that nothingness enters into the world. Nothingness is a negative condition in which *positive capabilities* reside, since the conscious Being is conscious of what it lacks, of what it could be, of what its possibilities are, of what its future might be. It's somehow all up for grabs. Humans are masters of their own existential choice, Sartre believes. The Being-for-itself, he says, doesn't desire what it is: it strives to be what it isn't. Only a conscious being has the capacity to distance itself from the world and reflect upon it, to introduce this gap, to affirm this nothingness, to comprehend it, to try to leap across it through its own praxis, through its own conscious power, through the magical power of its imagination.

This "gap" between the thing-world and the thinking world, between the world of objects and world of the conscious mind, is increasingly subject to collapse in our spectacular society. As Debord put it (cf. Chapter 1), the spectacular world of things is colonizing our brains with its thing-images, and is creating unity out of this separation. So, contra Jacques Rancière's claim regarding Debord, to engage in a politics of the counter-spectacle isn't to romanticize a world without separation but is to struggle to keep this separation alive. For in this separation, Sartre tells us, nothingness prevails, and within nothingness, within the power of the conscious mind understanding itself as separate from the world of things, possibilities reside, possibilities for addressing deficiencies, for creatively filling in the empty spaces of life. In this separation—what I've called a "space of slippage"—we might reinvent ourselves subjectively while creating a new world objectively, a new material world, a new physical and social structure. And so in this gap, in the nothingness that Sartre tells us exists in our world, that we bring into the world, we can begin to locate the realm of freedom, the realm of magic.

Thus the conscious Being, the Being-for-itself, is conscious of its own freedom. The crushing void of nothingness is in fact an opportunity for us to question, to doubt, to criticize, to fight and to take flight, to imagine alternatives, to act and to make choices. This freedom floats above any determinism, above any biological, psychological or social determinism, above any scientific Marxism or Freudianism, above anything imposed from above, anything that reduces or invokes some kind of inevitability; this freedom frees itself from the past, too, isn't weighed down by the past, and hence can reinvent, can create anew, create its own Macondo out of the free will of its Being-for-itself. Out of this free will arises the possibility of constructing a new *situation*, a meaningful totality from the standpoint of a free individual, who alone gives sense to their world, who creates the context and the content of what they do in this situation, and of how they live.[5]

It follows here, as it follows for any Magical Marxist project, that neo-communism cannot come *to* individuals by an abstract, predetermined law or logic—the logic of history, the science of history, the inner laws of the dialectic, etc.—but can only come *from* individuals who re-appropriate their subjective alienation (and/or material exploitation) by a collective praxis, a praxis which is the result of a unity of group and individual praxes. Or, as Sartre put it later in his *Critique of Dialectical Reason* (1960): "The group is *constructed* on the model of free individual action."[6] Elsewhere in this text (which Sartre always rated as his favorite and which celebrates its fiftieth anniversary at the time of writing) Sartre points out with typical abstruseness: "the unity of the group is immanent in the multiplicity of syntheses, of which each one is an individual praxis, and we have insisted on the fact that this unity is never that of a *made totality* but rather of a *totalization that makes itself*."[7] The promise of communism isn't born of any *external* objective logic, but is the inner will of thinking and acting individuals, of Beings-for-themselves, of real, everyday, concrete individuals who somehow find each other through a common cause, who define themselves as individuals in struggle, yet who also mobilize as individuals in a group, a group with a collective praxis, based on voluntary cooperation and a collective will and imagination.

Sartre says that those who try to fudge their freedom, who fear its consequences and run from the responsibility of being free, who seek to escape it by enslaving themselves, squirm with the malady he calls "bad faith" (*mauvaise foi*). We lie to ourselves, sell out, deny our dreams, take the easy option, and flee the anxiety of having to live up to our own potential, to our potential freedom. We act in bad faith by playing roles, Sartre says, like a waiter in a Parisian café conscious he's acting out a part, playing a game, ensuring he makes all the right movements, all the right gestures, and is solicitous about the customers' orders in an artificial way.[8] It is precisely because he is conscious of what he's up to that he is deceiving himself, is denying what it is to be a Being-for-itself, a free self. By contrast, to act in good faith is presumably to act as Remedios the Beauty acts in Macondo, with a consciousness that is totally free, totally natural, undetermined and hence lucid. Remedios the Beauty was a "symbol of subversion" (p. 165) because of her simplifying instinct; her consciousness was free of formalities because she obeyed no other law than the law of spontaneity. The conscious choices we Magical Marxists have to make in our lives and in our politics must be guided by precisely this unfettered imagination—like the imagination that created Remedios the Beauty, the imagination that produces a work of art, that re-appropriates our freedom and turns it into an œuvre. But this magical imagination will be something more than idealism, something more than simple wishful thinking and naive optimism.

A consciousness that cannot imagine, Sartre says, that is hopelessly mired in the "real," is incapable of the perception of unrealized possibilities. For Sartre, "the act of the imagination is an act of magic." It is magic because it conjures up imaginary forms, imaginary images, because free consciousness can always formulate the real constitution of an image and therefore posit imaginary images that are realizable possibilities.[9] We know these images exist but know that they do not yet really exist. Within this gap between the really real and the not-yet-real is the recognition that something is missing and that this something is also somehow attainable. Sartre frames the problematic as the double aspect of nothingness, as a slippage between two futures: a *real future* and a *future imagined*. The real future is like the real past, knowable because it is recognizable, because it is a future that merely continues what the past has bequeathed. This future is the future expected, already actual, since it doesn't take much imagination to herald its arrival. The real future is the business as usual of the past, a conservative future. It is what we don't have to imagine because we know it is already here, or about to be here soon. Taken thus, the real future is a kind of bad faith, a truncating of one's possibilities, an escape from freedom. To be free, Sartre insists, one needs to be able to pose a thesis about *irreality*. But, as ever, it necessarily has to be done by a consciousness that is conscious of something, that never ceases to be conscious of the object it doesn't yet have but knows exists somewhere in a distant unreality.

Resonances with the young Marx perhaps ring out, the Marx of 1844 who wrote about human "vital powers," about "passions" and "drives," about imagination as a "natural power" and how conscious life activity, our conceptual and imaginative drives, distinguish us from other animals. The fact that we can convert these drives into an active transformation of the objective world, as well as into a self-creation, means that we can produce ourselves *universally*, Marx said, not one-sidedly like other animals. Just as did Sartre, the young Marx claimed that these drives, these essential powers, this consciousness, always exist in relation to an object, to a desired object that lies outside of ourselves and which we "vigorously strive to attain."[10] Yet the specter of alienation forever haunts us, the specter of alienating activities, of the deadening division of labor, of stultifying work, endless drudgery, and mindless tasks that mean little or nothing to the doer but which cripple the imagination and numb our creative powers. If conscious activity is not "free," it can no longer transform anything. It's a consciousness without an object, says Marx, a consciousness that "is a mere means for our existence."[11]

Insofar, then, as consciousness can imagine, it needs to escape the narrow confines and deep factuality of the real world; it needs to be able subjectively to release itself from the world of alienation, from bad faith, from Being-in-itself. A consciousness that is for-itself can overcome the real, Sartre says, first of all through "affectivity" and then by "action," by conscious practice, by a filling of the void, a closing of the gap between the future real and the imagined future.[12] Sartre makes it clear that imagination isn't an empirical power, measurable or touchable; nor is it something that needs to be "added on" to consciousness in an ad hoc fashion. Rather, imagination is nothing less than a consciousness for-itself expressing itself in all its liberty. That's how imagination creates its own *real* image: *the imaginary*. The imaginary is another possibility in the existent, a non-existent real possibility. "The imaginary," says Sartre, "is in each case the concrete something towards which the existent is overcome."[13]

Architects and Bees: Releasing Human Vital Powers

In recent decades it's incredible how much the imagination seems to have disappeared from left consciousness, how its consciousness has wallowed hopelessly in the real, how it has been repressed by bad faith. It is the left's imagination, rather than the state, that seems to have withered away. We might wonder if the left has been successively defeated because it lacked the power of imagination or whether it is defeat that has thwarted its imagination, bullied it out of the battle of ideas, out of a possible imaginary future. In the case of Marxism, I suspect it's a touch of both, that a sort of negative dialectic has taken hold of our minds, reacting back to negate Marxism's own developmental life-spirit, its own evolution as a historical reality. But it's also true that some of the most innovative and imaginative Marxism has emerged from dark and depressing times, from fascism and war (cf. the Frankfurt School), out of prison camps and in exile (cf. Gramsci, Walter Benjamin, and Ernst Bloch). So how to explain the drying up of ideas? How to explain that hitherto long march of Marxism, permanently rewriting itself in the successive ruins of each epoch, suddenly stopping dead in its tracks? It seemed to stop dead in its tracks around 1979–80, with the advent of Margaret Thatcher and Ronald Reagan, and since 1989 this now stationary cripple, totally bereft of imagination, toppled almost completely along with those tumbling monuments and great walls.

The subsequent capitulation to bad faith, to realist actuality, and the apparent reluctance even to try to reach out into the nether-nether land of the normative, is tellingly exhibited by one of Marxism's most prominent mouthpieces, *New Left Review*, who recently toasted (or commiserated) its half-century on earth. The journal's lack of imagination, the disdain it shows towards little germs of new possibilities quietly incubating in the world, its obsession with scouring the political landscape for global oppositional forces, and nothing less, betrays the mandarin cynicism it contents itself with peddling: "To attend to the development of actually existing capitalism remains a first duty for a journal like *NLR*," it claims.[14] Since there are no "made totalities" around, let's forget about any totalizations in the course of making themselves. The mission, first and foremost, is simply empirical research, to monitor a failing global system, to soberly and coolly analyze capitalist machinations, to revel in clinical critical negativity.[15] All of which reveals the worst face of Marxism, a gutless and worthless variety, without a future, without hope, without hope of inspiring hope, without any discernible characteristics to pass on to anyone. Its only real engagement is an engagement in reproducing itself, of maintaining its own elite inner circle.

If Marxism wants to continue to play a losing game, it should go on doing things no differently, go on as *New Left Review* goes on, as a journal that doesn't document the future of Marxism only its past: a dead one. Marxism's future lies not in the hands of "official" Marxists, but with those who come from outside, who aren't poisoned by either sectarianism or the search for the purest theory, for the most rigorous rigor. The future of Marxism lies in the hands of oppositional social movements and in opportunist actions that break the mould of past battles, battles now long lost, no longer worth dwelling upon. The future of Marxism lies in a Marxism that forgets about its past and isn't so much interested in analyzing the present because it has already imagined the future—

it is already working towards that future, for and by itself. This Marxism does the only thing it can do in a situation of NO EXIT: *it gets going*, it imagines and re-imagines, it experiments here and now, it takes risks and talks in a language it has only just invented. Adherents and insurgents may not call themselves Marxists nor even communists; but their activism and engagement, their illicit subversion and overt radicalism, their desire for *autogestion*, for self-management and group praxis, for a community that lives somehow post-capitalistically, somehow compels them to become the best Marxists ever. It compels them to become "the worst of architects and the best of bees."

The phrase, of course, is Marx's own, from the beginning of the "Labor-Process" chapter of *Capital* Volume I. Marx's discussion here relates to the act of production, of labor-power at work, transforming nature, setting in motion "natural forces" that belong to our bodies, appropriating the materials of nature and adapting them to human needs. But, as Marx says, "we are not dealing here with those first instinctive forms of labor which remain on an animal level."[16] What we're dealing with is sophisticated and advanced labor, a form of production that can *imagine* beforehand the actual process of work and the product this work realizes. As Marx puts it: "At the end of every labor process, a result emerges which had already been conceived by the worker at the beginning, hence already existed ideally."[17]

Human beings, Marx says, don't only effect a change of form in the materials of nature; we also realize our own purpose in these materials. And this is a purpose we are conscious of, that conditions the mode of our activity. In effect, as a species, we become architects of our own destiny, of our own physical and mental forms, creating first in our imagination, in a plan or design, what's around us, making it empirical and real only afterwards. A spider puts to shame any human weaver, Marx says, and for any civil engineer or architect, a bee does likewise with its honeycomb. "But what distinguishes the worst of architects from the best of bees," says Marx, "is that the architect builds the cell in his mind before he constructs it in wax."[18] So even the weakest human imagination has one over other animals, even our weakest conceptions can be realized. Even the worst of architects—and if we look around our cities we see a lot of their work about!—can do something no bee can ever do. Marx, in short, is both cognizant of and wont to praise human mental powers of creation, the human capacity to formulate abstractions, to invent future scenarios, to conceive things in our fertile imagination before erecting them in reality. We do it in the capitalist labor process all the time, so why not in political life? What has happened to even the worst of architects of the left?

Those who have taken it upon themselves to create another sort of communal structure, another non-profit money-form, another mode of village life, another urban existence in an occupied building, those who have built their own housing alongside others, perhaps even rebuilt a whole neighborhood, those who have developed what Ivan Illich called "tools of conviviality," or have tried to imagine another destiny apart from the destiny handed down to them, one that they're told to await—these are the architects of a new society, and of a new Marxism of the future. For these people, their theoretical contestation boils down to practical experimentation, to an elaboration of alternative socialities germinating within the dominant society, of revolutionary reforms mixing imagination with practical will, somehow reforming the revolution, or at least living the revolution *now*. They're not waiting around for the right moment, when the conditions and contradictions are mature or fully developed; they're not waiting around for the Big Bang Revolution to come; they're creating it in a continuous process of experiment and adaptation. Very often these people aren't involved in, nor do they necessarily favor, a general insurrection; rather, they involve themselves in a sort of progressive political radicalization of their concept of life. It catches on, word gets around, and others experiment likewise, try their hand at it, opt out and tune in. A libertarian consciousness takes hold that is anti-capitalist at its core. If we look around our world today, these pockets of light and islands of possibility, little planets within a bigger planet, are springing up almost everywhere; and what they're trying to do is impart a new purpose to living, invent a new concept of what might be possible, and of what is necessary, based upon the active application of autonomous vital powers.

Marx makes it clear that imagination is a *vital power*; the power to imagine, and the role of the intellect to conceive and to analyze, is a vital force that only we humans have at our disposition; action, bodily force, conscious physical strength, is similarly a vital power; cooperation—human beings working together consciously according to a preconceived collective plan, using all our mental and physical energies—is again, for Marx, a vital power. Vital powers are sources of magic, of concrete, earthly magic. Marx was clear about where the magical force of a transformative politics would come from: *it would come from releasing these collective vital powers*. A new power arises, Marx says, out of the fusion of many forces into a single force; a new social force is developed when many hands cooperate in the same undivided operation.[19]

It's interesting to note how Marx actually recognizes a consciously conceived human project as something that both releases and stimulates our "animal spirits." In fact, in Marx's view, the role of preconception and imagination, of conscious purpose—and of the purpose of consciousness—is a "natural" complement to more instinctive, spontaneous impulses, to passions that unite us humans with other animals, and indeed with the plant world. (The vision almost sounds like a Wifredo Lam painting in which human, animal, and plant worlds merge incandescently as one.) Here, on the one hand, Marx wants to underscore the role of human imagination, our role as architects of our own destiny, as a priori agents of change, as super-brains leaping to freedom; yet, on the other hand, what's equally implied is that we shouldn't abandon our instincts either, our bee-like behavior, our spontaneous appropriation and re-appropriation, our sensuous being. In a future communist society, of whatever scale and capacity, the architect and the bee must find unity, must coexist, must imagine a counter-society amongst the honeycombs.

That a democratic society must be created and organized by conscious planning, by collective intervention first conceived in the imagination, is of paramount importance. Yet at the same time Marx knows that what he calls "real life"—and by that he means a society in which individuality is "fully developed"—is also characterized by novelty and contingency, by spontaneity and organic growth, by warm openness rather than icy routine. Thus human beings, Marx says, don't only affirm themselves intellectually in the objective world; we also do so—and need to do so—"with *all* our senses."[20] Any sense that's a prisoner of crude practical need, or dulled by mindless repetitive activity, is, Marx says, a "restricted sense." We must appropriate our relations with ourselves, and with others in our world, "in an integral way."[21] The senses must become "organs of our individuality" and "theoreticians in their immediate praxis." A "society that is *fully developed*," Marx claims,

> produces man in all the richness of his being, the rich man who is *profoundly and abundantly endowed with all the senses*, as its constant reality. It can be seen how subjectivism and objectivism, spiritualism and materialism, activity and passivity, lose their antithetical character, and hence their existence as such antitheses, only in the social condition; it can be seen how the resolution of the *theoretical* antitheses themselves is possible *only in a practical* way, only through the practical energy of man.[22]

One of the greatest impediments to the release of our vital powers is a society that not only creates work without purpose, but also organizes this work through a highly detailed and fragmented *division of labor*. The capitalist division of labor, which over recent years has projected itself on a truly international scale, has become so technologically advanced and so complex that most working people now function as mere appendages of machines, of assembly lines, cash tills, computer terminals of various shapes and sizes; these machines either make people toil longer and faster or else banish them from work altogether. This division of labor, Marx says, "compels each worker to spend on the work no more than the necessary time. This creates a continuity, a uniformity, a regularity, an order."[23] People thereby become tiny cogs in a mighty administrative and productive machine; specific and discrete agents of tasks whose sole purpose is usually to valorize capital, to aid commodity flows, to enhance profitability. The continuous appropriation of scientific knowledge by different fractions of capital has succeeded in converting people into "living" fixed capital, into organic dead labor; and each day at work reinforces this subordination; daily turnover time becomes the time of slow death, of non-recoverable bodily wear and tear. And even high-paying jobs for elite workers involve a detailed mental division of labor that's almost as deadening, almost as meaningless as the manual division of labor. Only the fat paycheck at the end of the month eases the emptiness.

Marx knows why the capitalist division of labor is so crippling and debilitating for people: "constant labor of one uniform kind disturbs the intensity and flow of man's animal spirits, which find recreation and delight in a mere change of activity."[24] But the problem isn't, as he sees it, a problem with the division of labor *per se*; breaking down tasks to organize work more efficiently, with greater coordination, both spatially and temporally, isn't in itself a pernicious idea. What is pernicious is the crudity with which it is currently realized, and particularly the *compulsion* it involves: one huge mass of people is confined to either manual torment or mental boredom, while another much smaller group monopolizes skills, dominates knowledge and expertise, and prospers from that domination and monopolization. This division of labor is pernicious in the sense that the real possibility of lightening the work load, spreading the burden, is transformed into its dialectical other, a system of repression and repetition, of obsessive and odious work. Work as the instrument of man only betokens man the instrument.

In an ideal imaginary state, new technology and the division of labor would have the capacity to free us from the drudgery of work; in reality, they have become "alien powers" frantically setting labor-power in motion, stifling true subjectivity, ushering in the "real subsumption" of life under the domain of capital. Here, even a lightening of the burden of labor through technology turns into "an instrument of torture, since the machine does not free the worker from work, but rather deprives the work itself of all content."[25] Work, we might say, becomes lean and stupid, at least for the bulk of the population. It follows that for any real freedom to be possible an alternative society wouldn't so much abolish the division of labor as neutralize it, socialize it, periodically switch tasks around, enabling people to vary their activity, letting them identify with this activity. Perhaps most crucial of all is to release the intensity and flow of the uniform activity itself, by translating productive gains from technology and the division of labor into *free time* or *working less*. Indeed, if there's one thing that can be gleaned from Marx here, it's that he regarded *time* as our most precious asset, as the wellspring of potential social riches, as something too important to let slip away unfulfilled. "Free time" is thus something vital for the full development of individuality, for self-unfolding, for expanding individual capacities, and for the creation and perpetuation of a better society. A communist society is a society in which time has been liberated, in which citizens have disposable time at hand, and where one's "second life" outside of the workplace becomes one's "real life."[26]

Imagination as "Most Damned Seriousness"

Such utopian yearnings actually assume the most pressing analytical concreteness in Marx's *Grundrisse*, in, for example, the long "chapter on Capital" he drafted between mid January and early February 1858. There, Marx posits a certain historicity at play: his "faith" in a utopian *might be* hinges on what will be. The development of communism will bloom through the "full development" of capitalism, through the historical development of its productive forces. The possibility of releasing ourselves from work, Marx says, comes about when living labor has materialized itself in machines, and when "the technological application of science" determines the entire productive character of capital. When the world of work is dominated by machines, when we become total appendages to new technology, when that technology "suspends" human beings from "the immediate form" of work, so that dead labor valorizes living labor (and not the other way around), then and only then, Marx says, will a new era become possible:[27]

To the degree that large industry develops, the creation of real wealth comes to depend less on labor time and on the amount of labor employed than on the power of the agencies set in motion during labor time, whose "powerful effectiveness" is itself in turn out of all proportion to the direct labor time spent on their production, but depends rather on the general state of science and on the progress of technology, or the application of science to production.[28]

That projection might already be with us. That "full development" of the productive forces is now an *is* not a *will be*: The world Marx described in those long nights of a February winter might be our world today. The society in which human ingenuity, imagination, scientific know-how, the vital powers of the human brain and hand have become objectified in fixed capital, in capital that apparently rules over us, may be the society in which we currently find ourselves. We have built a society that now enslaves us: we have quite literally become the worst of architects. Our brilliant imagination is objectified into an alien force; our "general intellect"—the collective accumulated powers of intellectual labor, of our brilliant doctors and scientists and thinkers—condemns us to a world forever besieged by crises, by misery and fatigue, by exploitation and depression. The communality and culmination of our vast knowledge, Marx says, has left us helpless.[29] And yet, despite all that, and seemingly counterfactually, Marx glimpses a warm-stream future lurking, a magical *might be*. Somehow, he makes the imaginative existential leap from a dire material reality to an almost Sartrean-like *ir*reality: in a little over ten pages of the *Grundrisse*, Marx projects the *immanent possibilities* in a world transformed into a vast form of fixed capital, *immanent possibilities* in a world in which the only labor that now really counts is no longer the labor of hard-ware but of thought-ware, of *immaterial* labor, of *cognitive* no-collar capitalism rather than blue-collar corporeal capitalism.[30]

Marx's realism here is magical in the sense that he doesn't just analyze what really exists; he imagines the unforeseen, he anticipates and initiates potential transformations already existing in the real, in mutated forms. His imagination is already plotting its own image, an *imaginary* communist future, presumably with its very own Imaginary Party, comprising workers who no longer work, who have been "suspended" from work, displaced from work whose "direct form" has ceased to be the "great well-spring of wealth." At that point, Marx says, "labor time ceases and *must cease* to be a measure of value, and hence exchange value must cease to be the measure of use value. The surplus labor of the mass has ceased to be the condition for the development of general wealth."[31] Marx draws several conclusions from this—complex conclusions—and tantalizingly leaves it to us to draw up a few more of our own.

To begin with, he says, "production based on exchange value breaks down, and the direct material production process is stripped of the form of penury and antithesis."[32] The debate around cognitive capitalism problematizes how this "classic" Marxian law of value, the theory of value Marx formulated in *Capital*, has become unhinged with the growth of immaterial labor, as high-tech, profit-laden, scientific, knowledge-based activities assume their own, apparently free-floating value dynamics within the overall economy, little of which can be stocked, quantified, formalized or objectified. There is thus, perhaps, little reason to doubt Gorz's words on the matter:

> By furnishing services, immaterial labor has become the hegemonic form of work; material labor is displaced to the periphery of the production process, or is summarily externalized. Although it remains indispensable and even dominant from a quantitative standpoint point, material labor has become a "subaltern moment" of the process. The heart of value creation is now immaterial labor.[33]

Other writers, like David Harvey, have convincingly shown how expanded and continued capital accumulation over the past couple of decades has had a marked penchant for *dispossession*, for asset stripping and commons plundering, for raiding the public coffers through privatization, for corporate fraud, and for rolling the dice on the stock market; it has shown zero commitment to investing in living labor in actual production.[34] What these theorists all show, or at least collectively imply, is that living labor might be a species en route to complete extinction. Marx himself puts it like this:

> Labor no longer appears so much to be included with the production process; rather, the human being comes to relate more as watchman and regulator to the production process itself ... He steps to the side of the production process instead of being its chief actor. In this transformation, it is neither the direct human labor he himself performs [that counts], nor the time during which he works, but rather the appropriation of his own general productive power.[35]

The tack Marx takes in the *Grundrisse* is that of an optimist, rubbing his hands gleefully at the prospect of material conditions "blow[ing] this foundation sky-high."[36] He sees a world that "suspends" labor, that revolves around "dead labor," around the production of social life under the control of the "general intellect," as pregnant with its contrary, as itself a "moving contradiction." Because, he says, it reduces the time of "necessary labor," and because here we have the wherewithal and ingredients for creating "the means of social disposable time," for being able "to reduce labor time for the whole society to a diminishing minimum, and thus to free everyone's time for their own development."[37] After all, real wealth, Marx reminds his readers, isn't command over surplus labor, but rather *disposable time outside that needed in direct production, for every individual and the whole society.*"[38] Disposable time, then, not labor time, is, for Marx, the measure of real wealth, a disposable time for the artistic, scientific development of the individual, a time for pastimes, for edification not putrefaction. Free time is "both idle time and time for higher activity," all of which will "transform its possessor into a different subject"; imagine, Marx says, "a human being in the process of becoming."[39] And yet, *nota bene,* "really free working"—e.g. composing, artistic endeavor, writing books, and other forms of "individual self-realization"—"in no way means that it becomes mere fun, mere amusement, as Fourier, with *grisette*-like naiveté, conceives it. Really free working ... is at the same time precisely the most damned seriousness, the most intense exertion."[40]

Anybody involved in any alternative project nowadays—
from Tarnac to Rio, from *banlieue* to *bidonville*, from landless
occupation to lawless re-appropriation—knows all too well that
opting out, that "free working," inevitably necessitates the most
damned seriousness. Participation entails commitment (lots of
evenings!), insecurity means doubt, lack of resources demands the
most intense exertion. To be sure, "liberated time," the Invisible
Committee says, "doesn't mean a vacation. Vacant time, dead
time, the time of emptiness and the fear of emptiness—this is the
time of work." With free time, conversely, "there'll be no more
time to *fill*, but a liberation of energy that no 'time' contains."[41]
In free time, the Sartrean leap to freedom is encountered, the
responsibility one must take for asserting one's freedom. We,
alone, are *responsible* for the meaning of the situation in which
we live; we, alone, give meaning to our world. Responsibility is
hard: we make a *conscious choice* to liberate ourselves, to rely
on ourselves, and then we have to take responsibility for the
choices we make. Still, this responsibility is *and has to be* a world
away from bourgeois/neo-liberal ideas about personal responsibility, about being responsible for the exploitation somebody else
inflicts upon us. Communist responsibility, by contrast, means
being responsible for self-assertion not for self-condemnation.

Chronicle of a Possible World Foretold

In a dream, time undergoes bizarre transformations; it no longer
remains linear but gets mangled up, compressed, and disjointed.
Things happen concurrently or ahead of time, out of all rational
sequence or consciously recognizable temporal ordering.
Everything becomes like a magical realist novel that begins with
its conclusion and then proceeds to work backwards as it goes
forwards, recounting its tale as a strange chronicle foretold.
Marxist utopian thought must now take on these strange characteristics, become a chronicle of a possible world foretold, a world
in which free time isn't squandered like work time, but is treated
with the most damned seriousness, the most intense exertion, the
greatest act of our imagination. There are two choices with respect

to this paradigm of a possible world foretold: either a chronicle of death or a chronicle of life: a *real future*, on the one hand, and a *future imagined*, on the other. Otherwise put: a "post-work" society in which the creation of wealth no longer equates to the employment of people contains both a knowable future full of threats as well as an *ir*real future of great opportunities; and neither option quite resembles those that Marx envisages in the *Grundrisse*.

A capitalist "post-work" society, our real future, seems less akin to work-as-an-economic-necessity than to work-as-an-ideological-and-political-urgency, a matter of preserving the stability and legitimacy of a system of work without workers, ensuring that workers (and ex-workers) remain consumers and somehow "embrace" the world of immaterial labor. Therein reside the threats: not least the threat that the desire for free time, the yearning to work less (a yearning a lot of the active workforce now seem to share), will be thrown back in people's faces, used as a pretext for the neo-liberal state to disengage, to promote "self-help" strategies as forms of self-reproduction and self-exploitation, as a means of social control: "we are all entrepreneurs!" Another threat is that joblessness, insecurity around work, part-time jobs, McJobs, temporary contracts and piecework tasks, performed casually and for little pay, translate into a never-ending, highly flexible pool of workers that enterprises can tap into or turn away at the whim of their business cycles. Here the menace of Marx's "industrial reserve army" looms: precariousness becomes the watchword for the "relative surplus population" of our day, for the continent worker progressively produced by the valorization of capital.[42]

This relative surplus population boils down to the huge mass of under-employed and sub-employed workers likely to be part-time, on-call, self-employed, on temporary contracts or workfare programs, who all succeed in making the official unemployment statistics look less dire than they actually are. These people are absorbed into an ever expanding "personal services industry," rendered even more ruthless and competitive by the burgeoning of temporary help agencies and contracting firms, coordinating the distribution of contingent labor-power whose supply and demand dances to the tune of outsourcing, cost-cutting companies. Temp agencies enable displaced workers to assume new careers floating between jobs. And not only have the numbers of people temping grown enormously over past decades, the temporary help business is itself a booming industry. (Manpower Inc., for example, is now a billion-dollar multinational company and the largest staffing agency in the world; it is technically the US's largest employer, too, hiring out 800,000 substitute workers each year. Moreover, with 4,100 offices in 82 countries, Manpower places 1.6 million people "in assignments" with more than 250,000 businesses worldwide annually.)

As at February 2010, the US has a giant black hole more than 10 million jobs deep. That's the number of jobs that would be needed to get the economy back to a "respectable" 5 percent unemployment level, the prevailing rate before the current downturn. With a growing population, and with more and more new people entering the labor market, the US would need to produce roughly 1.5 million new jobs every year—about 125,000 a month—to keep from sinking deeper into that black hole.[43] But even if some 600,000 jobs a month were created—more than double the pace of the 1990s—it would still take two years to fill in that gaping void. As even the most gung-ho neo-liberal economist will tell you, that's a rate of growth not sustained since the 1960s: it's a rate, in other words, that's a practical impossibility, even more so in an economy predicted to have *zero* growth for the foreseeable future. The possibility of a zero growth economy also stares Europe in the face and the continent seems afraid to stare back. In France, 10 percent of the population is now officially unemployed, some 2.8 million people (ILO figure, December 2009), and 100,000 people each month are added to the unemployment roster. In the UK, 2.4 million are officially unemployed (almost 8 percent of the population), and a further 1.4 million work under temporary contracts.

Yet amongst these threats reside certain possibilities, even truly revolutionary potentialities. And it's here that we encounter the *future imagined*, our possible dream state of a life foretold. In the UK, around 85 percent of part-timers don't want a full-time job, and there are many people who actively refuse to work supplementary hours, opting to downsize, to work less hours for less pay, and to live a little better in the meanwhile. "*Travailler plus pour gagner plus*" now reads like a quaint relic from another epoch; "*travailler moins, vivre mieux*" sounds more in tune with the zeitgeist. (This was, after all, always seen by Marx as the "fundamental imperative.") In times of crisis, the first thing enterprises do is slash jobs even more than they slash them when times are good. One's first reaction as a worker is "shit, a layoff, a pay cut, a reduction in hours..." The scenario is described in a still-valuable book, *Travailler deux heures par jour*, produced by the French collective "Adret"—"a mountainous land with a sunny exposure"—in the crisis-ridden 1970s. In one chapter, Charly Boyadjian, a young worker at a shoe factory in Romans, recounts what happened at his factory in late 1974 as the oil crisis started to bite. First of all, to cut costs, a brutal 48-hour "3X8" working week—in which an 8-hour shift is switched every week between morning, afternoon, and night-time—got reduced to 40 hours; then to 32, and later to 24. The initial worry, says Boyadjian, was about the inevitable loss of money. What to do? How to manage? Disaster strikes! But then, Boyadjian says, little by little, over the course of several weeks, all the workers noticed a change. Those who were previously exhausted began to feel better than before, more engaged with one another, more energized. Aggression diminished, too, and friendships developed. "It was in this period," Boyadjian says, "that contestation was born, because everyone had started to talk more ... you were less taken up in work, you discussed work ... you had a political discussion on a subject really important because somebody had sparked it."[44] After a while, those workers who had tried to top up their reduced earnings by working "*au noir*" stopped their informal activities, preferring to be with their families, "relearning how to live," how to relax, Boyadjian says. After the recession, many workers at the plant didn't want to revert to their old hours. And they'd become politicized around work, discovered something the union militants hadn't yet discovered, weren't rallying for. Just look, Boyadjian says, what effect reducing the working day has.

Imagine going all the way. Imagine, he says, "working two hours per day?" "It's important now to think about it, though it's sure not going to happen in one fell swoop."[45]

Perhaps, then, crises might be blessings rather than calamities? Perhaps we should embrace them by desisting from labor, and from consuming, and let the situation implode even more? Perhaps in times of crises, like the crisis that appears to be forever writ large nowadays, we can relearn how to do without work, like Boyadjian et al. did. In the US, twenty-somethings with college degrees are now apparently learning how to be "carefree," how to voluntarily switch jobs, on their own terms; they've reevaluated their career choices, as well as the whole notion of career itself, because they're intelligent enough to know that they might not have anything worth deeming "a career" anymore.[46] Since joblessness has lost a lot of its stigma in America, given that there are so many people unemployed, being out of work is no longer seen simply as a personal failing. In fact, there are a whole generation of twenty-somethings almost everywhere, especially young men, often young men of color, often young men who live in specific neighborhoods, who know they'll never work a salaried job. They know they can never count on either a pension or the "right to work" because they know all that is a fiction for them, a realism without any magic. Nor do they recognize themselves as "precarious" or belonging to any "*précariat*" because they would never define themselves in relation to work, to what "they do."

Perhaps, during crises, we can hatch alternative programs for survival, other methods by which we might not so much "earn a living" as live a living. Perhaps we can self-downsize or even refrain from work itself, and at the same time address a paradox that goes back at least to Max Weber: work is revered in our culture, yet at the same time workers are becoming superfluous; you hate your job and your boss, hate the servility of what you do, and how you do it, the pettiness of the tasks involved, yet want to keep your job at all costs. You see no other way of defining yourself other than *through work*, through what you do for a living, through the "honor" of being employed. Perhaps there's a point at which we can all be pushed over the edge, "set-free" as Marx said, voluntarily take the jump only to discover other aspects of ourselves, other ways to fill in the hole, to make a little money, to maintain our dignity and pride, and to survive off what Gorz calls a "frugal abundance." Perhaps it's time to get politicized around non-work. In opting out perhaps we can create a bit of havoc through refusing to work, turn absenteeism into a positive device, a will to struggle for another kind of work in which use value outbids exchange value. If capitalists can do without workers, then it's time workers realized that they can do without capitalists, that they can devise work without capitalists, even work without the state. What to do in a world without work? What to do with a great mass of unemployed, sub-employed, partially employed people who don't belong to a union or identify themselves with any class, let alone with each other? How to develop and incorporate them into a solidarity economy forged out of unbridled imagination and a lot of practical will?

We still hear voices on the left calling for full employment, still battling for a return to decent jobs for decent pay and decent benefits. I'm not so sure it operates that way anymore. Today, decent jobs are the rare exception, so rare in fact that it's safer to bet they no longer actually exist. If the left thinks otherwise then it's backing the wrong horse, channeling its energies in the wrong direction, going backwards not forwards, in a direction that's arguably more utopian than the vision of a society of free time. Now is the moment to change trajectory, to turn the tables, to transform a capitalist business ethic that downsizes individuals into a daring social ethic that upends capitalism.

6

BUTTERFLIES, OWLS, AND LITTLE GOLD FISHES: CONJURING UP REVOLUTIONARY MAGIC

But you're how many? I mean ... we, the group. I've no idea. One day there's two of us, another day ten. And sometimes there's 10,000 of us.

Cesare Battisti

Any system referring to human behavior not inspired by the poetic conditions of action is consigned to a miserable fate as a harmless pastime of the mind.

René Ménil

Soft Dreamers, Intellectual Anarchists

One of the most powerful and fundamentally subversive sensibilities in our society is the poetic sensibility. I write this near the end of *Magical Marxism* because never, perhaps, have we lived in such *un*poetic times, in an age that relegates the non-utilitarian to the car boot sale of our culture, to the distant hinterlands of a world whose sole inspiration is the crude application of "facts." One reason for this relegation of the poetic sensibility, and its relative marginalization in social life, may be that, secretly, power fears poetry, that it is somehow unnerved by the disruptive, magical energies of poetic thought, of poetic acts. Out loud, it laughs at poetry. In private, under its breath, power is wary of poetry because it speaks a language power can barely understand, acts in a way it can hardly fathom. Poetry resides somewhere else, somewhere inaccessible to power; it evokes sentiments, touches being, and speaks in a strange tongue. And sometimes it talks back to power, in its special voice, its spectral voice, with a spirit that can never be suppressed, can never be entirely silenced—try as power might. The unity of dream and action is reconciled in the poetic act, in the poetic moment, and that can produce its effect with the certainty of lightning...

*

In the early hours of one summer's morning, back in 1926, the poet-Marxist Henri Lefebvre was out marching in the French countryside, doing military service with a light infantry battalion whose men were singing war songs in the balmy July air. Lefebvre opposed these refrains with his own inner chant: "I embraced the dawn of summer...." Suddenly, Lefebvre says, "I glimpsed ten steps ahead of me, at the side of the lane, a lovely butterfly whose rose wings where damp; this prevented him from flying. I hastened myself, broke ranks, and took him as delicately as possible and placed him down on the embankment." Three seconds later, a corporal sticks a rifle butt in Henri's back. Then the captain, "high up on his nag," bawls: "*Chasseur* Lefebvre! 8 days in police detention." "This lad announces himself as a dangerous subversive element ... a soft dreamer, a savior of butterflies ... an intellectual anarchist...."[1] Soon afterwards, young Henri suffers the "severe punishment" of solitary confinement. Rotting there he ponders on the incident that would become a powerful romantic metaphor in his great brick-like, two-volume autobiography, *La somme et le reste*. He didn't regret anything, he said, didn't regret "the symbolic gesture" of "saving the tangible sign of poetry."[2] But he was furious nonetheless because he'd let himself seem weak, soft—worse, a dreamer—and there and then Lefebvre vowed he would become "more applied" as a warrior, harder, and more practical. If he dreamed, "it was of the subversive utilization of new science," he says. "I became ... precise, realistic, revolutionary." So if he later read Clausewitz, and if he soon envisaged writing a book called "Man and the Soldier," he "owed it all to a butterfly and a cruel captain."[3]

But not long after, although Lefebvre knew such a hardened stance had its merit for any left revolutionary, he knew as well that this wasn't really his style: the cold, realistic man of science he wasn't. As a wayward youth, years before his military service, the lad Lefebvre collected butterflies in the Pyrenean meadows near his hometown of Navarrenx; as a journeyman radical, he knew he would always remain a dreamer who came to their rescue. Butterflies, in short, were as flighty and as frivolous as Lefebvre himself, so light and breezy as to float away, to pollinate and come alive in the sunshine, in mid-summer. Indeed, butterflies symbolize a magical Marxist style that is will-o'-the-wisp, that's free, that thrives in the warmth, in natural light.

Butterflies are day-flying creatures that probe the air for scents, for balmy breezes, for nectar. Some species are migratory and travel vast distances, floating and fluttering over space, sometimes over thousands of miles (like the Monarch butterfly coursing between California and Mexico), orienting themselves using the sun's rays and heat. (Under cloud cover, butterflies perceive polarized light.) Butterflies are preeminently *anti*-science, too: their wing strokes, their flutters, cannot be easily accounted for within conventional steady-state aerodynamics. Butterflies dance to a different beat, to a different system of ducking and diving, a different kind of poetics, one frankly perplexing for Newtonian scientists. To be sure, butterflies aren't trippers like birds or bats; and even though their fluttering and wandering appears erratic, it isn't: butterflies merely avoid steady forward flight, steady linear advancement.

They say that butterflies personify a person's soul, that a butterfly floating around you means your lover is about to arrive on the scene. García Márquez's apprentice dreamer, Mauricio Babilonia, Meme's tragic mate from *One Hundred Years of Solitude*, was followed all his life by little yellow butterflies; they precede each of his courting appearances: "Meme saw them as if they had suddenly been born out of the light and her heart gave a turn" (p. 235).[4] Butterflies, meanwhile, symbolize "rebirth" into new life, after a period in a cocoon, an unleashing of freedom, an itinerant photosynthesis. This idea had a strong pull on Lefebvre himself, writing *La somme et le reste* in the wake of 1956 and the Soviet invasion of Hungary (which disgusted him), and after so many run-ins with the Stalinist hacks, finally "expelling himself" from the French Communist Party (PCF). ("*J'ai quitté le Parti par la gauche*," he enjoyed bragging.) "This book," he wrote in 1973, in an updated preface to *La somme et le reste*,

> speaks of deliverance, of happiness regained. Liberated from political pressure one exits from a place of suffocation, a man starts to live again, and to think. After a long period of asphyxiation, of delusion, of disappointments concealed ... look at him: he crawls up from the abyss ... He surges from the depths and surfaces, a little flattened by heavy pressures. He breathes in the sunshine, opens himself, displays himself and comes alive again.[5]

Marks of Subversion, Peace of the Spirit

Even during his 32 armed uprisings, all Colonel Aureliano Buendia really dreamed of was making little gold fishes in his workshop and giving Macondo an atmosphere of rural peace. When he'd succeeded in bringing calm to town, the colonel occupied himself for hours and hours with the alchemy his father had taught him, putting intricate little gold fishes together. "He had had to start thirty-two wars," his creator says, "and had had to violate all of his pacts with death and wallow like a hog in the dung heap of glory in order to discover the privileges of simplicity almost forty years later" (p. 142). In his workshop, the colonel no longer wished to talk about politics: his business henceforth was the shoestring enterprise of selling little gold fishes, created from melting down any scrappy morsel of gold, any coin or pot or pan he could get his hands on. People were baffled at first, not understanding how a fearsome fighter could retreat into an artisanal world of dedicated, small-scale manufacture. To many, his work seemed circular, "an exasperating vicious circle," a mere squandering of time, melting down gold coins only to convert them into delicate fishes. Actually, what interested the colonel wasn't so much the business as the *work*. The fishes became an outgrowth of his youthful poetic predilection, a fulfillment of his intrinsically artistic nature. He needed so much concentration to link the scales, to fit tiny rubies into the eyes, to laminate gills, to put fins and a hook at the end of each trinket, that during the day "there wasn't the smallest empty moment left for him." So absorbing was the attention required "by the delicacy of his artistry" that in a short time the colonel had aged more than during all the years of war. And yet, for all that, the implacable concentration had nonetheless rewarded the colonel with a contented "peace of the spirit" (p. 166).

He was no national hero, he insisted, just a simple artisan, one without memories, somebody who lost himself in the devotion to his art. One day, the colonel's mother, Ursula, brings his 17 estranged sons together, into their father's workshop; they'd arrived from the most distant corners of the coast and all bore with pride the name Aureliano. The colonel was amused by their wildness, and before they left gave each one of them a little gold fish, which, without him realizing it, had become a symbol of his effect on the world, a symbol of the revolutionary movement, even a shibboleth for conspirators and anarchists everywhere. Soon after, however, one by one, each son is murdered, violently executed by covert conservative forces still at large, still bearing a grudge, still conspiring to kill off entirely the Buendia legacy of radical liberalism.

When the colonel himself discovers that people are buying his gold fishes not as pieces of jewelry but as collector's treasure, as relics of a once great leader, of a once great ideal, he is disgusted and stops selling them. (Towards the end of *One Hundred Years of Solitude*, after the colonel's death, an army officer enters his old workshop with José Arcadio Segundo; the former is mesmerized by the room's odor, by an atmosphere long protected by a strange supernatural light. In an old tin pot, they discover 18 little gold fishes, dusty but intact. "I'd like to take one, if I may," he asks José Arcadio Segundo. "At one time they were a mark of subversion, but now they're relics." Segundo gives him a little fish and the officer put it in his shirt pocket "with a childlike glow in his eyes.") The colonel kept making his gold fishes, two each day in fact, and when he'd finished 25 of them, he would melt them down and start all over again, working day and night, totally absorbed, without thinking about anything or anyone, without even thinking about himself. He would eventually try to melt down every single fish he could retrieve, so determined was he to prevent reification, to prevent them becoming symbols of myth and political disillusionment. In becoming relics, dead things coveted by avaricious collectors, they lost their integrity as human artifacts, as objects that continued to breathe, symbols of living, concrete labor—works of work not works of business.

Where Butterflies Roam: the Politics of Space

If, for the colonel, making the little gold fishes meant another concept of the allocation of *time*, the time for creating use value as opposed to exchange value, then the poetics of the butterfly is a veritable poetics of *space*, of commanding space, of floating over any space you want to, flitting from one place to another, resting somewhere for a while, pollinating space; the butterfly is a fitting symbol for a Marxist like Henri Lefebvre who shifted historical materialism from its basis in industrial production to the activity of *producing space*, to the right to the city, to a revolution that would somehow be both urban and geographical. Of course, to float from space to space in our culture is a lot more difficult for a person than for a butterfly. Often walls confront us, prevent us from entering somewhere, deny us access, force us to move someplace else, far away from the action, to places and spaces where there's little nectar or pollen. Indeed, we live in a culture in which space itself has been commodified, has become a piece of merchandise, a thing to speculate on, to buy and sell, rent out, monopolize and colonize, tear down and reshape. These days, the free movement of the butterfly is a human ideal not an actual fact.

Over the past few decades, strange things have happened to our spaces, particularly to our urban spaces. Spaces in which people could once wander and linger, in public and in common, have steadily been transformed into spick and span privatized zones whose clients are exclusively the well heeled. Once shabby yet decent mixed neighborhoods have become homogenized and gentrified, unaffordable for former occupants, and for most people apart from the super rich who all seem to look the same, dress the same, consume the same. Our cities are becoming banal playgrounds for real estate corporations and financial institutions, for young executives and tourists, for upscale services and for the highest bidder. Former grubby industries have gone bust or cleared out overseas, to someplace cheaper, somewhere more easily exploitable. Post-industrial enclaves now displace people spatially while reshaping them temporally, fostering insecure and under-paid work and over-worked workers—busboys and valets, waiters and barmen, cleaners and security guards—who all need several jobs just to pay the bills. A denial of space here equates to a pilfering of time, to a widening disjuncture between where people live, or where they can afford to live, and where they can still find a job, to the hours wasted journeying in lock-jammed traffic or doing mammoth hikes, frequently on foot. Never have people traveled so much to do a thing so rare.

In the late 1960s, Lefebvre was pretty adamant that, in the twenty-first century, cities would replace factories as the central node of analysis and struggle for Marxists. Cities would be major sites of capital accumulation, on the one side, and of organized revolt, on the other. Just as ordinary people are exploited and downsized at work, so, too, Lefebvre said, will they be exploited and downsized where they live. Physical removal from decently paid jobs, with decent contracts and benefits, will be "complemented" by their physical removal from decent neighborhoods, with decent rents and services. Liberalism once extracted surplus value by exploiting people at the workplace; neo-liberalism now extracts its cut by dispossessing them in their living space, by sequestering the commons, by re-appropriating the centers of our cities. For Lefebvre, accordingly, a new Marxist humanism must be founded on a new right, on a right to the commons, a *right to the city*, which will emerge like a "cry and demand," he says, like a militant call-to-arms.[6]

This isn't any pseudo right, Lefebvre assures us—nothing like the toothless rights found in the UN's Universal Declaration of Human Rights from 1948; neither is it a simple visiting right, a right to take a tourist trip down memory lane, to gawk at a gentrified old center, enjoying for the day a city you've been displaced from. No, this right, says Lefebvre, can only be formulated as a transformed and renewed right to urban life itself, a right to renewed centrality. There can be no city without centrality, no urbanity, Lefebvre believes, without a dynamic core, without a vibrant, open public forum, full of lived moments and "enchanting" encounters, disengaged somehow from the logic of exchange value.

The right to the city must magically bolster the right to space, the right to land, because all of that enables people's right to self-affirmation and self-unfolding. This right to space, moreover, is tantamount to the right to living space and the right to a livelihood. Millions of rural smallholders across the globe are each year thrown off their land by big agribusiness, by the development of corporate export farming; these people lose the means to feed themselves as well as the means to make a little money; so they migrate to the city in search of work that's increasingly disappearing, migrating to an alien habitat they can little afford or understand. At the same time, former urban dwellers, trapped in insecure labor markets, are progressively edged out of a center they, too, can barely afford and no longer understand. Thus a push-pull effect takes hold, a vicious dialectic of dispossession, sucking people in and spitting people out, pretty much in the same breath, forcing old timers and newcomers alike to embrace each other out on the periphery, out in a zone of social marginalization, in assorted ZUS the world over,[7] where they're mutually stuck between the rock and the hard place, space-less and rights-less. Just as capitalism prospers from *abstract labor* at the workplace, so too does it grow and flourish through the production of *abstract space*, through a material landscape of office blocks and luxury apartments, of shopping malls and boutiques, museums and global markets. And where abstract space reigns few butterflies roam.

Making Gold Fishes: The Politics of Time

We ought to remember that Colonel Aureliano Buendia spent many, many years battling for his right to free time, for his right to work without wage-laboring. He struggled for his right to pass his time as he wanted, to engage in the creation of something, to affirm himself artistically, to find an outlet to express himself, to feel *ontologically* attached to what he did, to how he worked. It's true that for most people going out to work each day gives structure to their lives, gives "stability" to their week, enables them to engage with society, to mingle in the outside world and become public beings. In our culture, the sphere of "non-work," or, more specifically, non-paid work, is looked down upon; it is traditionally the sphere of "domestic labor," a woman's place that many housewives with kids know only too well isn't just the sphere of endless chores (without pay), but is equally one of isolation and solitude, boredom and disconnection, especially for those women living in suburbs or on the periphery of our big cities. It's clear, therefore, that Marx's radiant dream in the *Grundrisse* of reducing work time mustn't result in a free time that is *empty time*, in a time cut off from space, from a social and physical environment that creates sociability, that has supportive structures and promotes autonomous cooperation as well as autonomous activity.

The colonel himself needed fulfillment somehow, needed something to replace his former day job as a warrior. If you take steady work away, stop doing what you once did every day, what do you replace it with? How to fill in the pores of a liberated day? Here, in a somewhat different guise, we again encounter the problem of negativity, of Marxists being better able to engage in war than in peace, better able to react rather than recreate, more adept at negating than at proposing new activities to fill time once the battle might be won; or else they're not able to see how it's possible *to engage in peaceable activities while still engaging in war*. One battle certain factions of the European left have been engaged in over recent decades, a battle that attempts to kill two birds with one stone, is that of replacing wage-labor with a "social income" or a "revenue of existence." The social income, so adherents like Gorz and Hardt and Negri maintain, is an income to meet the needs of *citizens* rather than *workers*; it's a basic, unconditional income guaranteed to every person, irrespective of occupational situation, irrespective of availability and willingness to work, an income which would enable anybody, should they so desire, to make little gold fishes in a quiet workshop somewhere. The social income is simply an allowance due to you as a human being living on planet earth now, a planet where automation and fixed capital has replaced your living labor, has made you superfluous in the workplace, has made vast gains in productivity at your expense, generating huge profits for a few people who've barely worked at all. The social income is thus a form of *payback time*, something owed to you when necessary production involves only a limited quantity of labor and very few hours of actual work.

Proponents of a social income point out that it isn't a replacement for unemployment benefit: it isn't compensation doled out by the state to any person who demonstrates they need it. The sum wouldn't be designed to create dependency, nor to be a safety net addressing social exclusion; rather it should foster autonomy, help spark a profusion of new, creative activities as well as a self-unfolding of the person, since the deadening urgency and psychological stress of finding paid work to make ends meet is lifted. People could afford to take risks, to experiment with their lives; their basic cost of living would be assured, given to them as a right not as alms. For sure, those who wanted to top up this income, through part-time employment, could readily do so; yet, in general, the social income is a social dividend designed to release people's creative dispositions, to release people from the burden of work-as-we-once-knew-it. It would try to wean people away from their former wage-work habits, from their old work obsessions and fears, creating in its stead a new norm of free time, of the damn serious exertion of making little gold fishes.

Some leftists have endeavored to show how a social income is already feasible, demonstrating its practical policy efficacy today, that it is already a *realistic* option in a world where productivist logic—be it capitalistic or formerly communistic—has tellingly broken down. Sufficient monies could be gleaned, supporters say, through assorted fiscal measures like progressive income taxes, revisions in Value Added Tax (VAT), to say nothing about imposing a Tobin tax on financial transactions, wherein a less than 1 percent penalty could muster over 4 billion dollars each year.

Strategies of this kind could equip governments with the necessary resources to take action should the political will be there, should they be pressured into acting now, before it's too late, before our society has completely gone down the pan.

Be that as it may, one might justifiably ask if the idea of a social income here represents social reform or social repair? Is it meant to transform or to bail out a failed capitalist system? Won't a social wage within capitalism just be a jumped up replacement for being on the dole? Moreover, by demonstrating the efficacy of a social income, by showing how it can be achieved now, under capitalism, the left seems to want to take capitalists on at their own numbers game, converting vital human experience into the language of quantitative spreadsheets and cost-benefit analyses. Is this the left on the offensive or is it really a timid defensive strategy? Why should the left feel the need to prove to states and to companies that they can afford to pay up without losing out, without threatening their bottom-line, without losing votes?[8]

Needless to say, every sensible person knows that the state and capital can afford to cough up. Everybody knows that a social income is possible, that a change in our current logic of work and productivist paradigm is both necessary and urgent. Yet perhaps the point here isn't defensive economics at all, but offensive politics, a matter of getting organized, of individual and collective struggle, of inventing free time *now*, of experimenting *now*. Only via such an active, creative route now will people discover who they are, how much they're really worth, and how much they can take back: businesses will never give anything up without being forced to. But here again we encounter another problem, perhaps *the* biggest problem, with the social income debate. For it will strike many as odd that autonomous leftists who've (rightly) expressed utter fear and loathing of the state, and whose ideals about communism invoke an *absolute* (not relative) autonomy from the state, should somehow want to allow the state back into daily life, even if only through the backdoor. They wish, on the one hand, to smash the state, to break its oppressive grip, its oppressive apparatus, yet, on the other hand, they also want to reform the state, want it to come to everybody's rescue, to provide and orchestrate a social income. The state is exploitative, we hear (and know), it's an agent of neo-liberal capital, lubricating the "free" market flows of contemporary capitalism; and yet, suddenly and somehow, the state is to become providential, caring for all ordinary people, socially responsible. This doesn't quite stack up. How will this state come about? Whose state will it be? Is this emancipatory state with its social income a prelude to social transformation, or is the inception of a social wage in itself the first act of a futuristic communist state? Either way, it's hard to see how autonomists can have it both ways, how they—we—can invoke unfettered self-determination at the same time as demand the state provide the necessary means for that self-determination. It's hard to know if this social income policy is a form of reformism that will permit the revolution or a revolution that will permit reformism.

The debate over a social income is, then, arguably lame and rather futile, especially when there are so many other more meaningful and pressing struggles and campaigns to be waged. Intelligent people today, progressive and politically savvy people, those who want to change the world, perhaps even a few Marxist people, all know that with regard to getting things done, to really achieving social change, the capitalist state is a hindrance rather than a help. People cannot rely on the state to provide them with anything: politicians are either bought off or too afraid of harming their careers; and even the well-meaning ones whose heads are full of bright reforms and new visions rarely get anywhere in the "democratic" political process. (Guy Debord's proclamation from 1988 not only still stands but perhaps rings even more true: "For the first time in contemporary Europe no party or fraction of a party even tries to pretend that they wish to change anything significant.")[9]

Becoming autonomous, asserting Magical Marxism, thus means that any new experiments in living, any new collective affinities and fidelities, any new forms of solidarity and citizenry, will have to come without subsidies and will need to be impenetrable to state interference, to state intervention. The neo-liberal state will never give us the time of day, let alone any free time during the day. In the final analysis, we who still care have nobody other than ourselves to rely on to create this free time, nothing but our own collective imagination and capacity for cooperation, nothing but our own vital powers. We already knew the revolution would never be televised; now, too, we know it will never be funded.

Float Like a Butterfly: Taking Back the Land

Butterflies give another sense to the concept of a *floating* relative surplus population, those masses of men and women living in our cities and countryside, those who labor insecurely and whose position in society is forever precarious and marginal. It's these floating butterflies who'll be the new rank-and-filers as well as the new vanguard of any Magical Marxist politics. And the crucial sites of their dialectical flight and fight won't be so much factories and industrial plants as the streets and squares and slums of our megacities, the villages, haciendas and jungles of our countryside. These diverse peoples will intersect and intermingle somewhere in space; they'll belong to an Imaginary Party still in the making, without any solid defining base or any obvious leadership; and they will assert, in their different ways and languages, a right to the city and a right to control the land in which they find themselves, the land they are absent from, the land which is theirs. Their modus operandi won't involve any well-established organization, nor will it likely mean negotiating via any formal institutions (at least in the first instance). Rather, their activism will be *direct* and their means of communication will be virtual as well as actual, transmitted by both word of right and word of might. Their power will emerge through their numbers, through the vital power of their cooperation, the power of their inexorable *swarming*. The flutter of the butterfly will be irrepressible and its pollen will be cast almost everywhere there's a fresh breeze, almost everywhere the balmy wind blows.

This floating butterfly surplus population is ubiquitous and its numbers are growing, its ranks expanding, emitting ominous signs of what might be, of what's perhaps in store. People are emerging out of their cocoons after much suppression, breathing in new life, with new expectations, in the ruins and debris of the permanent crisis. They aren't demanding more pay like they once did, or even expressing a desire to continue to work at all; they have a fresh repertoire of new clarion calls: "TAKE BACK THE LAND" ... "THE RIGHT TO THE CITY" ... "THE RIGHT TO SELF-MANAGEMENT" ... "THE RIGHT TO AUTONOMY." Participants are organizing mass occupations of underused and overused land, of empty buildings and vacant lots, of abandoned villages and pillaged properties, in the First and Third Worlds (Worlds that are often social rather than explicitly geographical, and can coexist with one another in the same region), wrestling over and struggling for any space or place they can get their hands on, anywhere that has been repossessed and regressed by capital and impounded by the state.

Rank-and-filers are emerging from assorted layers of society, from the middle stratum downwards, from its Lazarus layers, beyond the confines of a working class, beyond the residues of a lumpenproletariat, beyond anything fixed because the identities of these peoples are constantly changing as they react and remake themselves. Their ranks encompass working and non-working people whose subjectivities somehow convey a collective desire to objectively exist in space, to have one's place. In the US, the "Take Back the Land" movement is a phoenix that's progressively rising out of the ashes. Now a national campaign, Take Back the Land's principles and passions are pretty universal and transnational: grassroots organization, identifying vacant public land, foreclosed homes and healthy-yet-abandoned buildings, moving people into them, homeless people as well as modest-means working people, liberating land and securing housing for those who need it most, for those dispossessed.[10]

When the real estate market was booming, gentrification similarly boomed across America, skyrocketing rents and property values; when crisis hit and the speculative bubble burst, banks called in over-inflated debts and builders stop building, luxury premises stayed unfinished or empty and homes got repossessed; mortgage default soon became an American contagion. At the same time as people got kicked out, the banks were conveniently bailed out. Thus the goal of Take Back the Land: not the simple reformism of old, nor merely to pressure government into building more public housing, more affordable units, but rather to create a new relationship to land, a new land reform movement, a new radical and positive human right. That's why "taking back" also signifies "opting out"; people have had enough with the old ways of doing stuff and losing; they want to explore their own new ways. And campaigners unanimously agree: government is an integral part of the problem to be overcome.

Meanwhile, the "Right to the City" has become a global cry and demand, just as Lefebvre anticipated, just as he dreamed of long ago. Now, it bears the radical abbreviation "RTTC," which has rapidly taken hold as an unofficial planetary charter, a right to the global city, a right to any city for its citizens. RTTC are the "normative letters"—as James Joyce might have said— of a potentially revitalized left that also stand for Here Comes Everybody (HCE),[11] because this is a banner taken up everywhere around the world, everywhere the effects of a decomposition of work and of living space strike. RTTC are the normative letters of planet urban, our planet, *the* social environment to which everybody is indeed coming and which everybody is somehow shaping. In the US again, the RTTC alliance is constructing bridges between production and reproduction, between housing activists and insecure service workers, recognizing that neo-liberal economic policies create "lean" cities as well as "lean" enterprises, knowing full well how "rationalization" and "privatization" don't just affect work but disrupt all aspects of daily life.

As a consequence, lean production through fixed capital and the downsizing of living labor is underwriting a relatively new urban process we might label "lean urbanization." In lean urbanization a city is actively downsized, assumes the status of a business enterprise, whose successes are typically measured by competitiveness, by its ability to balance its budget, to operate efficiently, to maximize its service provision, *at minimum cost.* Cost trimmings through contracting-out public services, through tendering contracts to low-balling service employers, whose labor force is invariably underpaid, overworked and temporary, enable city and national governments to transfer monies from wage-earners to employers, from workers to financiers, from living labor to the dead labor found all around us in the built environment. Savings from public coffers get re-channeled via subsidies and rent holidays to the private sector to construct and reconstruct urban space itself, the all-too-familiar material landscape of office buildings and shopping malls, marinas and waterfront developments, upscale housing and sporting arenas, Olympic villages and spectacular architecture. Thus exploitation of living insecure labor gets capitalized quite literally in space, in fixed, if not always solid, form.[12]

The RTTC alliance suggests that enough is enough, that a process of *taking back* is underway, a reclamation of what once belonged to the people. "RTTC" are the normative letters that try to turn the tide of the looting and re-routing of public riches, of common goods, like city streets—like the right to space and fresh air and fresh water—that's been a financial bonanza for certain factions of the bourgeoisie. Now, the taking back of the city affirms a higher right, a right to *de*-dispossession, a right to *re*-possession of the commons, a *re*-publicization of what Hardt and Negri call the *commonwealth*.[13] The RTTC alliance shifts the terrain of debate around rights onto an entirely different plane, onto a more normative plane, perhaps onto a more Marxist plane. By "rights," it's pretty evident that the RTTC movement has something else in mind than the UN's Universal Declaration of Human Rights. "Everyone," Article 25 of that Declaration says, "has the right to a standard of living adequate for the health and well-being of himself and his family, including food, clothing, housing and medical care." But meanwhile Article 17 claims, with its two clauses: "(1) Everybody has the right to own property alone as well as in association with others; and (2) No one shall be arbitrarily deprived of his property." Both Articles are, of course, salient for any discussion on the right to the city. Yet, for any Marxist, these two rights are directly contradictory, contradictory in a bourgeois sense: the right to property deprives the poor of a place in the center of the city, yet apparently nobody can be deprived of their right to property, thus of their right to the city.

Everybody has a right to adequate housing and well being, but property owners have the private right to deny such a universal right, because no one can deprive them of their property.

It's striking how much this contradiction resembles the contradiction Marx sets out in "The Working Day" chapter of the first volume of *Capital*. It's likewise striking how much the RTTC movement follows Marx's logic about how a "reconciliation" might be possible, how a right to the city might be enacted. The dialogue Marx constructs between capitalist and laborer around the length of the working day, barely four pages long, contains the kernel of Marxian political thought and demonstrates very vividly how questions of "rights" have no universal meaning, have no foundational basis in institutions; nor are they responsive to any moral or legal argument: questions of rights, including rights to the city, are, first and foremost, questions about *social power*, about who wins. "The capitalist takes his stand on the law of commodity-exchange," Marx says.

> Like other buyers, he seeks to extract the maximum possible benefit from the use-value of his commodity. Suddenly, however, there arises the voice of the worker, which had previously been stifled in the sound and the fury of the production process: "The commodity I have sold you differs from the ordinary crowd of commodities in that its use creates value, a greater value than it costs. That is why you bought it. What appears on your side as the valorization of capital is on my side an excess of expenditure of labor-power."[14]

What the capitalist gains in labor, Marx says, by putting his employee to work for as long and as hard as possible, for the maximum duration of the working day, the worker loses "in substance," through damaging their health and well being. "Everybody has a right to their property," the UN Declaration of Rights has it, and no one can be deprived of this inalienable right. "The capitalist," Marx says, sticking tight to the UN's credo, "maintains his right as a purchaser when he tries to make the working day as long as possible, to make two working days out of one. On the other hand, the peculiar nature of the commodity sold implies a limit to its consumption by the purchaser"; so the worker responds in kind, and likewise clings on to the UN's Declaration: "the worker maintains his right as a seller when he wishes to reduce the working day to a particular normal length."[15] Consequently, Marx concludes, there is here an "antinomy of right against right, both equally bearing the seal of the law of exchange," and both equally bearing the seal of the UN's Declaration of Human Rights.

And yet, for Marx, "between equal rights *force decides*." Hence the struggle for rights isn't something granted from above, isn't acknowledged through the courts, or granted because it's morally correct; instead, for those who have no rights, it's something that is *taken*, that involves struggle and force. As such, one must struggle for one's right to the city; nobody is going to give it to the displaced and to the banished, to the RTTC movement. The right to the city must be taken by force, through practical action, through organized militancy, permanent subversion, and militant optimism. That's the only means by which one creates a Marxian truth, obtains a Marxian right: through action, through the force of Here Comes Everybody, through the Imaginary Party taking bloom.

Of Time, Space, and Citizens

Together, Taking Back the Land and the Right to the City are staking out new spaces of slippage: they're exploding amid the implosion of supposedly solid social forms. These movements are staking out beachheads for creative agency and new subjectivities in the *global banlieues* of post-industrial malaise. Therein, new modes of organizing and autonomous strategies are being engineered in directions that not only try to reclaim space, but also attempt to liberate time, to reclaim time, to create free time politically as well as use free time politically, in the building of new social movements. The double-aspect is mutually reinforcing. The politics of free time can also free up time for politics and politicking. These actions are pinpointing the way forward, even if the paths they indicate remain dimly lit with horizons obscured. (Here, for sure, butterflies fly using polarized light.) Since 1995, one program emerging out of France that's been pioneering a novel escape route is the so-called *Réseau de Citoyenneté Sociale* (Social Citizenship Network), which conducts its activities through assorted "*Maisons de Citoyenneté Sociale*," or Social Citizenship Centers. At first, these centers, set up in neighborhoods *défavorisés*, were essentially youth centers dealing with the unemployed, particularly young men, those either displaced from the labor market or with little hope of ever entering it. However, these centers weren't regular state institutions, nor were they advice centers aimed at finding work for young people, for getting them into, or back into, the wage-labor grind; instead, they were imaginative schemes to help the unemployed restore confidence in their own capacities and potentialities, offering programs and training and modest financial assistance so that young people could develop their own activities in an independent manner.

Interestingly, what began as "*Maisons des chômages*," "Centers for the Unemployed," soon reached out and took onboard the growing numbers of precariously *employed* people, partially employed young women and young men, together with students, retirees, and even *sans papiers*. The project quickly renamed itself "Center of Social Citizenship," upping the ante, recognizing how disenfranchisement isn't just economic, effecting work life, but is social and political as well, effecting all aspects of community life. In Toulouse's Center of Social Citizenship, one of the most innovative, issues of political re-empowerment and liberated work prompted the formation of *L'académie du temps libéré* (The Academy of Liberated Time), an educative space designed to foster debate and incubate ideas around a solidarity economy of auto-production and autonomous self-management.

Holding forums with young people, talking to them, creating pedagogic dialogues, helping them to organize and coordinate themselves, became direct acts of politicization and *conscientization*: they led people to understand how they might become, not dispensable and disposable labor-power, but able-bodied citizens involved in an economy of free time. As such, this program isn't so much equipping participants to re-enter the labor market as to create their own labor markets, ones with a different value theory. Social citizenship, says Anne Dreuille, one of program's directors, "unnerves all forms of corporate, unionist and party political representation. We're interrogating the whole model of work based on salaried employment, calling into question petty, poorly paid jobs [*petit boulots*], which exploit people with little power or efficacy to desist ... [But] to refuse petty jobs," claims Dreuille, "is also to resist. To want to create something else is to prove that we wish to work differently." For Dreuille, the project's aim, above all, is both ideological and practical: to move from a "recognition" of the problem to "resisting" it; it's a quest in which unemployed people can bloom as "jobless-creators."[16]

One question that never ceases to come up is: "Why work?" Collectively addressing this question, figuring out practical alternatives to wage-labor, to time-wasting abstract labor, to empty time, and inventing a new economy that de-economizes exchange, frees up time, involves a new social configuration, and that reclaims space, is to threaten the capitalist system with *mass demobilization*. Should this ever come about, civilization would be brought to its knees rather quickly, more quickly than perhaps one would imagine. Or perhaps not, if we could really imagine it, if we could really initiate it. Such a dramatic assault would need to incorporate a politics of time as well as a politics of space, a two-pronged radical attack in which activists become furtive double agents, time-travelers as well as space cadets, voyagers and protagonists in a new Marxist quantum gravity. No passports would be necessary in these rites of passage from one liberated commune to another, from one reclaimed space-time zone to another. But, as the Imaginary Party pointed out in its own neo-communist manifesto, "for us it's not about *possessing* territory. Rather, it's a matter of increasing the density of the communes, of circulation, and of solidarities to the point that the territory becomes unreadable, opaque to all authority. We don't want to occupy the territory, we want to *be* the territory."[17]

Magical action, magical practice, should bring its own time-space relations into existence, should invent its own time-space continuum, its own economy of time as well as its own self-management of space. "Every practice," the Imaginary

Party says, "brings a territory into existence ... a territory of child's play, of lovers, of a riot; a territory of farmers, ornithologists, or *flaneurs*. The rule is simple: the more territories there are superimposed on a given zone, the more circulation there is between them, the harder it will be for power to get a handle on them."[18] Self-organization, in short, superimposes its own space-time relations over the state's cartography, over the state's office hours, scrambling and blurring them, undermining and overriding them, by-passing them as it produces its own secession, its own fields, factories, and workshops, as well, of course, as its own butterflies and little gold fishes...

The Bird of Minerva and Black Magic

If *Magical Marxism* is any kind of dream book, it's evident that we can't entirely expunge the night-time; we can't have a dream politics without also having darkness, without the falling of dusk. If butterflies express our daytime frivolity, our floating fortunes, our wish-images and daydreaming passions, then the owl of Minerva symbolizes our darker desires, a truth cradled by the security of nightfall. The Joycean Here Comes Everybody, after all, finds its collective force in the psychic nooks and crannies of nocturnal life, where things go bump, where knowledge resides, where the famous Hegelian bird-sage makes its silent swoop, where the gray in gray of social theory begins to paint itself black.

If Henri Lefebvre is Marxism's multicolored butterfly, its night owl, its Grand Duc, is surely Guy Debord, the prince of darkness whose critical and creative powers come into their own only at the fall of dusk. "In the midwinter nights of 1988, in Paris's square des Missions Étrangères," as Debord drafted his *Comments on the Society of the Spectacle* at his nearby rue du Bac apartment, "an owl would obstinately repeat his calls ... And this unusual run of encounters with the bird of Minerva, its air of surprise and indignation, did not in the least seem to constitute an allusion to the imprudent conduct or various aberrations of my life."[19] Debord liked owls and seemed to identify himself with them: their secrecy and wisdom, their nocturnal qualities and melancholy, their consecration by Hegel, all somehow inspired him. In his *Correspondance*, which stretches to a hefty seven tomes, Debord often alludes to their calls. At Champot, his rural retreat in the Auvergne, "every evening," he wrote Gérard Lebovici (March 8, 1978), "one hears in a wood that surrounds us the call of the bird of Minerva. Given that 'knowledge will never come,' it's comforting to know that at least it doesn't reside too far away."[20]

The spirit of the night owl and the wandering butterfly negate and create together, are both pessimistic and optimistic, the moon and the sun. In their dialectical antithesis and explosive synthesis they express the critical and constructive powers of Magical Marxism itself, of negating and creating, of the phoenix rising out of the ruins, utopia out of dystopia. "What acceptable paradise can we extract from so many ruins," an adolescent Debord asked, "without falling into them?"[21] How can magical Marxists paint a society like Matisse, with gorgeously evocative primary colors, or like Wifredo Lam, with his voluptuous tropical nether-nether world, without devouring its children as in Goya's dark paintings, where blackness overwhelms everything? In Goya, Debord knew there's no light only lightning. He knew that night meant security and that it's the dawn one should fear, daylight, for then the enemy closes in. "Up! Or you are lost," Mephisto warns Faust near the end of Part I of Goethe's devilish compact. "Prating and waiting and pointless wavering. / My horses are quavering, / Over the sky creeps the dawn..." "What did the darkness spawn? / He! He! Send him away!"[22]

And as night falls on *Magical Marxism*, too, as its own shades of gray in gray gather, let us not forget that banishing darkness is to negate Marxism itself, is to do away with its *black magic*, with its sympathy for the devil, with its elemental creative powers, not just its destructive powers which are always more obvious. The ruling classes forever want to send away the darkness, to banish it and condemn it as "evil," to flood it with artificial light and climatized air, with a false brightness of lies, with ersatz sterility. Yet to talk of a black magical Marxism is to conjure up, and to try to tap, a certain "primitive" spirit that's within us, a certain "natural" spontaneous energy that lies dormant within everybody, a wildness and a plenitude, a *vital* power in the fullest sense of the term. To invoke the "primitive" is, then, to invoke something denigrated in our "advanced" culture, a spirit whose flaming passion has been doused amid widespread affluence and material gadgetry.

To say this isn't, however, to reify "primitive cultures," to reify the exoticness of the Caribbean or Latin America, or of the Brazil where I pen these words; rather, it's to suggest that "primitive thought" isn't the exclusive domain of specific faraway peoples, with traditional life-forms, but is a structure of feeling that's appropriate to all of us, that defines our poetic impulses, our primal desires, our radical spirit. Part of André Breton's post-colonial brilliance was to recognize this, showing how the darkness of the primitive actually exists as the "interior voice" within each human being. "In periods of great social and moral crisis," he said in 1943, in Haiti, during a speech whose venue is now likely reduced to ruins, "I believe it is indispensable that we enquire into primitive thought, to rediscover the fundamental aspirations, the incontestably authentic aspirations of mankind."[23]

While the primitive resides within all of us, and while it implies some sort of cosmic liaison between human beings, animals, plants, and the stars, sometimes a demonic liaison, it's also an everydayness present in the sensual, in the erotic, in the vital, in a joyous accord of love, of friendship and camaraderie. It's rarely found, for instance, in societies of riches and abundance where invariably *zombies* roam, those mythical archetypes which in Haitian voodoo bespeak of the living dead, a being condemned not to death but to life, a being with a vague, dull, almost glazed look in their eyes, eyes without sparkle or fire, without imagination or culture, twenty-first-century eyes. Zombies feed on the blandest of diets and the fog of forgetfulness and insensibility has made them unaware of their condition, the generalized condition we call our life today, circa 2010, after a history that other zombies tell us has ended, has expended all its creative capacities to invent something else, to organize its political, economic, and cultural life differently. It's true that in Haitian voodoo a zombie "is a beast of burden exploited mercilessly by his master who forces him to toil in the fields, crushes him with work, and whips him at the slightest pretext."[24] The Haitian surrealist poet and novelist, René Depestre, thinks the history of colonialism and slavery is "a process of generalized zombification of mankind."[25] Here I'm suggesting something different: that a role reversal has somehow taken place, that it's the masters themselves who've turned zombie, the ruling classes who now have those dull, twenty-first-century eyes.

To make the leap from zombie-hood, the leap out of our insomnia plague, into a world of magical desire and dream-images, into a living, troubling world of magical politics and potions, is, in a nutshell, the real point of *Magical Marxism*. It's a call to sneak about subversively, to summon up the magician, to enter into another realm of reality, a raw, vivid, marvelous reality, like in a García Márquez novel, or in a Lam canvas like *The Jungle*, which hangs in the lobby of New York's Museum of Modern Art, near the cloakroom, waiting to enter onto the main stage,[26] a giant 2 meter by 2 meter image with its delirious symbolism, its voodoo motifs, its Cubist multidimensionality. Four or maybe five figures with contorted arms and legs, evoking bamboo shoots or sugar cane, beckon you inside; twisted body parts, buttocks and breasts, faces that look like totems, like haunted half-moons, like African masks, menace; hands lurk with scissors behind palm leaves and Bougainville trees; human, animal, plant, and flower worlds cohabit in one exotic and erotic landscape of colors and forms all syncopating to some distant drum beat, like the drummer who wants to reclaim the streets. Yellows and greens, blues and blue-greens, blue-blacks and yellowy-oranges make up a vast kaleidoscope composed with the same frantic passion, with the same ordinary madness, that Marxists now need to compose their magical politics. What I'm asking is that we make this leap together, that we leap out of one jungle, that of our current life, into another more primitive jungle, a more imaginative and richer one, richer in the *Grundrisse*'s sense of riches. Maybe what *Magical Marxism* is really saying is that we should let *The Jungle* somehow leap into us, try to live out its primitive anarchic vitality, let it enter into us, body and soul, for keeps.

"Specters" of Magical Marxism

Strategically, organizationally, there's another implication of black magic: its *haunting* capacity, its *threatening* vitality, its ability to cast spells, to disappear and reappear. Its scariness is based upon a certain spectrality, like the veil of mystery the Imaginary Party envelops itself in, its capacity to create an anonymity, an absence that unnerves the powers-that-be, that hints that somewhere, somehow, someone is plotting something and power isn't quite sure who or where it is. Magical Marxists need to revel in this primitive spectrality, in the specters of its black magic, foster them somehow, use them as part of our arsenal to disrupt, to frighten society's rulers; let us use invisibility and absence, let us conjure up black magic to keep them guessing, to keep them haunted; let us gather like owls of Minerva and organize at the falling of dusk; let us continue to conjure up revolutionary specters of Marx, and let them continue to put the fear of God into those God-fearing bourgeoisie.

Jacques Derrida, in his ingenious reading of Marx's *Manifesto* and *Eighteenth Brumaire*, was undoubtedly correct to think that "specters" of Marx pose a threat to the bourgeois order, and that these specters are multiple and will never stop posing a threat. Let them threaten... When I first read Derrida's *Specters of Marx* not long after its English publication, I thought the book deliberately obscurantist, even ridiculous, and later wholeheartedly endorsed the critiques voiced in *Ghostly Demarcations* by Marxist scholars of more classical persuasions.[27] But after re-reading *Specters of Marx* recently, with more than 15 years hindsight, somewhat older and hopefully a bit wiser, Derrida's intervention struck me as brilliant. Although I think his specters still run rampant more on the page than in everyday life, never quite managing to leap from between the deconstructed lines into political life, Derrida's notion of a "New International" does share a lot of similarities with the Imaginary Party, and with the kind of non-class, broad-based alliances I've sketched out in this book. "The New International," says Derrida, is a link of affinity, suffering and hope, a still discreet, almost secret link, as it was around 1848, but more and more visible, we have more than one sign of it. It is an untimely link, without status, without title, and without a name, barely public ... without contract, "out of joint," without coordination, without party, without country, without national community, without co-citizenship, without common belonging to a class. The name of New International is given here to what calls to the friendship of an alliance without institution among those who, even if they no longer believe or never believed in the socialist-Marxist International, in the dictatorship of the proletariat, in the messianic-eschatological role of the universal union of the proletarians of all lands, continue to be inspired by at least one of the spirits of Marx or of Marxism. It is a call for them to ally themselves, in a new, concrete and real way, even if this alliance no longer takes the form of a party or a workers' international, in the critique of the state of international law, the concepts of State and nation, and so forth: in order to renew this critique, and especially to radicalize it.[28]

On that basis alone, on the basis of this magnificent passage, Derrida's text will mature well and is worthy of another close reading today. Meanwhile, as for those diehard Marxist materialists, those who draw their non-ghostly demarcations, it's clear to me now that they never did understand how to party (small "p") at a great raucous wake...

In a very real sense, specters of Marx haunt the bourgeois order more than ever; they have come alive again and again, weighing like a nightmare on the brain of the living, like voodoo, like black magic, returning in transubstantiated forms, more alive than before, because nowadays they're no longer singular or insti-tutionalized specters, no longer dictatorships of the proletariat, state-managed, state-staged. They're no longer obvious or visible, like the specters of old that never really scared anyone, save their own people. Now, these specters are unaffiliated and nonaligned phantoms, and they're everywhere, underground and over-ground, everywhere that there are anti-capitalist spirits, everywhere there are people who form alliances to resist global capital, who invent something new out of progressive citizenships and novel comings together, beyond the state, beyond class, beyond work. Nowadays, the black magical Marxism haunting the bourgeois holy order is a freer Marxism, a Marxism that's broken from its institutional fetters, its dogma machine, its parties and cells, from its unions and official purveyors. Here, at last, we see ghosts who are not dead, who are beyond death, and who continually walk through walls.

In believing in specters, in seeing them, in becoming multiple specters ourselves, we can now perhaps more easily believe in a de-materialized Magical Realist Marxism; we can begin to believe in the sort of agenda we set ourselves at the outset of this book: we can see another reality because we believe in it, because we can now imagine it, conjure it up in our heads, make it real. We can believe in a Marxism that's not just critical analysis, a Marxism that's liberated from debates about class and the role of the state, about the dictatorship of the proletariat. We can believe in a Marxism that no longer calls itself "scientific" and gives up on the distinction between form and content, between appearance and essence. We can believe in a Marxism that stakes out the contours of a new dream-like reality, a materialist fantasy, a fantastic materialism, a Marxism that utters sighs of disenchant-ment with the present yet affirms the most tenacious nostalgia for dreams of the future. Now, perhaps, we can believe in a Marxism that advocates a more free-floating and ethereal political vision, a more phantasmal radicalism. Now, we can believe in a Marxism that opens up the horizons of the affirmative and reaches out beyond the dour realism of critical negativity.

A maverick Marxism, to be sure, one that will doubtless upset the purists, raise hackles in their learned journals and amongst their select coterie—should they deign to even pay even scant attention to what's gone on here. But this is a plea made from the inside, made by a "believer" who wants to knock down a few more walls that cut Marxism off, that hermetically seal it off from outsiders, from potential allies and unwitting fellow-travelers, to reclaim it from those who've encased it and made it rigid and thus *breakable*. Making it magical, making it fleeting and floating like a butterfly or an owl, more open in its de-materialized flexibility, is to make Marxism more pliable and stretchable, light but never lightweight, frivolous but never fickle; above all, it makes

Marxism *unbreakable* because there will never be anything set in stone or cast in concrete, no giant monuments or ego edifices, nothing that towers above people.

A Marxism thus opened up, that doesn't insist upon its chosen standard bearers or its messianic history-makers, is a Marxism without an identity complex, without a fragile identity that it needs to defend so guardedly, so preciously. It's a Marxism that can drop such defensiveness because it goes on the offensive, because it has an uncanny ability to access directly our latent magical state. A Marxism not repressed by the factuality of the external world because its energies come from the inside, from the subjective world, an interior world in which the collective energies of people don't give themselves over to abstractions of any type, to anything holy or hallowed. Magical Marxists break out of pre-history because we're already living out history, acting now, making it happen in the present, embarking on a permanent revolution in which action is forever convulsive. For as darkness gathers across our valley of dreams, all Magical Marxists know, if they know anything at all, that Marxism needs to be CONVULSIVE or it won't be...

NOTES

Preface

1. John Hutnyk, *Bad Marxism: Capitalism and Cultural Studies*, Pluto Press, London, 2004. When I first proposed the present book to Pluto, Hutnyk generously suggested in his reader's report that the book "skates the utopian edge of reason and politics, which we would do well not to forget, can also be the refuge of comrades."

2. The "amongst other things" is borrowed from John Berger's essay "Ten Dispatches About Place," *Le monde diplomatique*, August 2005. "Somebody enquires: Are you still a Marxist?" Watching four burros graze in a field on a bright mid-summer's day, seeing them roll about on their backs and stand motionless, time slows down, says Berger. They stare back at the English writer, propped up against an apple tree, size him up, and wander away, heads down, ears missing nothing. "I watch them," he says, "eyes skinned. In our exchanges such as they are, in the midday company we offer one another, there is a substratum of what I can only describe as gratitude. Four burros in a field, month of June, year 2005. Yes, I'm still amongst other things a Marxist." Berger's piece helped convince another donkey-lover that this silent wisdom might also somehow be Marxist. (Cf. Andy Merrifield, *The Wisdom of Donkeys*, Walker Books, New York, 2008.)

3. Guy Debord, *Panegyric Volume One*, Verso, London, 1991, p. 48.

4. Carl von Clausewitz, *On War*, Everyman Library, New York, 1993, pp. 474–9.

5. This brilliantly intelligent cinematic set piece from 1981 has a romantic dreamer and a realist skeptic dialogue over dinner in a New York restaurant. The screenplay, written by Wallace Shawn and André Gregory, is available in book form and warrants close scrutiny. "You see," explains Gregory, "I keep thinking that we need a new language, a language of the heart, a language where language isn't needed—some kind of language between people that is a new kind of poetry, that is the poetry of the dancing bee, that tells us where the honey is. And I think that in order to create that language we're going to have to learn how you can go through a looking-glass into another kind of perception, in which you have that sense of being united to all things, and suddenly you understand everything." (Wallace Shawn and André Gregory, *My Dinner with André*, Grove Press, New York, 1981, p. 95.)

6. Subcomandante Marcos, "The Fourth World War has Begun," *Nepantla: Views from the South*, Vol. 2, No. 3, 2001, p. 570.

7. Gabriel García Márquez, *One Hundred Years of Solitude*, Picador Books, London, 1978, p. 125.
8. Guy Debord was another big fan of *My Dinner with André*, confessing his admiration of Louis Malle's film to the French writer Morgan Sportès in the late 1980s. Christophe Bourseiller's *Vie et Mort de Guy Debord* (Plon, Paris, 1999) recalls Debord's numerous meetings with Sportès in assorted Parisian bars chosen by Debord (p. 525). The interesting revelation about Debord's fondness for the film elicits only a couple of throwaway lines and is never followed up by Bourseiller.
9. Shawn and Gregory, *My Dinner with André*, pp. 91–2.
10. Shawn and Gregory, *My Dinner with André*, pp. 93–4.
11. Shawn and Gregory, *My Dinner with André*, pp. 94–5.

Introduction

1   John Cassidy, "The Return of Karl Marx," *The New Yorker*, October 1997, p. 248.
2. Militant was a Trotskyist faction of the British Labour Party who dominated Liverpool municipal politics after its dramatic electoral victory in May 1983. Militant councilors reigned almost supreme in the city until 1987, during which time they imposed their own brand of hard-edged, confrontational socialism, frequently clashing with Margaret Thatcher's Tory government over budgeting and rate-capping, at the same time as they clashed with trade unions and Neil Kinnock's Labour Party. For more details, see Peter Taaffe and Tony Mulhearn, *Liverpool: A City that Dared to Fight*, Fortress Books, London, 1988; cf. Michael Parkinson, *Liverpool on the Brink*, Policy Journals, Hermitage, 1985.
3. Herbert Marcuse, *One Dimensional Man: The Ideology of Industrial Society*, Routledge and Kegan Paul, London, 1964.
4. "News from Nowhere" still thrives along Bold Street as a women's cooperative. But back then it was located in a frayed, marginal zone, near the Mersey Tunnel entrance, actually next to a fascist "Soldier of Fortune" store, whose clientele periodically lobbed bricks through the bookstore's window. From time to time, the bookstore's clientele would respond in kind. Ah, those were the days!
5. After almost 40 consecutive years of teaching Marx's *Capital*, Harvey has finally written up his lectures, and published them in handy book form, there for everybody to ponder over. The text is a step-by-step guide for old-hats and newcomers alike, and is a vital resource for anyone interested in understanding our world's innumerable crises and instabilities. See David Harvey, *Introduction to Marx's Capital*, Verso, London, 2009.
6. I transcribed the experience in article form: see Andy Merrifield, "Marx@2000.com," *Monthly Review*, November 2000, pp. 21–35; cf. Jeff Byles, "Dialectical U," *The Village Voice*, January 23, 2001. It's true about my generation's failings; it's only with hindsight that this has become apparent. Just as the 1960s generation never saw the coming of the early 1970s' economic crises, and even if they had were powerless to do anything

about them, my generation failed to halt the New Right backlash in the 1980s, leaving us powerless to prevent the neo-liberal long march throughout the 1990s.

7. Karl Marx, *Capital I*, Penguin Books, Harmondsworth, 1976, p. 481.

8. David Harvey, *The New Imperialism*, Oxford University Press, Oxford, 2003; see especially Chapter 4. John Berger, whose novels are often so subtle and multilayered, still knows how to call a spade a spade. He pulls no punches in labeling our current system: "economic fascism." "Today, in the age of globalization," he writes, "the world is dominated by finance not industrial capital, and the dogmas that define criminality and the logic of incarceration have radically changed. Prisons have always existed, of course, and more and more are getting built. But prison walls henceforth have a different goal. What constitutes the feeling of incarceration has been transformed." (John Berger, *Dans l'entre-temps: réflexions sur le fascisme économique*, Indigène éditions, Montpellier, 2009, p. 10.)

9. Harvey, *The New Imperialism*, p. 148.

10. Harvey, *The New Imperialism*, p. 148.

11. Guy Debord, *Comments on the Society of the Spectacle*, Verso, London, 1991, p. 16, original emphasis. This text, of course, is Debord's sequel to *The Society of the Spectacle*.

12. Debord, *Comments on the Society of the Spectacle*, p. 24.

13. García Márquez, *One Hundred Years of Solitude*, p. 75. Hereafter page references to the novel are given in the text.

14. *The Coming Insurrection*, Semiotext(e), Los Angeles, 2009, p. 23. *L'insurrection qui vient* was originally published in France in 2007 under the authorship of "The Invisible Committee." I'll return to its suggestive "neo-communist manifesto" in Chapter 2.

15. Eduardo Galeano, *The Book of Embraces*, W.W. Norton & Co., New York, 1991, p. 223.

16. Galeano, *The Book of Embraces*, p. 223.

17. Karl Marx, "The Eighteenth Brumaire of Louis Bonaparte," in Robert Tucker (ed.), *The Marx–Engels Reader*, W. W. Norton & Co., New York, 1978, p. 597.

18. Marx, "The Eighteenth Brumaire," pp. 597–8, emphasis added.

19. García Márquez often said that literature, for him, should be a poetic transformation of reality; perhaps it's possible to see politics in this same light? In the first volume of his memoirs, García Márquez poses a related question: why is a thinker like Friedrich Engels only taught as a boring political economist rather than an inspiring lyric poet? García Márquez refers to Engels' *The Origin of the Family, Private Property, and the State*, and suggests that it's really an "epic poem of a beautiful human adventure." (Gabriel García Márquez, *Living to Tell the Tale*, Alfred Knopf, New York, 2003, p. 192.)

20. Aimé Césaire, "Calling the Magician: A Few Words from a Caribbean Civilization," in Michael Richardson (ed.), *Refusal of the Shadow: Surrealism and the Caribbean*, Verso, London, 1996, pp. 119–20

21. Plato, *The Republic*, Everyman Books, New York, 1935, pp. 305–6.

22. Sigmund Freud, *The Interpretation of Dreams*, Avon Books, New York, 1965. See especially pp. 201–2, 214–15.

23. Karl Marx, *Capital III*, Lawrence & Wishart, London, 1959, p. 465.

24. Marx, *Capital III*, p. 472, emphasis added.

25. Marx, *Capital III*, p. 466, emphasis added.

26. André Gorz, *Farewell to the Working Class*, Pluto Press, London, 1982, p. 67.

27. Henri Lefebvre, *Critique of Everyday Life, Volume One*, Verso, London, 1991, p. 21.

28. Alejo Carpentier, "On the Marvelous Real in America," in Lois Parkinson Zamora and Wendy Faris (eds.), *Magical Realism: Theory, History, Community*, Duke University Press, Durham, 1995, p. 85.

29. Carpentier, "On the Marvelous Real in America," p. 86. "What is the history of Latin America," Carpentier had asked, "if not a chronicle of the marvelous in the real." It was this idea, the idea of *lo real maravilloso*, that eventually became synonymous with "magical realism," and the early writings of Carpentier are now taken as prologues to what we recognize today as the Magical Realist genre. Apparently, after having read and been so impressed with Carpentier's *Explosion in a Cathedral* (1962), García Márquez decided to toss in the trash an earlier draft of *One Hundred Years of Solitude* and begin again. *Explosion in a Cathedral*, entitled *El Siglo de las Luces* (*The Century of Light*) in the original Spanish, transports us back to colonial Guadeloupe and Haiti in the wake of the French Revolution. The novel focuses on a young orphan, Esteban, and his relationship with the mysterious subversive pirate Victor Hugues, a prototypical Colonel Aureliano Buendia. Esteban is dazzled by the revolutionary 1790s Caribbean, as republican ideals reach enslaved people's *outre-mer*; he's dazzled by magical streets and pageants, by hearsay and underground fervor, by secret clans and associations, by music and women, by corporal and political excesses. In amongst it all, Esteban finds for a while an intoxicating liberation, a total transformation of his erstwhile sickly self: "Do you want to work for the revolution," somebody asks him. "He responds yes, with pride, with enthusiasm, adding that he won't allow his fervor, nor his desire to labor for liberty, to be put in any shadow of doubt." (Alejo Carpentier, *Le siècle des lumières*, Gallimard, Paris, 1962, p. 140.)

30. Carpentier, "On the Marvelous Real in America," p. 86. *Amadís of Gaul* is a masterpiece of Castilian medieval fantasy from 1508, staple reading for a youthful Don Quixote; *Tirant le Blanc* is a 1490 Valencian romantic epic that cast a magic spell on a pre-*Don Quixote* Cervantes. Carpentier himself has been criticized for his "conception of an independent American sensibility" and for his "extremely ungenerous appreciation" of European surrealism. According to Michael Richardson, in his useful introduction to *Refusal of the Shadow: Surrealism and the Caribbean* (Verso, London, 1996, especially pp. 12–13), this reveals Carpentier's refusal to engage with the dynamic way different cultures interact, cross-fertilize, and transform one another. Magic, in other words, exists everywhere there's a perceptual twist to reality, and goes beyond any singular culture, should there be such a thing as singular culture anyway.

31. Karl Marx, "The Economic and Philosophical Manuscripts," in *Karl Marx: Early Writings*, Penguin, Harmondsworth, 1974, p. 326.

32. Johan Huizinga, *Homo Ludens: A Study of the Play Element in Culture*, Beacon Press, Boston, 1955, p. 26.

33. Huizinga, *Homo Ludens*, p. 195.

34. Huizinga, *Homo Ludens*, p. 206.

35. Huizinga, *Homo Ludens*, pp. 210–11.

36. Gabriel García Márquez, "The Solitude of Latin America," 1982 Nobel Prize for Literature Lecture; http://nobelprize.org/nobel_prizes/literature/laureates/1982/marquez-lecture.html

Chapter 1

1. Even though *The Society of the Spectacle* and *One Hundred Years of Solitude* are quintessential 1960s books, their authors admit to coming of age in the 1950s. In *Considérations sur l'assassinat de Gérard Lebovici*, Debord says he wasn't converted by the street skirmishes of May 1968; "I am an older bandit than that," he claims; "1968 was a date that came to me much later." (See Guy Debord, *Œuvres*, Gallimard-Quarto, Paris, 2006, p. 1564.) A lot of Debord's political muckraking fomented during the 1950s, through Lettrist and early Situationist rebel-rousing, and through experimental films and radical urbanism. If anything, Debord's disposition was more classical, more baroque: his Marxism went back to the future from the seventeenth century. As for García Márquez, his political awakening similarly occurred in the 1950s, specifically in the spring of 1959, when he went to Cuba as a young journalist to write a series of articles "about a guy half out of his mind" trying to overthrow the Batista regime. Several months afterwards, Castro's efforts were consummated and in the 1970s a friendship deepened between the former-lawyer-cum-revolutionary and the future Nobel Laureate. Also in the 1950s, García Márquez toured the Eastern Bloc and wrote an article called "The Iron Curtain," in which he expressed his disapproval of what was happening there. The Soviet model of socialism, with its dogmatism and chasteness was the antithesis of his Marxist ideas and wasn't for Latin America, García Márquez said. Thus Debord and Márquez find common ground over their incredulity towards Soviet-style socialism.

2. Guy Debord, *Correspondance volume 2: septembre 1960–décembre 1964*, Librairie Artheme Fayard, Paris, 2001, p. 279.

3. Debord, *Correspondance volume 2*, p. 307.

4. This is a well-known passage from *The Society of the Spectacle* (Black & Red Books, Detroit, 1970), from Thesis #9: "Dans le monde *réellement renversé*," Debord says in his original French, "le vrai est un moment du faux." Debord's italics, as we'll soon see, are vital, because he's telling us that, nowadays, falsity *really is* the truth, that this falsity is in no way a faux reality, that it is real reality: such is the spectacle's grip, such is our perceptual take on its reality, that we have now normalized this topsy-turvy world as our ordinary, everlasting condition of life.

5. Lautréamont, "Les Chants de Maldoror," in *Œuvres Complètes*, Éditions Charlot, Paris, 1946, p. 289.

6. Lautréamont, "Les Chants de Maldoror," p. 292, p. 251.

7. Gabriel García Márquez, *The Fragrance of Guava: Plinio Apuleyo Mendoza in Conversation with Gabriel García Márquez*, Verso, London, 1983, p. 72.

8. García Márquez, *The Fragrance of Guava*, pp. 30–1.

9. Marx, *Capital I*, p. 284.

10. García Márquez knows plenty about dictatorships: he has lived through a good number of Latin American despots, like Rojas Pinilla in his native Colombia, and has written about them as well, like his monstrous Caribbean tyrant in *The Autumn of the Patriarch*, first published in Spain in 1975, in the autumn of another pathological fascist, General Franco. *The Autumn of the Patriarch* gives poetic meaning to Debord's concept of the concentrated spectacle: "none of us had ever seen him," García Márquez writes, "and even though his profile was on both sides of all coins, on postage stamps, on condom labels, on trusses and scapulars, and even though his engraved picture with the flag across his chest and the dragon of the fatherland was displayed at all times in all places, we knew that they were copies of copies of portraits that had already been considered unfaithful ... yet we knew that he was there, we knew it because the world went on, life went on, the mail was delivered, the municipal band played its retreat of silly waltzes on Saturday under the dusty palm trees." (Gabriel García Márquez, *The Autumn of the Patriarch*, Avon Books, New York, 1976, p. 10.) Some might consider García Márquez a bit too intimate with another tyrant, a real life one: Fidel Castro. Often critical of Castro's regime, García Márquez nonetheless remains an optimistic advocate of Cuba, pointing out its continental significance as a beachhead against US hegemony. "It is my duty to serve the Latin American revolution however I can," García Márquez remarked in 1997, "and concretely, to serve the defense of the Cuban Revolution, which is one of the most basic obligations for any Latin American revolutionary right now." (Cited in A. Esteban and S. Panichelli, *Fidel and Gabo: A Portrait of the Legendary Friendship Between Fidel Castro and Gabriel García Márquez*, Pegasus Books, New York, 2009, p. 69.)

11. García Márquez, *The Fragrance of Guava*, p. 73.

12. Cf. Eduardo Posada-Carbo's essay "Fiction as History: The *Bananeras* and Gabriel Márquez's *One Hundred Years of Solitude*," *Journal of Latin American Studies*, No. 2, May 1998, pp. 395–414. Posada-Carbo raises concerns about the scrupulousness of García Márquez's rendering of the banana worker's massacre and his fidelity to "real" historical reality. Posada-Carbo "challenges" the idea that *One Hundred Years of Solitude* can be used an "historical source," claiming the evidence points to a handful of deaths not to the 3,000-odd García Márquez invokes. Moreover, rather than any "conspiracy of silence," Posada-Carbo says that García Márquez's "legendary" version has now generally been adopted as "official history." Yet while Posada-Carbo's article cheers for a provable realism in the light of fictive representation, it ends up emphasizing precisely the sort of thing its author wanted to avoid: that we can never know for sure the absolute "facts." Michael Wood, author of a monograph on García Márquez's great

book, puts it well: "the texture of the novel is made up of legends treated as truths—because they are truths to those who believe them—but also ... of real facts that no one believes in." (Michael Wood, *García Márquez: One Hundred Years of Solitude*, Cambridge University Press, Cambridge, 1990, p. 58.)

13. Marx, *Capital I*, p. 165.

14. John Holloway, *How to Change the World Without Taking Power: The Meaning of Revolution Today*, Pluto Press, London, 2002; see especially Chapters 4, 5, and 6. Holloway devotes three whole chapters to fetishism.

15. Holloway, *How to Change the World Without Taking Power*, p. 36.

16. It's important to stress that the insomnia plague doesn't represent a form of classical Marxist "false consciousness." A more precise and subtle understanding would perhaps invoke Louis Althusser's notion of ideology: the insomnia plague is "a representation of the imaginary relationship of individuals to their real conditions of existence." (Louis Althusser, *Lenin and Philosophy and Other Essays*, New Left Books, London, 1971, pp. 152–65.) Ideology, says Althusser, is something eternal, without history. There's nothing unreal about ideology or about the insomnia plague, even though at the same time neither directly corresponds to reality either. Nonetheless, like ideology, the plague somehow *makes allusion* to reality and constitutes concrete individuals as social subjects.

17. See Jacques Rancière, *Le spectateur emancipé*, Éditions la fabrique, Paris, 2009.

18. Clausewitz gained combat experience in the Napoleonic era. He served time as a Prussian field soldier, was captured by the French in 1806, rose to the rank of major-general at 38, and played a major role in the resurrection of Prussia and the final defeat of Napoleon in 1815 at Waterloo. Clausewitz operated equally effectively in Berlin's intellectual circles. His approach to war was distinctly dialectical, and he brought into his account the frailties of human nature and the complexity of the physical and psychological world. In the 1970s, Debord invented a war board game called *Kriegspiel*, which he joked "may well be the only one of my works that anyone will dare acknowledge as having some value" (Guy Debord, *Panegyric*, Verso, London, 1991, p. 64). Its strategic and tactical relations followed Clausewitz's theory of classical warfare, where two armies, with infantry, cavalry and foot and horse regiments, confront one another like white and black confront each other in chess. The goal of the game is, however, serious: "the complete destruction of the military potential of the other."

19. Carl von Clausewitz, *On War*, Everyman Library, New York, 1993, p. 471.

20. Guy Debord and Alice Becker-Ho, *Le jeu de la guerre*, Gallimard, Paris, 2006, p. 148.

21. Marx, *Early Writings*, p. 422.

22. This is the magical Debordian rejoinder to Jacques Rancière, and singularly the best route any spectator can take towards emancipation.

23. Of Chinese origins, the Cuban-born artist Lam (1902–82), also a Spanish Civil War veteran, blended European surrealist and cubist motifs with Afro-Caribbean myth and totemism. His most famous painting, the 2 meter by 2 meter *The Jungle* (1943), has stood in the lobby entrance of New York's

Museum of Modern Art (MoMA) since 1945. Lam's vivid imagery was inspired by the magic of tropical culture—by its exotic vegetation, birds, and atmosphere, by its primal dance rhythms and primitive rituals. One-time friend of Picasso and the surrealists André Breton and André Masson, as well as Aimé Césaire and Situationist artist Asger Jorn, Lam was fêted by Alejo Carpentier as an artist who really understood the Latin American "marvelous real." Later in life, Lam also did a series of lithographs for García Márquez's short story, the poem in prose, "The Last Voyage of the Ghost Ship" (1976). One of the things Lam's *Jungle* and García Márquez's *One Hundred Years of Solitude* have in common is their spontaneous candor. Colors and words dance vividly in front of us with a freshness of vision. Both works are achieved by men at the top of their game, more or less the same age—40 years old—still full of boundless energy and perhaps some naivety, yet not self-conscious of what they're doing. Their modus operandi is instinctive, impromptu: they're making it up as they go along, giving free reign to unbridled impulse, to an art of pure creation; there are political lessons to derive from this. Their respective canvases are vast and complex, erotic and voluptuous, mad and chaotic, scary and darkly incandescent, bursting with metaphor, even with political metaphor. Lam's art, André Breton once said, "showers with stars the BECOMING that must be human well-being." Even Louis Althusser waxed lyrical about Lam: "I discovered him. I've known Lam forever. He was born before us, the world's oldest painter; and the youngest." If Magical Marxism has a portrait painter, a portrait of itself in action, that artist would surely be Lam.

24. Early Macondo bears an uncanny resemblance to David Harvey's dream-state at the end of one of his best books, *Spaces of Hope*, perhaps emphasizing how journeying beyond the spectacle is really going back to the future. The year is 2020, even though it sounds a lot like 2009; a stock market collapse has driven pension funds and banks under; after widespread crop failure and environmental havoc, a meltdown leads to a period of anarchy out of which the ruling class is overthrown and new radical communities organize themselves around egalitarian bioregions. Private property is abolished and soon a transformed spirit pervades the new social order, quicker than anyone would have ever imagined beforehand. Play, aesthetics, and the pursuit of intellectual and personal passions begins to flourish, and people engage in unrepressed "spirit-talk." Above all, there are "no banks and insurance companies to run our lives, no multinational companies, no lawyers, no stockbrokers, no vast bureaucracies, no professors of this or that, no military apparatus, no elaborate forms of law enforcement." (David Harvey, *Spaces of Hope*, California University Press, Berkeley, 2000, p. 280.)

25. Henri Lefebvre, "Theoretical Problems of *Autogestion*," in *Selected Essays on State, Space, World*, ed. Stuart Elden and Neil Brenner, Minnesota University Press, Minneapolis, 2009, p. 148.

26. "In any place and moment in which *autogestion* is spontaneously manifested," says Lefebvre, "it carries within itself the possibility of its generalization and radicalization; but at the same time it reveals and crystallizes the contradictions of society before it." (Lefebvre, "Theoretical Problems of *Autogestion*," p. 147.)

Chapter 2

1. See "Entretien avec Julien Coupat: La prolongation de ma detention est une petite vengeance," *Le Monde*, May 25, 2009.

2. See "Liberating Lipsticks and Lattes," *New York Times*, June 18, 2009; and "The Insurrectionary Style," *The New Yorker*, June 16, 2009.

3. *The Coming Insurrection*, Semiotext(e), Los Angeles, 2009, p. 9. All page references are to the Semiotext(e) edition. The Invisible Committee's "Introduction" to the English translation was written in January 2009 and didn't appear in the original French version.

4. "Liberating Lipsticks and Lattes."

5. In a wonderful irony, after Beck introduced the book to his 3 million or so viewers, and after he proclaimed it "the most evil book I've read in a long, long time," *The Coming Insurrection* soared to No.1 on Amazon's bestseller list. (See "A Book Attacking Capitalism Gets Sales Help from a Fox Host," *New York Times*, March 14, 2010.)

6. Cf. "Considérations sur l'assassinat de Gérard Lebovici," in Debord, *Œuvres*, p. 1539.

7. Debord actually uses the expression "*insurrectional style*" (original emphasis) in *The Society of the Spectacle* (Thesis #206), describing the young Marx's "style of negation" from *The Poverty of Philosophy*. See Debord, *Œuvres*, p. 853.

8. See Luc Boltanski, "Situationist Inheritors"; http://tarnac9.wordpress. com/2009/05/12/situationist-inheritors

9. Poet-boxer, Dadaist, and wild-man "deserter of seventeen nations," Cravan set sail one morning in 1918 in a small fishing boat into the Gulf of Mexico; his craft breezed out to sea, dipped on the horizon, and nobody ever saw him again. For details of Cravan's short life and everlasting thought, see my "The Provocations of Arthur Cravan," *The Brooklyn Rail*, June 2004; www.brooklynrail.org/2004/06/books/the-provocations-of-arthur-cravan. In a fascinating novel, *Arthur Cravan n'est pas mort noyé* (Grasset, Paris, 2006), Philippe Dagen reinvents Cravan's shadowy world of flight and eternal dislike, bringing him back to life in Geneva during the 1960s, claiming he didn't drown in 1918, that it was yet another prank from an arch-*mystificateur*.

10. The interview is downloadable in English translation: http://tarnac9. wordpress.com/2009/05/28/interview-with-julien-coupat. Gérard Coupat, Julien's father, says of the affair: "They are turning my son into a scapegoat for a generation who have started to think for themselves about capitalism and its wrongs and to demonstrate against the government... The government is keeping my son in prison because a man of the left with the courage to demonstrate is the last thing they want now, with the economic situation getting worse and worse. Nothing like this has happened in France since the war. It is very serious." (Cited in Jason Burke, "France Braced for Rebirth of Violent Left," *Observer*, January 4, 2009.)

11. See http://trucadire.com/files/documents/PV-SDAT.pdf

12. Giorgio Agamben, "Terrorisme ou tragi-comédie," *Libération*, November 19, 2008; www.liberation.fr/.../0101267186-terrorisme-ou-tragi-comedie

13. Another striking thing about *The Coming Insurrection* and the arrests of Julien Coupat and the Tarnac Nine relates to the role of radical publishing today: whether writing (and publishing) a book is the same as doing in kind, whether to provoke on the page is enough to make one guilty of the act. Nowadays, it's perhaps too messy to ban a book when you can just as easily arrest its supposed author. Even the publishers, Éditions la fabrique, headed by veteran *gauchiste* Eric Hazan, had to face state heat. Anti-terrorist police called Hazan in for questioning and subjected him to four hours of abusive interrogation demanding to know the author's identity. Needless to say, Hazan refused to comply.

14. Agamben taught Coupat at Paris's École des hautes études for a while and collaborated in Coupat's short-lived journal *Tiqqun*. An English version of *The Coming Community* was published by Minnesota University Press in 1993, translated by one half of *Empire*'s duo, Michael Hardt.

15. Coupat's hard-line francophone *Tiqqun* shouldn't be confused with Michael Lerner's Jewish-American liberal *Tikkun*.

16. *Tiqqun*, No. 1, 1999, p. 50. See *"Thèses sur le Parti Imaginaire."*

17. James Joyce, *Ulysses*, Modern Library edition, New York, 1946, p. 327 ("Cyclops," Chapter 12).

18. Joyce, *Ulysses*, p. 55. In 2004, the *Théorie du Bloom* from *Tiqqun* appeared in stand-alone book form (*Théorie du Bloom*, Éditions la fabrique, Paris, 2004).

19. "Théorie du Bloom," *Tiqqun*, No.1, 1999, p. 25. Throughout *Tiqqun*, the Debordian concept of spectacle always appears upper-case as Spectacle.

20. *Tiqqun*, No.1, p. 35. Cf. Herman Melville, *Bartleby*, Dove Books, New York, 1990, p. 19. In a 1993 essay called "Bartleby, or on Contingency," Agamben was one of the first contemporary theorists to shine philosophical and political light on the rebellious law-copyist Bartleby (see Giorgio Agamben, *Potentialities: Collected Essays in Philosophy*, Stanford University Press, Stanford, CA, 1999, pp. 243–71). Bartleby's refusal as a form of quiet negation and political potentiality has been emphasized more recently by Michael Hardt and Antonio Negri in *Empire* (Harvard University Press, Cambridge, MA, 2000) and by Slavoj Žižek in *The Parallax View* (MIT Press, Cambridge, MA, 2006). One interesting commentary on Bartleby that pre-dates them all is Gilles Deleuze's postscript to Flammarion's 1989 French translation of *Bartleby*. Deleuze's approach is literary based, but is interesting politically because he draws out the radical lineage—the radical "formula"—connecting Melville's Bartleby, Dostoevsky's underground man, Musil's Ulrich, and Kafka's Gregor Samsa. Each was a person without qualities or particularities who conveyed a "new logic," says Deleuze, or rather leads us towards another logic that has little to do with reason (Gilles Deleuze, "Bartleby, ou la formule" in Herman Melville, *Bartleby*, Flammarion, Paris, 1989, p. 191). "Bartleby isn't sick," Deleuze writes, "but the doctor of an American malady, the medicine man, the new Christ, a brother to us all" (p. 203).

21. Jean-Paul Sartre, *L'existentialisme est un humanisme*, Gallimard, Paris, 1996, p. 39.

22. *The Coming Insurrection*, p. 34.

23. *The Coming Insurrection*, p. 44. This chimes more with Benjamin Péret's hard-edged Great Refusal and poetry of non-coincidence: "*Je ne mange pas de ce pain-là*" ["I won't stoop to that"], his well-known militant surrealist verse from 1936. "I've stolen all I could," Péret tells us, "from shops whose windows I smashed!"

24. *The Coming Insurrection*, p. 41, p. 42.

25. Karl Marx, *Grundrisse, livre 3: chapitre du capital*, Éditions Anthropos 10–18, Paris, 1968, p. 343.

26. *The Coming Insurrection*, p. 95.

27. *The Coming Insurrection*, p. 15, p. 16.

28. *The Coming Insurrection*, p. 99.

29. See André Gorz's persuasive essay, "A New Historical Subject: The Non-Class of Post-Industrial Proletarians," in *Farewell to the Working Class*, Pluto Press, London, 1982, p. 67.

30. Someone once asked Henri Lefebvre if he was really an anarchist: "No," he said. "I'm a Marxist, of course, so that one day we can all become anarchists." (Cited in Ed Soja, *Thirdspace*, Blackwell, Oxford, 1996, p. 33.)

31. See Alberto Toscano, "The War Against Preterrorism: The Tarnac Nine and *The Coming Insurrection*," *Radical Philosophy*, No. 154, March/April 2009.

32. Gorz, *Farewell to the Working Class*, p. 68.

33. Gorz, *Farewell to the Working Class*, p. 75.

34. Gorz, *Farewell to the Working Class*, p. 11.

35. *The Coming Insurrection*, p. 98.

36. See Ivan Illich, *la convivialité*, Éditions du Seuil, Paris, 1973, especially Chapter 2, "La reconstruction conviviale," pp. 26–49.

37. *The Coming Insurrection*, p. 98.

38. *The Coming Insurrection*, p. 110.

39. *The Coming Insurrection*, p. 116. At the end of *Vers le cybernanthrope* (Denoël, Paris, 1971, pp. 211–13), Lefebvre suggests that the insurrection will vanquish by a new style, homemade and home-baked, at once organized and spontaneous, valorizing desire and passion, pitting slingshots against tanks, nets against armor, and clatter against chatter.

40. *The Coming Insurrection*, pp. 112–13.

41. *The Coming Insurrection*, p. 114.

42. The mask incident is recounted in Juana Ponce de León's "Editor's Note" to Subcomandante Marcos's selected writings, *Our Word is Our Weapon*, Serpent's Tail Books, London, 2001, p. xxvi.

43. *The Coming Insurrection*, p. 113.

44. *The Coming Insurrection*, p. 112.

45. *The Coming Insurrection*, p. 125.

46. Louis-Auguste Blanqui (1805–85) spent half of his life rotting in French jails because of his threatening utopian communist ideals. He came of age between the revolutions of 1830 and 1848. Marx and Engels admired Blanqui's writings and activism and Marx saw him "as the heart and head of the French proletarian party" (see Marx's letter to Dr. Watteau, November 10, 1861). Blanqui's most magical text, however, is the proto-New Age *L'éternité par les astres* (*Eternity through the Stars*) (1872). For a great source of Blanqui's

voluminous writings, nearly all of which were scribbled clandestinely behind
bars, see www.marxists.org/reference/archive/blanqui/index.htm

47. Blanqui, *Textes choisis*, Éditions sociales, Paris, 1955, pp. 217–18.
48. *The Coming Insurrection*, p. 128.
49. The words are General Moncada's from *One Hundred Years of Solitude*
(p. 135), addressed to Colonel Aureliano Buendia, fearing that such was
the latter's loathing of despotism that he'd turn into Macondo's most brutal
despot.
50. *The Coming Insurrection*, p. 101.
51. *The Coming Insurrection*, p. 102.
52. *The Coming Insurrection*, p. 104.
53. *The Coming Insurrection*, p. 104.
54. Gorz, "Nine Theses for a Future Left," in *Farewell to the Working Class*,
p. 2.
55. *The Coming Insurrection*, p. 108.
56. *The Coming Insurrection*, p. 109.
57. When Cuba lost access to Soviet oil, fertilizers, and export market in the
early 1990s it faced virtual ruin and a very immediate crisis: feeding its
population. Cubans initiated a "Special Period" to create a low-energy
alterative and developed a system of organic urban agriculture that has
since helped resolve its food security problems. Cuba's city gardens are now
renowned and provide lessons for creating a radically low-tech healthy future
food system.
58. *The Coming Insurrection*, p. 96.
59. Ernst Bloch, *The Principle of Hope, Volume One*, MIT Press, Cambridge
MA, 1986, p. 75.
60. André Gorz, *Misères du present, richesse du possible*, Éditions Galilée, Paris,
1997, p. 11, emphasis added. Gorz, of course, is speaking of an Exodus from
the society of wage-labor, that hastens the end of our alienated "salaried
society." At times, Gorz suggests that this Exodus is a metaphor, a metaphor
of a concrete utopia, a symbol of a departure for a promised land, one
yet-to-be invented—or, better, one invented *only* through the process of
departure. "Utopia has the function of letting us stand back," he says; "it
permits us to judge what we are doing in the light of what we should do."
61. Palmares was the best-known *Quilombo*, near Recife in Northeastern Brazil;
in its hey-day it had a population of around 30,000 renegade ex-slaves.
Palmares endured for almost the whole of the seventeenth century.
62. *The Coming Insurrection*, pp. 12–13.
63. *The Coming Insurrection*, p. 98.

Chapter 3

1. Daniela Issa, "Praxis of Empowerment: Mística and Mobilization in Brazil's
Landless Rural Workers' Movement," *Latin American Perspectives*, Vol. 34,
2007, p. 125.
2. In the radical imagination, mística figures much in the same vein as Raymond
Williams' "structure of feeling": as a meaning and value actively lived and

felt. "We are talking about characteristic elements of impulse," Williams wrote, "specifically affective elements of consciousness and relationships: not feeling against thought, but thought as felt and feeling as thought: practical consciousness of a present kind, in a living and inter-relating continuity." (Raymond Williams, *Marxism and Literature*, Oxford University Press, Oxford, 1978, p. 132.)

3. Hobsbawm, cover blurb for Jan Rocha's and Sue Branford's *Cutting the Wire: The Story of the Landless Movement in Brazil*, Latin American Bureau, London, 2002.

4. In April 1996, 19 MST members were massacred by the military police, and 69 wounded, in what started as a peaceful protest in the Amazonian state of Pará. The event, now as mythical as the banana workers' massacred from *One Hundred Years of Solitude*, caused national and international outcry, and prompted one of Brazil's largest criminal cases, graphically documented by Amnesty International and still largely unsettled.

5. Cited in Issa, "Praxis of Empowerment," p. 129. *Lonas pretas* are the black plastic tarpaulins used as makeshift tents; they signify the initial stage of a land occupation and for the MST are loaded with deep meaning and powerful symbolism. So, too, is the MST's red flag, with its map of Brazil and two peasant laborers, a man and a woman. As for seeds, they represent the land and farming and subsistence, hope of things to come, growing in the future, of fertility and food for the generations to come. Seeds have utopian connotations, but, as every organic farmer knows, are also susceptible to inclement weather. Much of what drives MST activism is collective memory and the creation of a symbolic, largely imaginary universe, all of which magically transforms the life-and-death realism of their plight in Brazil.

6. Cited in Abdurazack Karriem, "The Rise and Transformation of the Brazilian Landless Movement into a Counter-Hegemonic Political Actor: A Gramscian Analysis," *Geoforum*, Vol. 40, 2009, p. 319.

7. Issa, "Praxis of Empowerment," p. 130.

8. Federico García Lorca, *In Search of Duende*, New Direction Books, New York, 1955, p. 52.

9. William Wordsworth, "Preface to *Lyrical Ballads*" (1800), in *The Complete Poetical Works of William Wordsworth*, Houghton Mifflin & Company, New York, 1932, p. 791.

10. Wordsworth, "Preface to *Lyrical Ballads*," p. 791, emphasis added.

11. Wordsworth, "Preface to *Lyrical Ballads*," pp. 795–6.

12. Wordsworth, "Preface to *Lyrical Ballads*," p. 795.

13. Wordsworth, "Preface to *Lyrical Ballads*, p. 790.

14. Walter Benjamin, "Hashish in Marseilles," in *Reflections: Essays, Aphorisms, Autobiographical Writings*, Schocken Books, New York, 1978, p. 141, p. 144.

15. Benjamin, "Hashish in Marseilles," p. 142.

16. Walter Benjamin, "Surrealism: The Last Snapshot of the European Intelligentsia," in *Reflections*, p. 190.

17. Vladimir Lenin, *One Step Forward, Two Steps Back (The Crisis in our Party)*, Progress Publishers, Moscow, 1978.

18. Rosa Luxemburg, "Leninism or Marxism" in *The Russian Revolution, and Lenin or Marxism?*, University of Michigan Press, Ann Arbor, 1961, p. 94.

19. Luxemburg, "Leninism or Marxism?", p. 94.

20. Luxemburg, "Leninism or Marxism?", p. 92.

21. Luxemburg, "Leninism or Marxism?", p. 94.

22. Henri Lefebvre, *L'irruption, de Nanterre au sommet*, Éditions Anthropos, Paris, 1968, p. 79. The text is translated into English under the title *The Explosion*, Monthly Review Press, New York, 1969. In June 2005, the British Labour government authorized a ban on all impromptu protests within a half-mile "exclusion zone" around Westminster. Some Members of Parliament say protests are an "eyesore"; loudspeakers distract them from their work and piles of placards reputedly pose "security risks." Henceforth, under this new exclusion legislation, police have to authorize any demonstration, and anyone staging an unauthorized spontaneous protest can be arrested.

23. Mike Davis, "Planet of Slums: Urban Involution and the Informal Proletariat," *New Left Review*, March–April, 2004, pp. 29–30. See also Mike Davis, *Planet of Slums*, Verso, London, 2006.

24. Lefebvre, *L'irruption*, p. 81.

25. Lefebvre, *L'irruption*, pp. 81–2.

26. Lefebvre, *L'irruption*, pp. 82–3.

27. Henri Lefebvre, *The Survival of Capitalism*, Alison and Busby, London, 1976, p. 100. "There must be an objective," Lefebvre says, "a strategy: nothing can replace political thought, or a cultivated spontaneity." Curiously, when Lefebvre published *La survie du capitalisme* in 1973, he included several essays that had already figured in *The Explosion* [*L'irruption, de Nanterre au sommet*], including "Contestation, Spontaneity, Violence." Alas, the English version removed these repetitions, denying Anglophone audiences the chance to muse on the reason for the doubling up. The subtitle of *The Survival of Capitalism* perhaps offers clues: "Reproduction of Relations of Production." Five-years on from '68, the capitalist system had not only withstood "subjective" bombardment, it had "objectively" begun to grow, too. The essential condition of this growth is that relations of production can be *reproduced*. In a nod to Althusser, Lefebvre's text is less exuberant in its revolutionary hopes, and enters into the world of institutional analyses; yet it's obvious he can't quite resist toying with the idea of spontaneity and contestation throwing a spanner in the apparatus of societal reproduction.

28. Lefebvre, *L'irruption*, p. 172.

29. Stendhal, *Racine and Shakespeare*, cited in Henri Lefebvre, *Introduction to Modernity*, Verso, London, 1995, p. 239. Stendhal (1783–1842) was the penname of Henri Beyle, whose romantic novels, especially *Scarlet and Black* (1830) and *The Charterhouse of Parma* (1839), brought him fame and fans. Stendhal dedicated his works to "the happy few," and coined the term "Beylism" as his philosophical credo for the pursuit of happiness. His dedication may have been an allusion to Shakespeare's *Henry V*: "We few, we happy few, we band of brothers." Interestingly, Shakespeare's phrase would feature in Guy Debord's film version of *The Society of the Spectacle* (1973). Following the caption of "we happy few," the frame flashes to wall

graffiti at an occupied Sorbonne, circa late 1960s: "Run quickly, comrade, the old world is behind you!"

30. The idea of a "Smart Mob" comes from Howard Rheingold, the virtual communities guru whose influential book, *Smart Mobs: The Next Social Revolution* (Basic Books, New York, 2002), is the bible of disaffected computer geeks who've transformed themselves into hackers, mobile IT activists, and connected citizens now coalescing around autonomous lifestyle communities. Smart Mob keywords are: "mobile communication," "pervasive computing," 'wireless networks," and "collective action." As Rheingold puts it in his own summary of the book: "The people who make up smart mobs cooperate in ways never before possible because they carry devices that possess both communication and computing capabilities. Their mobile devices connect them with other information devices in the environment as well as with other people's telephones. Dirt-cheap microprocessors embedded in everything from box tops to shoes are beginning to permeate furniture, buildings, neighborhoods, products with invisible intercommunicating smartifacts. When they connect the tangible objects and places of our daily lives with the Internet, handheld communication media mutate into wearable remote control devices for the physical world."

31. "Protests Powered by Cell-phone," *New York Times*, September 9, 2004.

32. Peter Waterman, "International Labor Communication by Computer: The Fifth International," Working Paper Series No.129, Institute of Social Studies (ISS), The Hague, The Netherlands, July 1992.

33. Waterman, "International Labor Communication by Computer," pp. 3–4.

34. In a fundamental sense, "hackers" can "crack" open computer systems and gain access to them, sometimes covertly, by circumventing security devices. Hackers are generally united in their dislike of corporate monopolization of information technology and digital media, and usually share a profound anti-authoritarian impulse in their development and propagation of free software.

35. André Gorz, *L'immatériel: connaissance, valeur et capital*, Éditions Galilée, Paris, 2003. See, especially, Chapter III, "Vers une société de l'intelligence?" In September 2007, the 84-year-old Gorz and his terminally ill wife Dorine ended their days together in a joint-suicide pact. Gorz's poignant memoir, *Lettre à D* (2006), a postscript to their undying companionship (undying even in death) became a bestseller in France; sparse and elegant, this text exhibits all the qualities of what Magical Marxism should be: a tale of love in the time of social theory.

36. Gorz, *L'immatériel*, p. 93.

37. Gorz, *L'immatériel*, p92

38. Cf. Sarkozy's Presidential campaign mantra from March 2006: "*Travailler plus pour gagner plus!*" As a recent *Le Monde* "Dossier & Document" indicates, the majority of French now recognize the bankruptcy of the Sarkozy equation: as economic crises deepen into everyday life, layoffs and increasing job insecurity are the order of the day. Most workers prefer to reduce their hours of work, and many, "to the great chagrin of the unions, prefer to battle for a severance cheque than preserve a job already condemned." ("Travail: Le temps des révoltes," *Le Monde dossiers et documents*, No. 389, septembre 2009.) Cf. Chapter 5 below.

39. Peter Glotz, *Die beschleunigte Gesellschaft*, cited in Gorz, *L'immatériel*, p. 92.

40. Gorz, *L'immatériel*, p. 98.

41. Marx, *Capital I*, p. 443, emphasis added. Marx's discussion on "Cooperation" (Chapter 13) is worthy of closer inspection, it still having a lot to say about the relationship between technological advancement and collective human potentiality, and this not only in its capitalistic guise. "When the worker cooperates in a planned way with others," says Marx, "he strips off the fetters of his individuality, and develops the capabilities of his species" (p. 447).

42. Marx, *Capital I*, p. 449.

43. Oekonux is an amalgam of "OEKOnomie" (Open Source Economy) and Linux, the free software project conceived in the early 1990s by Finish computer scientist Linus Torvalds. Torvalds wanted to free up intellectual resources from corporate control and create a non-alienated knowledgebase available to all. Linux continues to pioneer a new ethic with respect to work, money, and an exchange-value economy. See www.oekonux.org

44. See www.krisis.org

45. "Free Software and GPL Society: An Interview with Stefan Merten," 2001; http://subsol.c3.hu/subsol_2/contributors0/mertentext.html

46. "Free Software and GPL Society: An Interview with Stefan Merten." The German *Selbstentfaltung* is close to the French *épanouissement personnel*, a sort of personal blossoming and blooming, and closer, too, to the Imaginary Party's "theory of Bloom" (see Chapter 2). For that reason, I prefer to keep Stefan Merten's somewhat clunky translation of "self-unfolding" because it denotes something in motion, something in the process of becoming, of opening out, of flowering; it's also a newer, fresher-sounding label for expressing a post-industrial becoming, replacing the jaded Marxian concept of "self-development."

47. Robert McChesney, a leading American left activist and media analyst, is, however, right to underscore the "hardware" stumbling block. To get real digital freedom, McChesney claims, our "ultimate goal is to get rid of the media capitalists in the phone and cable companies, which are state created monopolies, and to divest them from control." The cell-phone companies are similar obstacles. "The one thing the phone and cable companies are good at," McChesney says, "is buying off and controlling politicians. They aren't any good at the actual business of telecommunications service provision." (Robert McChesney, "Media Capitalism, the State and twenty-first century Media Democracy Struggles," *The Bullet*, August 2009; www.socialistproject. ca/bullet/246.php)

48. Unsurprisingly, the loony US right hasn't taken these human potentialities sitting down, and fearing the worst of all fears—an attack on its bottom-line—dismisses the Free Software movement as a Marxist plot to overthrow America. Thus, the so-called "Heartland Institute," which offers "market-based approaches to environmental protection, privatization of public services, and deregulation in areas of property rights," claims: "Net neutrality [the Free Software movement] divests control over the Internet from the private sector to the government. And in typical Marxist fashion, innocuous words—the language of neutralism and liberty—cloak an agenda that would crush American freedom." (See www.webcitation.org/5kkEOK2lI)

49. Marx, *Capital I*, p. 449.
50. Marx, *Capital I*, p. 460.
51. "Free Software and GPL Society: An Interview with Stefan Merten."
52. Pekka Himanen, *The Hacker Ethic and the Spirit of the Information Age*, Random House, New York, 2001. Himanen's book, since translated into dozens of languages, has an epilogue by his Berkeley mentor, the sociologist Manuel Castells. In my own book, *Metromarxism: A Marxist Tale of the City* (Routledge, New York, 2002), I was critical of Castells' reification of technology in the trilogy *The Informational Age*. Himanen, however, has demonstrated how technology doesn't have to decouple from social relations, nor does it have to kowtow to the corporate sector. Indeed, technology, as Himanen shows, can have all the normative qualities that Castells denounces in his mammoth text. "Theory and research," says Castells, "in general as well as in this book, should be considered as a means for understanding our world, and should be judged exclusively on their accuracy, rigor and relevance." (Manuel Castells, *The End of the Millennium*; Volume 3 of *The Informational Age: Economy, Society and Culture*, Basil Blackwell, Oxford, 1996, p. 359.)
53. Theorists like Gorz have also been at the center of debates in Europe about a "revenue of existence," about a "social income" or "guaranteed income," which isn't a handout from the state or a disguised form of dependency like unemployment benefit. Nor is it a top-up for a low-wage economy, hence a state subsidy for tight employers. Rather, a social income is an assertion of a "right to a social existence," to an income that guarantees a "self-unfolding," as well as an acknowledgement that a salaried work society is finally, both ecologically and socially, kaput. Gorz finds in the social income movement an extension of the hacker ethic: "For the vast majority of unemployed, it is no longer a question of defending an illusory return to full-employment, but to invent, and experiment in, the full employment of life." (Laurent Guilloteau, cited in Gorz, *L'immatériel*, p. 101.)
54. Interview with Himanen, *Libération*, May 25, 2001; www.freescape.eu.org/biblio/article.php3?id_article=129
55. For an interesting discussion of the hacker ethic in terms of new work relations and modes of direct cooperation, see Pascal Jollivet, "L'éthique hacker de Pekka Himanen," *Multitudes*, mars–avril 2002, pp. 161–70.
56. Henri Lefebvre, "Theoretical Problems of *Autogestion*," p. 147.
57. The neo-liberal marketplace, of course, is the domain of non-innovative, un-dynamic state-constructed monopolies whose essential strength lies not in the products they make (if they still make any products), but in the manner in which they successfully destroy opposition and throttle competition. And they are able to do so because they buy off politicians and exploit every subsidy and tax break they can scrounge off the state, while spreading the myth that they are champions of the free market.

Chapter 4

1. Franz Kafka, *The Castle*, Minerva, London, 1992, pp. 59–60.
2. Debord, *Comments on the Society of the Spectacle*, p. 9.

3. Cf. Vinay Gidwani's interesting discussion in "Capitalism's Anxious Whole: Fear, Capture and Escape in the *Grundrisse*," *Antipode: A Radical Journal of Geography*, Vol. 40, 2008, pp. 857–78.

4. G. W. F. Hegel, *Phenomenology of Spirit*, Oxford University Press, Oxford, 1977, p. 19.

5. The magnificent positivity of the *Grundrisse*, for example, comes when Marx makes his own leap of the imagination, when he shrugs off the shackles of Hegel's *Logic*. In a little over ten pages, Marx reaches out to Fourier and projects the wealth of a futuristic communist society predicated on disposable time, on free time outside of production (see Karl Marx, *Grundrisse*, Penguin, Harmondsworth, 1973, pp. 699–712).

6. Still, Spinoza was Marx's favorite philosopher and it's noteworthy how frequently the idea of the "positive" crops up in Marx himself, most regularly in his early writings, especially in "The Economic and Philosophical Manuscripts" (1844). There, Marx speaks of creating a "*positive* community" (*Early Writings*, p. 347), a community that is a "*positive* expression" of communism (p. 345), a community in which there's "*positive* supersession" of private property (p. 349); the re-appropriation of human life, for Marx, is "therefore the *positive* supersession of all estrangement" (p. 349) (emphases added). At that point, Marx says, "a *positive* humanism, *positively* originating in itself, comes into being" (p. 395, emphasis added). Moreover, in the same text Marx roots for Feuerbach in the latter's opposition to the Hegelian "negation of the negation," endorsing Feuerbach's justification for taking "the *positive*, that is sensuously ascertained, as his *starting-point*" (pp. 381–2, emphases added).

7. Holloway, *Change the World Without taking Power*, p. 169.

8. Holloway, *Change the World Without Taking Power*, p. 167.

9. Holloway, *Change the World Without Taking Power*, p. 167.

10. Antonio Negri, *The Savage Anomaly*, Minnesota University Press, Minneapolis, 1991, p. 158.

11. Negri, *The Savage Anomaly*, p. 156. Negri also helps delineate Hegel's thought from Spinoza's. Spinoza's philosophy, says Negri, has nothing to do with either negation or mediation; in Spinoza, the role of spontaneity isn't "blocked" by a closed logical system of contradictory articulation. There simply is "no sordid game of mediation" (p. 141), only a pure affirmation actually defined by spontaneity, which "reproduces itself with increasing intensity at always more substantial levels of being" (p. 47).

12. Bloch, *The Principle of Hope, Volume One*, p. 210.

13. Bloch, *The Principle of Hope, Volume One*, p. 197.

14. Bloch, *The Principle of Hope, Volume One*, p. 200.

15. Bloch, *The Principle of Hope, Volume One*, p. 206.

16. Bloch, *The Principle of Hope, Volume One*, pp. 209–10.

17. Mariana Mora, "Zapatista Anti-Capitalist Politics and the 'Other Campaign': Learning from the Struggles for Indigenous Rights and Autonomy," *Latin American Perspectives*, Vol. 34, No. 2, 2007, p. 69.

18. Both cited in Mora, "Zapatista Anti-Capitalist Politics," p. 70.

19. Michael Hardt and Toni Negri, *Commonwealth*, Harvard University Press, Cambridge, MA, 2009, pp. 236–48.

20. David Harvey, "Commonwealth: An Exchange," *Artforum*, November 2009, p. 258.
21. R. J. Spjut, "Defining Subversion," *British Journal of Law and Society*, Vol. 6, No. 2, Winter 1979, pp. 254–61. Citation from p. 254.
22. Spjut, "Defining Subversion," p. 256.
23. Spjut, "Defining Subversion," p. 261.
24. Friedrich Nietzsche, *Thus Spoke Zarathustra* in *The Portable Nietzsche*, Viking Press, New York, 1954, p. 160.
25. Saul Padover (ed.), *The Letters of Karl Marx*, Prentice-Hall Inc., Englewood Cliffs, New Jersey, 1979, original emphasis.
26. Marx, "Ricardo's Denial of General Over-Production. Possibility of a Crisis Inherent in the Inner Contradictions of Commodity and Money," Chapter XVII of "Theories of Surplus Value," in Tucker (ed.), *The Marx–Engels Reader*, pp. 443–4.
27. Hilary Wainwright, "Porto Alegre: Public Power Beyond the State," in Sue Branford and Bernardi Kucinski, *Lula and the Workers Party in Brazil*, New Press, New York, 2005, p. 113; see also Hilary Wainwright, *Reclaim the State: Experiments in Popular Democracy*, Verso, London, 2003.
28. See Patrick Bond, "The World Social Forum," in Rupert Taylor (ed.), *Third Sector Research*, Springer, New York, 2010, pp. 327–36.
29. Walden Bello, "The Forum at the Crossroads," *Foreign Policy in Focus*, 2007; www.fpif.org/fpiftxt/4196
30. Along with events at the *Usina do Gasômetro*, other sessions were held at the city's assorted municipal buildings. Sometimes these events coincided with one another; oftentimes people knew of neither. Meanwhile, unadvertised meetings being staged in PT as in the Portuguese-friendly satellite towns like Canoas and São Leopoldo merely compounded the sense of dislocation and disunity.
31. Cf. David Harvey, *The Enigma of Capital*, Profile Books, London, 2010.
32. Giorgio Agamben, *Homo Sacer: Sovereign Power and Bare Life*, Stanford University Press, Stanford, CA, 1998, p. 8.
33. Cf. Bessompierre, *L'amitié de Guy Debord, rapide comme une charge de cavalerie légère*, Les fondeurs de briques, Saint-Sulpice-La-Pointe, 2010.

Chapter 5

1. See Peter Lang, *LETS Work: Rebuilding the Local Economy*, Grover Books, Swanley, Kent, 1994.
2. See Michael Linton, "The LETSystem Design Manual" (August, 1994); www.gmlets.u-net.com/design/dm1^3.html
3. "Speculative Realism" is a new, emergent branch of radical philosophy that's now capturing the imagination of young philosophers. Championed by Quentin Meillassoux (a French philosopher based at Paris's École Normale Supérieure) and Ray Brassier (a Brit based at the American University in Beirut), Speculative Realism interrogates the "correlationism" that has preoccupied philosophers since the beginnings of philosophy itself: what is the relationship (or correlation) between the subject and object, between the

thinking mind and the external world? Speculative Realism tries to steer a course between what Graham Harman calls "the robotic chains of reasoning" of the Analytical School and the "non sequiturs, lack of clarity, and poetic self-indulgence" of contemporary continental philosophy (see Harman's *Prince of Networks: Bruno Latour and Metaphysics*, re.press, Melbourne, 2009; see also Meillassoux's *After Finitude: An Essay on the Necessity of Contingency*, Continuum Books, London, 2008; and Brassier's *Nihil Unbound: Enlightenment and Extinction*, Palgrave Macmillan, Basingstoke, 2008). Much of the excitement and promise of Speculative Realism lies in the way it explores different brands of knowledge and action outside of empirical forms and transcendental norms, suggesting that there are other possibilities besides the Hobson's choices of Hume versus Kant, Marxist materialism versus Hegelian idealism, or hard-edged realism versus flaky po-mo constructivism. The ontological terrain, in other words, is a lot more open, a lot more floating than has hitherto been credited, even if Speculative Realism still clings onto a distinctively realist (i.e. non-human) anchoring, doubtless a little too realist for José Arcadio Buendía's fantastical tastes.

4. Jean-Paul Sartre, *L'être et le néant*, Gallimard, Paris, 1943, p. 33.

5. For Sartre, "situations" are loaded with all kinds of profound existential meaning: you are never entirely free in a situation, he says, but you can change the situation, make choices in it, imagine other situations, construct other situations. The idea of situations struck a loud chord with Debord, too, in his Situationist (and earlier Lettrist) years. Both these groups sought to hijack certain urban situations, to detonate them, modify them, push the limits of their internal logic to create situations with new internal logics. "The new Beauty will be THE SITUATION," Debord said in 1954, "that is to say, provisional and lived" (see Guy Debord, "Réponse à une enquête du groupe surréaliste Belge," in *Guy Debord présente POTLATCH (1954–1957)*, Gallimard, Paris, 1996, p. 42).

6. Jean-Paul Sartre, *Critique de la raison dialectique, Tome 1*, Gallimard, Paris, 1960, p. 544, original emphasis.

7. Sartre, *Critique de la raison dialectique, Tome 1*, p. 432, emphasis added.

8. Sartre, *L'être et le néant*, pp. 98–9.

9. Jean-Paul Sartre, *L'imaginaire*, Gallimard, Paris, 1940, p. 239, p. 343.

10. Cf. Marx, "The Economic and Philosophical Manuscripts," *Early Writings*, pp. 389–90.

11. Marx, "The Economic and Philosophical Manuscripts," *Early Writings*, p. 328.

12. Sartre, *L'imaginaire*, p. 355.

13. Sartre, *L'imaginaire*, p. 359.

14. Susan Watkins, "Editorial: Shifting Sands," *New Left Review*, January–February 2010, pp. 5–27.

15. A line from André Gorz's *Letter to D* (Polity Press, London, 2009, pp. 72–3) comes to mind in this regard, a personal admission by Gorz that seems to capture the whole *façon de vivre* of the left: "I am comfortable with the art of failure and annihilation, not with the art of success and positive affirmation." Of course, Gorz would, through his wife Dorine, eventually learn how to

love and affirm the affirmative; his lessons on personal as well as political liberation are lessons we can all learn together.

16. Marx, *Capital I*, p. 283.
17. Marx, *Capital I*, p. 284.
18. Marx, *Capital I*, p. 284.
19. Cf. Marx, *Capital I*, Chapter 13: "Cooperation," p. 443.
20. Marx, "The Economic and Philosophical Manuscripts," *Early Writings*, p. 353, original emphasis.
21. Marx, "The Economic and Philosophical Manuscripts," *Early Writings*, p. 351.
22. Marx, "The Economic and Philosophical Manuscripts," *Early Writings*, p. 354, original emphases.
23. Marx, *Capital I*, pp. 464–5.
24. Marx, *Capital I*, p. 460.
25. Marx, *Capital I*, p. 548.
26. Thus the nonsense of Lenin's fascination with Frederick Taylor's "scientific management" principles, through which Lenin wanted to "fill in the pores" of the frantic Soviet working day.
27. Marx, *Grundrisse*, especially pp. 699–700.
28. Marx, *Grundrisse*, pp. 704–5.
29. Marx, *Grundrisse*, p. 700.
30. The perils and possibilities of so-called "immaterial labor" and "cognitive capitalism" have prompted lively debate amongst Marxists and post-Marxists. The best-known exponents, and perhaps its most blatant optimists, are Hardt and Negri who, beginning with *Empire* (2000), uphold "the general intellect" of the multitude as the virtual vanguard of revolutionary transformation. "The central role previously occupied by the labor power of mass factory workers in the production of surplus value is today increasingly filled by intellectual, immaterial, and communicative labor power. It is thus necessary to develop a new political theory of value that can pose the problem of this new capitalist accumulation of value at the center of the mechanism of exploitation (and thus, perhaps, at the center of potential revolt)." (Hardt and Negri, *Empire*, p. 29.) See, too, Negri's earlier *Marx Beyond Marx* (Autonomedia, New York, 1989), which offers some imaginative "lessons on the *Grundrisse*," particularly on the role of subjectivity and agency in Marx. Other key sources on this debate are Gorz's *L'immatériel* (2003) and Yann Moulier Boutang's excellent collection, *Le capitalisme cognitive: La nouvelle grande transformation* (Éditions Amsterdam, Paris, 2007). Much of the action around cognitive capitalism dovetails with that of "hacker ethics" and a "guaranteed social income."
31. Marx, *Grundrisse*, p. 705, emphasis added.
32. Marx, *Grundrisse*, pp. 705–6.
33. Gorz, *L'immateriél*, p. 17.
34. See, especially, Harvey, *The New Imperialism*, Chapter 4.
35. Marx, *Grundrisse*, p. 705. According to Norbert Bensel, Director of Human Resources at the German car manufacturer Daimler-Benz, workers now equate to "business associates." "The most creative businesses," he says, "are ones with the greatest numbers of intimate relations ... Business

associates are an important part of the business's capital ... Their motivation, their know-how, their capacity to innovate and their social and emotional competence, are a growing factor in the evaluation of their work ... This will no longer be evaluated in terms of number of hours on the job, but on the basis of objectives attained and quality of results. They are entrepreneurs." The citation comes from *The Coming Insurrection*, p. 47. Interestingly, Gorz, in *L'immatériel* (p. 14), also furnishes the same quotation, which is where, I suspect, the "Invisible Committee" first spotted it.

36. Marx, *Grundrisse*, p. 706.
37. Marx, *Grundrisse*, p. 708.
38. Marx, *Grundrisse*, p. 706, original emphases. Marx is here citing an anonymous pamphlet published in London in 1821 called *The Source and Remedy of the National Difficulties, deduced from principles of political economy in a letter to Lord John Russell*. The nameless author is widely believed to have been a disciple of David Ricardo.
39. Marx, *Grundrisse*, p. 712.
40. Marx, *Grundrisse*, p. 611.
41. *The Coming Insurrection*, p. 104, original emphasis.
42. Cf. Marx, *Capital I*, pp. 794–802.
43. See Don Peck, "How a New Jobless Era will Transform America," *The Atlantic*, March 2010, p. 44.
44. Charly Boyadjian, "Le temps en '3X8'," *Travailler deux heures par jour*, Éditions du Seuil, Paris, 1977, pp. 25–6.
45. Boyadjian, *Travailler deux heures par jour*, p. 29. It's important to remember, however, that these two hours aren't hours in which people are still disempowered in work, still alienated and stupefied. "Nobody," said Simone Weil ironically, "would accept being a slave for two hours a day; slavery, for it to be accepted, ought to last long enough each day to completely break a man." (Simone Weil, *La condition ouvrière*, Gallimard folios essais, Paris, 2002 [1934].)
46. Peck, "How a New Jobless Era will Transform America," p. 46.

Chapter 6

1. Henri Lefebvre, *La somme et le reste, Tome II*, Éditions La Nef de Paris, Paris, 1959, p. 428.
2. Lefebvre, *La somme et le reste, Tome II*, pp. 428–9.
3. Lefebvre, *La somme et le reste, Tome II*, p. 429.
4. One night, trying surreptitiously to get into a bathroom where Meme, "naked and trembling with love," awaited him, a guard shot Mauricio down from the drainpipe. A bullet that lodged in his spinal column reduced Mauricio to bed for the rest of his life. He died of old age in solitude, "tormented by memories and by the yellow butterflies, who did not give him a moment's peace" (p. 238).
5. Henri Lefebvre, *La somme et le reste*, Bélibaste, Genève, 1973, p. 11.
6. Cf. Henri Lefebvre, *Le droit à la ville*, Éditions Anthropos, Paris, 1968, p. 120.

7. ZUS are "*Zones Urbaines Sensibles*," the French euphemism for problematic neighborhoods, "sensitive" areas with "sensitive" populations; the term is generally synonymous with the peripheral *banlieues* in which 4.5 million French people face poverty, employment, and insecure work. In French ZUS, official unemployment rates for men between the ages of 15 and 24 currently run at 41.7%; most young men living in ZUS face the reality of probably never being able to find stable work.

8. Gorz senses the danger with this kind of dabbling, too. In a letter addressed to the Belgian political philosopher, Philippe Van Parijs, responding to the latter's article "Why Surfers Should be Fed" (*Philosophy and Public Affairs*, No. 20, 1991, pp. 101–31), which outlines a "liberal case for an unconditional basic income," Gorz writes: "Why does this line of thinking provoke a certain malaise in me? Because the argument here bases itself at the level of quasi-algebraic logic, and questions of justice aren't reducible to that. Justice starts out from a normative ideal, which precedes all possible rationalization. You can shift from the normative to a logical and judicial formalization, but you cannot begin from logical rationalization and then move in the opposite direction." (André Gorz cited in Philippe van Parijs, "De la sphère autonome à l'allocation universelle," in Christophe Fourel [ed.], *André Gorz: un penseur pour le XXIe siècle*, La découverte, Paris, 2009, p. 173.)

9. Debord, *Comments on the Society of the Spectacle*, p. 21.

10. "Take Back the Land" started out in Miami in 2006 when a handful of activists and homeless people seized control of a vacant publicly owned lot in the Liberty City section of Miami, establishing a self-run shantytown called Umoja (Unity) Village, constructed out of discarded plywood and packing palettes, tin roofs and cardboard boxes, and housing 53 displaced residents. The village was held for six months before a mysterious fire burnt it to the ground. Nonetheless, these actions attracted sympathetic audiences nationwide, sparking a larger campaign against capital investment through gentrification, predatory loans, and enticing financial packages, on the one hand, and capital divestment through housing foreclosures, abandonment, and repossession, on the other. Take Back the Land received added lift from Michael Moore's recent film, *Capitalism: A Love Story*, which featured activist Max Rameau and highlighted the successes of the Miami occupations and eviction defenses.

11. Cf. James Joyce, *Finnegans Wake*, Faber and Faber, London, 1966, p. 42: "The great fact emerges that after that historic date all holographs so far exhumed initialled by Haromphrey bear the sigla H.C.E. and ... to his cronies it was equally certainly a pleasant turn of the populace which gave him as sense of those normative letters the nickname Here Comes Everybody. An imposing everybody he always indeed looked, constantly the same as and equal to himself and magnificently well worthy of any and all such universalisation."

12. See Andy Merrifield, *Dialectical Urbanism*, Monthly Review Press, New York, 2002, especially Chapter 4.

13. The metropolis, Hardt and Negri say, "inscribes" the multitude's past, "its subordinations, suffering, and struggles," while it "poses the conditions,

positive and negative, for its future." In the "era of biopolitical production," they add, "the metropolis increasingly fulfils the role as the inorganic body of the multitude" (Hardt and Negri, *Commonwealth*, p. 249). The metropolis, then, is rightly conceived as the site of the production of a new urban commons, as well as the site where urban social movements and work-based autonomous politics can fruitfully conjoin.

14. Marx, *Capital I*, p. 342.
15. Marx, *Capital I*, p. 344.
16. See the very interesting collection edited by Anne Dreuille, *Les aventuriers de l'économie solidaire: entre reconnaissance et résistance: la quête des chômeurs-créateurs*, L'Harmattan, Paris, 2001. The citation comes from page 187. The book includes touching testimonies from the young people who participated in the project. It also includes a short offering from André Gorz, who saw the "Academy of Liberated Time" as an "embryonic form" of a potential new relationship to work, and a mode of life that's somehow "*de*-economized" in surplus-value terms.
17. *The Coming Insurrection*, p. 108, original emphases.
18. *The Coming Insurrection*, p. 108.
19. Debord, *Panegyric*, p. 51.
20. Guy Debord, *Correspondance volume 5: janvier 1973–décembre 1978*, Librairie Arthème Fayard, Paris, 2005, p. 452.
21. Guy Debord, *Marquis de Sade a des yeux de fille*, Éditions Fayard, Paris, 2004, p. 57.
22. Goethe, *Faust*, Anchor Books, New York, 1963, p. 421. "He! He! Send him away!" is uttered by Gretchen, and the "He" in question is Mephisto.
23. Breton cited in Richardson, *Refusal of the Shadow*, pp. 23–4.
24. Alfred Métraux, *Le Vaudou haïtien*, cited in Richardson, *Refusal of the Shadow*, p. 26.
25. Richardson, *Refusal of the Shadow*, p. 27.
26. The Chinese-American poet, John Yau, thinks that the location of Lam's "ethnic" painting is telling, that to see it we "must wait in the cloakroom": "the artist has been allowed into the museum's lobby," says Yau, "but, like a delivery boy, has been made to wait in an inauspicious passageway near the front door." (See John Yau, "Please Wait in the Cloakroom," *Arts Magazine*, No. 63, December 1988.) This past June (2010), after extensive refurbishments had taken place at the Museum of Modern Art, I returned to the mid-town gallery. Now, Lam's canvas has finally entered the main stage, to a prime site on the fourth floor, in the thick of the Americas' modern art.
27. See Jacques Derrida, *Specters of Marx: The State of the Debt, the Work of Mourning, and the New International*, Routledge, New York, 1994; and Michael Sprinker (ed.), *Ghostly Demarcations: Symposium on Jacques Derrida's Specters of Marx*, Verso, London, 1999.
28. Derrida, *Specters of Marx*, pp. 85–6.

NAME INDEX

SUBJECT INDEX